MORE BIBLICAL EVIDENCE FOR CATHOLICISM

By

Dave Armstrong

Companion to
A Biblical Defense of Catholicism

© 2002 by Dave Armstrong. All rights reserved.

No part of this book may be reproduced, stored in a retrieval system, or transmitted by any means, electronic, mechanical, photocopying, recording, or otherwise, without written permission from the author.

ISBN: 0-7596-7072-2

This book is printed on acid free paper.

1stBooks - rev. 12/17/01

Most biblical citations are from the Revised Standard Version of the Bible (© 1971) and New Revised Standard Version (© 1989): both copyrighted by the Division of Christian Education of the National Council of the Churches of Christ in the United States of America. All emphases have been added.

For further related reading, see the author's award-winning website: *Biblical Evidence for Catholicism* (http://ic.net/~erasmus/RAZHOME.HTM)

...contend for the faith which was once for all delivered to the saints. (Jude 3)

Table of Contents

Dedication		vii
Foreword: by Dr. Scott Hahn		ix
Introduction		xi
Chapter One	Biblical Indications as to the Definition of the Gospel and the Nature of Sacramentalism	1
Chapter Two	Fictional Dialogues on *Sola Scriptura* ("Bible Alone"), the Real Presence, and Penance	7
Chapter Three	Is Catholicism Half-Pagan?	16
Chapter Four	Sin and Sinners in the Catholic Church: Disproof of its Ecclesiastical Authority?	20
Chapter Five	Denominationalism and Sectarianism	26
Chapter Six	Catholicism is Neither Pelagian Nor Semi-Pelagian (The Nature and Extent of Human Effort in Salvation)	30
Chapter Seven	"Is This God?": Biblical and Philosophical Reflections on the Blessed Eucharist	35
Chapter Eight	Why the Catholic Mass is Not Idolatry	48
Chapter Nine	The Old Testament, the Ancient Jews, and *Sola Scriptura*	52
Chapter Ten	Was the Catholic Church an Avowed Enemy of Holy Scripture in the Middle Ages or at any Other Time?	61
Chapter Eleven	Insurmountable Practical Problems of *Sola Scriptura*	69
Chapter Twelve	Dialogue on the Alleged "Perspicuous Apostolic Message" as a Corollary of *Sola Scriptura*	83
Chapter Thirteen	Dialogue on the Logic, Epistemology, and Practical Application of Catholic Infallible Authority	93
Chapter Fourteen	Dialogue on Biblical Arguments for Purgatory	102
Chapter Fifteen	A Biblical and Theological Primer on the Veneration of the Blessed Virgin Mary, Her Sinlessness, and Her God-Ordained Function as Mediatrix	107

Chapter Sixteen	Mary the Mediatrix: Biblical Rationale and Deeper Reflections and Explanations	117
Appendix One:	My Respect for Protestants	132
Appendix Two:	My Odyssey From Evangelicalism to Catholicism (Transcript of a Radio Interview)	139
Appendix Three:	150 Reasons Why I am a Catholic (Featuring 300 Biblical Evidences Favoring Catholicism)	150
Appendix Four:	Catholicism and Orthodoxy: A Comparison	168

Dedication

To my family: my beautiful and cherished wife Judith Ann Kozora, my wonderful parents, Graham and Lois Armstrong, and my three fabulous children: Paul David, Michael Brendan, and Matthew Newman. I heartily thank them all for their unwavering love, support, patience, and understanding.

Particularly, I would like to dedicate this book to my first daughter, soon to be born: Angelina Rose, and to our four children in heaven, whom we eagerly look forward to meeting on the glorious day when we behold our Lord Jesus Christ face to face: Maria Judith (conceived in May 1989), Thomas Wesley (November 1989), Renee Therese (June 1992). and Ryan Francis (October 2000).

Though they never lived on earth, they are more alive than we are, and will live forever in bliss with their Father in heaven. May we always remember that God creates an eternal soul whenever a conception occurs, and that we are merely pilgrims passing through this vale of tears, destined for a far better place, provided that we remain faithful till the end.

Her children rise up and call her blessed; her husband also, and he praises her; "Many women have done excellently, but you surpass them all." Charm is deceitful, and beauty is vain, but a woman who fears the LORD is to be praised. Give her the fruit of her hands, and let her works praise her in the gates.

(Proverbs 31:28-31; RSV)

What was wonderful about childhood is that anything in it was a wonder. It was not merely a world full of miracles; it was a miraculous world.

(G.K. Chesterton, *Autobiography*)

A child is a pledge of immortality, for he bears upon him in figure those high and eternal excellences in which the joy of heaven consists, and which would not thus be shadowed forth by the all-gracious Creator, were they not one day to be realized.

(Venerable John Henry Cardinal Newman, *Miscellanies*)

Foreword
(Dr. Scott Hahn)

When I began investigating the claims of the Catholic Church in the early 1980s, there were relatively few popular books on the market written explicitly to present the case for the Catholic Church *vis a vis* Protestant beliefs. In the last two decades Catholic apologetic resources have proliferated. I am grateful that more and better tools are consistently being made available for the work of building up the Church, the kingdom of God on earth.

More Biblical Evidence for Catholicism is one such helpful building tool. In this book, David Armstrong has supplied useful information to engage those who are not enemies, but brothers and sisters who seek the fullness of God's family in the Catholic Church. This book provides information that can help lower barriers between Catholics and non-Catholics by exchanging information and perspectives on doctrinal issues such as *sola scriptura*, the Eucharist, and salvation. It can prepare Catholics to give a clearer answer for the hope that is within them (1 Pet. 3:15).

Reading this book needs to be accompanied by a significant amount of prayer. No amount of information or argumentation alone opens the heart to the grace of God. And the grace of God does not merely call us to intellectual assent to truths. We need to encounter Truth in the depths of our hearts, and answer His call to deny ourselves, take up our cross and follow Him (Mt. 16:24).

Introduction

This work is intended as a companion piece and continuation (in terms of the general category of reasoning or apologetics) of my first book, *A Biblical Defense of Catholicism*. Once again my purpose is to accumulate biblical arguments in support of distinctively Catholic doctrinal positions, with Protestant readers particularly in mind (as well as Catholics not overly familiar with the Bible).

I also touch upon the closely-related subjects of *sola Scriptura* (the Protestant notion of *Scripture Alone*), the Catholic Church's high regard for Holy Scripture, and critiques from our separated Christian brethren with regard to matters of ecclesiology (Church) and Tradition (i.e., the twin Catholic counter-principles to *sola Scriptura*), primarily in chapters nine through thirteen.

Additionally, a fair degree of emphasis has been devoted to certain common and erroneous charges against the Catholic Church (chapters three, four, six, and eight) and to dialogue (back-and-forth discussion), so that readers can have a sense of interaction with opponents of various Catholic doctrines, and how they might be answered from Scripture, history, and reason.

Appendix One, "My Respect for Protestants," is my heartfelt attempt to make it crystal clear that my own arguments and critiques are never intended in a personal, or "anti-Protestant" fashion. One can disagree on particulars, while still largely respecting (even admiring) persons who hold to a Christian view other than one's own (yet not compromising one's own beliefs at all). I felt very strongly about making my ecumenism (which I consider as perfectly complementary to my apologetics) a matter of public record.

Almost all of these chapters came about as a result of challenges and dialogues undertaken via e-mail and Internet lists and bulletin boards, from mid-1996 through to mid-2000. My first book was much more heavily-researched and oriented towards use as a "reference," whereas the present work is more expository, informal, "essay-ish," and conversational in nature, due to the circumstances in which most of the writing occurred (thus there are far fewer footnotes, by design).

A Biblical Defense of Catholicism tended somewhat toward the catechetical, descriptive end of the theological spectrum; here I am trying to get further *behind* the thought and rationale of Catholic theology—to explore its "worldview" or underlying assumptions a bit more thoroughly, and even—sometimes—the epistemology of the Catholic believer (i.e., *why* and *how* they believe what they do: the *process* of acquiring that knowledge, or possible, theoretical rationales for it).

This exploration of underlying presuppositions and premises is especially true of the last two chapters on Mariology, which delve into very deep spiritual and theological matters (no doubt quite inadequately, but one has to start somewhere, and I am learning much myself, as I ponder, meditate, and jot down my own thoughts).

I find that my own thoughts are greatly stimulated by direct challenges. Traditionally, Catholic apologetic endeavors have usually been counter-reactions to views which arose and competed with the accepted, received doctrines and teachings of the Catholic Church. Mariology developed in reaction to Nestorianism. Trinitarianism developed as a result of Sabellianism and Arianism.

The doctrine of Christ (particularly, His Two Natures) was, in the long run, better understood by the early Church and "fine-tuned" because of the dangers to orthodoxy posed by the heresies of Monophysitism and Monothelitism. St. Augustine developed his ecclesiology and theology (particularly with regard to grace) in the course of his disputes with the Donatists, Pelagians, and Manichaeans.

The details of all those noble and necessary battles waged for Mother Church are unimportant at the moment; my point is that much of theology, as well as apologetics, is done in the "heat" of competition and challenge. These confrontations help us to strengthen and better understand our own opinions and beliefs (or, conversely, to repudiate them if they are found wanting).

This has been very much my experience on the Internet. I love the challenges which have come my way, and I my own faith has been greatly strengthened when the arguments I produced in the course of dialogue (ultimately almost wholly derived from the Bible itself or past defenders of the Catholic faith) withstood attacks and therefore provided further support for the Catholic position.

It has always been this way for Christians who are out in the "world," in the marketplace of ideas, contending for the faith. Jesus disputed with the Pharisees and other religious authority figures of His time, and—sadly—His own townspeople. St. Paul—as Scripture informs us—routinely "argued" and "reasoned" with both Jews and Greeks.

The Church Fathers opposed many false teachings and presented a positive message of the Gospel in the (altogether biblical) context of the one, holy, catholic, and apostolic Church. I seek to follow their example and offer up my own meager contributions to the defense of Catholicism. I would like to share with readers some of what I have learned in my various dialogues and debates.

My thoughts and arguments throughout the book are not always (indeed, not usually) thoroughly-formulated, nor do I think they are even necessarily always successful, by any means. I am happy to leave that judgment of success or failure to the reader.

My intention is to provide examples (especially in the dialogue chapters) of a Catholic grappling with opposing views and attempting to give an orthodox, magisterial Catholic response. These are real-life encounters, or at the very least, essays which were written with competing ideas and premises and worldviews (several of which I used to hold myself) very much in mind at all times.

I hope and pray that I have done justice to the topics I have dealt with, and that I have—in some small way—helped others to understand some things better, by God's grace. I am not a theologian, and have no formal theological training (though a great deal of informal training, these past twenty years). But perhaps that is preferable for my purposes, since (hopefully) I can express these points on a more popular level (assuming I do have correct beliefs concerning them), as opposed to a strictly academic, scholarly level.

I have never claimed to be a scholar, because I am not, and I reiterate that again here, lest anyone misunderstand the level of ambition for what I am presently attempting to do. I appreciate when someone thinks that I do possess such credentials (occasionally I receive such feedback), and it is flattering. But readers looking for the "latest research" or absolute rigor and documentation of every claim made will not find it here. Plenty of books can offer that (such as those by Dr. Scott Hahn), and I heartily recommend them, and use them myself, all the time. But I am trying to do something a little different.

My strength of argument exists only insofar as my reasoning and exposition is in harmony with both Sacred Scripture and Sacred (Apostolic) Tradition. I hope that I am completely in accord with those sources of true Christian dogma (I certainly always try to be). They can quite hold their own: truth has that inherent power.

Our job as Catholic apologists is to communicate these truths accurately and in terms that our target audience can *understand*, and to show that they are more plausible and worthy of belief, in so doing. The Catholic apologist mainly tries to remove obstructions or roadblocks, and to help clear up misunderstandings and erroneous "debris" which often surrounds Catholic teaching and the Catholic Church.

I also pray that our Lord God will help readers discern any of my own errors or inadequate charity, manner, or presentation, which got mixed in with the "passing-on" of true Christian Tradition, and will "discard" them like the bone of a delicious chicken leg, or the seeds of an apple.

Chapter One

Biblical Indications as to the Definition of the Gospel and the Nature of Sacramentalism

Many non-Catholic Christians maintain that Catholics are not Christians at all. I define *Christian* in terms of "orthodoxy," "creed," "confession," and "doctrine," as opposed to a "wheat and tares," "individual commitment to Christ" or "metaphysical" sense. Both sets of assumptions are valid in their own sphere, yet one must utilize some objective doctrinal criteria in order to define any belief system.

I wish to examine the question as to what constitutes the *gospel*. I am operating under the premise that a group which accepts and believes in the gospel is rightfully deserving of the title *Christian*. Curiously, many Protestants want to define the gospel in the strict sense of "justification by faith alone." The Bible, however (which most Protestants adhere to as their ultimate authority in matters of Christian belief), is very explicit and clear that this is not the case at all.

For example, we know what the *gospel* is because we have a record of the apostles preaching it immediately after Pentecost. St. Peter's first sermon in the Upper Room (Acts 2:22-40) is certainly the gospel, since 3000 people became Christians upon hearing it (2:41). In this speech he utters not a word about "faith alone."

He instructs the hearers, rather, to *repent, and be baptized... so that your sins may be forgiven* (2:38). So, immediately after the resurrection, at the very outset of the "Church Age," an apostle teaches sacramentalism and baptismal regeneration—doctrines which are anathema to most evangelical Protestants.

St. Paul defines the gospel in Acts 13:16-41 as the resurrection of Jesus (verses 32-33), and in 1 Corinthians 15:1-8 as His death, burial, and resurrection. When Paul converted, straightaway he also got baptized, in order to have his *sins washed away* (Acts 22:12-16).

Biblical factors such as these caused people like Martin Luther and John Wesley and their denominations (Lutheranism and Methodism), and other communions such as the Anglicans and the Church of Christ, to retain this doctrine of baptismal regeneration.

Furthermore, when the rich young ruler asked Jesus how he could be saved (Luke 18:18-25), our Lord, accordingly, didn't say "just believe in Me with faith alone." Rather, He commanded him to perform a "work," to sell all that he had. Jesus also rewards and grants salvation at least partially according to works and acts of charity, rather than on the basis of faith alone (or, *sola fide*): (Matthew 16:27, 25:30-46—note conjunction *for* in 25:35).

Therefore, the explicit scriptural proclamations and definitions of the gospel strikingly exclude "faith alone," and other actions by Jesus and the apostles contradict it by force of example. From these facts we conclude that the gospel is—as St. Paul teaches—**the death, burial and resurrection of Jesus**. This is the "good news" (the literal meaning of *gospel*), not some technical theory of salvation (or, soteriology).

Even common sense would dictate that this *good news* is comprised of Jesus' redemptive work for us—the great historical drama of His incarnation and atonement, not forensic, "legal," imputed justification. And the Prophets foretold these *events*, not a fine-tuned theory of *application* of those events to the believer. How could a mere theological abstract reasonably be called "good news"?

This seems clear enough, yet many otherwise brilliant, learned Protestant scholars, radio preachers, prominent pastors, and so forth, falsely accuse ecumenical Protestants of "betraying the gospel" by their attempts to cooperate and have fellowship with Catholics as much as possible, and to find common theological ground (which is, of course, very considerable).

For these reasons and many others, it is (once one presupposes biblical inspiration and authority) impossible to read Catholicism (as a set of doctrines and dogmas) out of the Christian faith, since both sides fully accept all the supernatural facts of Christ's divinity and man's fallenness and believe that salvation comes solely as a result of His atoning work on our behalf—always ultimately His work of grace, whether or not works enter into the equation.

The contrary is the heresy of *Pelagianism* (works-salvation, or "self-produced salvation"), which was (in all its various forms) condemned by the Catholic Church in A.D. 529 at the Second Council of Orange (following St. Augustine). The Council of Trent in the 16th century also condemned these false notions of how salvation is attained. Yet the myths stubbornly persist.

Also, both sides agree that good works ought to be present in every Christian's life, whether they are required for salvation (as the sign that saving grace and faith is truly present), or done in gratitude for salvation already accomplished. But if the devil wants to keep Christians divided, he has—sadly—had a very easy time doing it.

I was asked by a Protestant in the midst of an e-mail dialogue, "What is your hope of salvation?" I answered: "Jesus." The universal *Catechism of the Catholic Church*, in its section #169, states that: "Salvation comes from God alone..." The *Catechism* goes on to speak of the role of the Church as "our teacher in the faith," but not "as if she were the author of our salvation."

My friend continued, asking, "This is the question of the Gospel. Is your salvation by grace alone through faith alone in Christ alone? Or is it grace plus something, faith plus something and Christ plus...?" I replied: "It's not 'grace +'

anything. Rather, it is the elementary, eminently biblical recognition that *faith without works is dead* (James 2:14-26), and that we possess a 'faith that works' (1 Thessalonians 1:3, 2 Thessalonians 1:11, Titus 1:15-16). **All salvation and all good works whatever ultimately derive from God's enabling and necessary grace alone.**"

Catholics and Protestants both hold to the gospel, as biblically defined above. We differ on questions of justification, which is the application of salvation and the gospel and Jesus' work to the individual, not the gospel itself. Nor is TULIP[1] (Calvinism) the gospel, strictly speaking. The key is the absolute primacy of grace and the utter condemnation of Pelagianism in both systems.

There are, of course, major differences between the two camps, but on the central tenets of Christianity (e.g., doctrine of God, the life and works of Jesus, centrality of grace, the Bible, the fallenness of man, the total inability of man to save himself, creation, judgment, heaven and hell, etc.) we are in agreement. Catholics regard anyone baptized with a trinitarian formula to be a Christian.

We can "fight" vigorously (yet amiably and respectfully) over our many disagreements, but there should be no division over whether we are brothers in Christ, or concerning the nature of the gospel.

Similarly, evangelical Protestants—of the "low church" or non-denominational variety especially—, oftentimes exhibit an antipathy to matter as a conveyor of grace (or "blessing"). In other words, they tend to deny the *sacramental principle*. This hearkens back in some respects to the Docetic heresy, with traces of Nestorianism and Donatism.

Non-Catholic and non-Orthodox Christians frequently express the notion that matter is a step down, a "reduction" of Christ's atonement: a sort of "matter vs. spirit" outlook. Catholics (and Orthodox and many Anglicans and Lutherans) believe that this view collapses when scrutinized in scriptural and reasoned depth.

The incarnation of Jesus, which made the atonement possible, was the event in salvation history which raised matter to previously unknown heights. God took on human flesh! Given that all created matter was "good" in God's opinion from the start (Genesis 1:25), and now is "glorified" further by the wonder of the incarnation, why is it that such beliefs are still held? What is the scriptural basis? And this occurs, curiously, even though most non-sacramental Protestants would not deny the goodness of matter per se.

Ritual and "physicality" were not abolished by the coming of Christ. Nor was the atonement purely "spiritual." Quite the contrary! It was as physical as it could

---

[1] TULIP = Total Depravity, Unconditional Election, Limited Atonement, Irresistible Grace, and Perseverance of the Saints

be, as well as obviously spiritual. Protestants speak of "the blood," and rightly so (see Revelation 5:9, Ephesians 1:7, Colossians 1:14, Hebrews 9:12, 1 Peter 1:2, 1 John 1:7, etc.).

It was the very suffering of Jesus in the flesh, and the voluntary shedding of His own blood, which constituted the crucial, if not essential aspect of the propitiatory atonement. One can't avoid this. *By his bruises we are healed* (Isaiah 53:5).

The New Testament is filled with incarnational and sacramental indications: instances of matter conveying grace. The Church is the "Body" of Christ (1 Corinthians 12:27, Ephesians 1:22-3, 5:30), and marriage (including the sexual act) is described as a direct parallel to Christ and the Church (Ephesians 5:22-33, especially 29-32). Jesus even seems to literally equate Himself in some sense with the Church, saying He was "persecuted" by Paul, after His resurrection (Acts 9:5).

Not only that, there is the whole repeated strain in St. Paul's thought of identifying with Christ and His sufferings, very graphically and literally, or so it would seem: 2 Corinthians 4:10, Philippians 2:17, 3:10, 2 Timothy 4:6, and above all, Colossians 1:24; cf. 2 Corinthians 1:5-7, 6:4-10, 11:23-30, Galatians 2:20, 6:17, Romans 12:1.

Matter conveys grace often in Holy Scripture: baptism confers regeneration: Acts 2:38, 22:16, 1 Peter 3:21 (cf. Mark 16:16, Romans 6:3-4), 1 Corinthians 6:11, Titus 3:5. Paul's "handkerchiefs" healed the sick (Acts 19:12), as did even Peter's shadow (Acts 5:15), and of course, Jesus' garment (Matthew 9:20-22) and saliva mixed with dirt (John 9:5 ff., Mark 8:22-25), as well as water from the pool of Siloam (John 9:7). Anointing with oil for healing is encouraged (James 5:14).

Then there is the laying on of hands for the purpose of ordination and commissioning (Acts 6:6, 1 Timothy 4:14, 2 Timothy 1:6) and to facilitate the initial outpouring of the Holy Spirit (Acts 8:17-19, 13:3, 19:6), and for healing (Mark 6:5, Luke 13:13, Acts 9:17-18). Even under the Old Covenant, a dead man was raised simply by coming in contact with the bones of Elisha (2 Kings 13:21).

Sacramentalism is merely the Incarnation extended, just as the Church is. No a priori biblical or logical case can be made against sacramentalism or a literal Eucharist on the grounds that matter is inferior to spirit and/or indicative of a stunted, primitive, "pagan" spirituality or some such similar negative judgment.

Closely related to the denial of the sacramental principle is the common non-Catholic Christian notion that one can *do absolutely nothing* to contribute to their salvation (including any sacraments, sacramentals, fasting, almsgiving, etc.), even if these acts are construed (as they are in Catholicism) as originating in God's enabling grace, and regarded as merely cooperating with God, Who alone saves.

Such pious acts are viewed as a denial of Christ's work on the cross rather than the outworking or *application* of the redemption in the Christian life. From this view, it would seem to logically follow, then, that one couldn't do anything to *lose* their salvation, either, including wicked sins. That would entail the doctrine of eternal security, which not all Protestants accept.

There is an inherent tension in a view which would require *absolutely no human effort*. For "doing nothing at all" would also include such things as the altar call, the sinner's prayer, joining of a fellowship, public confession of repentance, renunciation of former sinful activities, and other commonly-accepted evangelical Protestant practices. These things are still free acts of the will, thus *doing* something.

Amidst all the esoteric, technical, theoretical, hair-splitting, abstract theological arguments which take place, the simply-ascertained fact remains that every Christian must follow Jesus with all their "heart, soul, strength, and mind," perform good works, and try to live a righteous life.

The theologians grapple with the proper place of these things in the schema of salvation. They get paid for it, and can devote their lives to that worthy endeavor. As for us common folk, we are commanded to love Jesus and our fellow man (as Jesus loved us), and that should be sufficient. We are to be disciples, not philosophers.

Repentance and a heartfelt commitment to Christ and Christianity involves many acts. One must stop engaging in immoral sex, and that is doing something. Or they must ditch drugs, and that is doing something; or if they repent and stop cheating on income tax returns, that is doing something, etc.

It would be difficult to prove that such activities as outlined above are not *doing* anything (after all, even changing one's mind or will is doing *something*). And baptism is included in that, whether one adopts the non-sacramental position or not. Regardless of what one believes takes place with the water, a person still *did* something. And we were commanded to **do** so by Jesus. Holy Communion (whatever one believes) is included as well. Jesus commanded it, and we *do* it.

The comeback or concession to this is that indeed it may be admitted that we do certain things, but that our doing them doesn't *improve* our faith, but rather, merely *proves* it. In other words, our actions (from this perspective) have no bearing on our state of grace or ultimate salvation.

But this is a distinction without a difference, in my opinion. Both Catholics and Protestants of all stripes agree that, for instance, baptism is *necessary*. So the practical result is the same, in the lives of committed Christians: faith is present, and also the act of baptism, whether of the individual past the age of reason, or else by the parents acting in the infants' stead. All the abstractions in the world might be made about all these acts not being part of salvation / justification, but only sanctification, yet the fact remains that we are commanded to do these things, and most Christians indeed do them. The Catholic point in all this is that faith and works go hand in hand, and ought not to be separated, **not** that one is saved by any work.

Again, there is no *practical* difference between this and "orthodox" evangelical Protestantism, which holds that good works will inevitably follow in the life of any person who is "saved" or of the Elect (whichever paradigm is preferred). Christians of all types are far more concerned with orthodoxy (*correct doctrine*) than they are with orthopraxis (*correct practice*), but the biblical view places equal emphasis on both.

It is objected that a requirement to do anything for salvation somehow denigrates or denies Jesus' complete work on the cross for our salvation. But this is not true at all. Catholics believe that the work which only He could do needs to be appropriated to human beings by means of their freely given consent (even though God initiates *that* as well—see, e.g., Philippians 2:13).

Otherwise, God becomes the author of evil, since there would be no human free will to assent to follow God and accept His work for us; thus the ones who end up in hell are there *only* because of God's express decree, and it couldn't have been otherwise. As soon as free will is accepted, the *do* comes in with it. There is no way out of this, either biblically or logically. To deny it would be (as a logical end-result) to fall into sheer determinism.

Or it might be argued that repentance, submission, and faith are all "inward," not external acts. Whether they are inward or outward is irrelevant to the discussion at hand. Persons are still *doing* something. And they are doing it irregardless of whether God is the cause of those actions or not (which He is, in the sense of making them possible in the first place, and in His Providence).

The whole point is that we **cooperate** with God's grace, because the *do* resides in the will, not mere externality or "physicality." When one decides within himself to give up a particular sin, that is one of the most consequential acts he could do. Reducing "acts" to the external is an almost Pharisaical way of looking at the human will and human responsibility.

Chapter Two

Fictional Dialogues on *Sola Scriptura* ("Bible Alone"), the Real Presence, and Penance

Sola Scriptura

Catholics accept Church authority and a reliable, divinely-protected Tradition, whereas Protestants ulimately "pick and choose" which traditions are to their own particular denominational taste. This is arbitrary in two ways:

1) There is really no cogent, non-arbitrary method for Protestants to determine which tradition is true (e.g., the New Testament Canon) and which is false (e.g., Marian doctrines);

2) The notion of authority in Protestant ecclesiology is inadequate for the task of proclaiming "authoritatively" which tradition is true, and the grounds will be circular in any event:

Protestant (P): X is a true, biblical doctrine because it is biblical.

Catholic (C): According to which denominational tradition?

P: Ours.

C: How do you know your tradition is true, and that others which contradict it are false?

P: Because we are the most biblical.

C: How do you know yours is the most biblical?

P: Because our exegesis is the most all-encompassing and consistent, and true to the clear teaching of Scripture.

C: But the other Protestant traditions claim the same superiority...

P: I must say in love that they are wrong.

C: How do you know they are wrong? Don't Protestants try to be tolerant of each other's "distinctives," especially in "secondary" issues? Yet you are calling fellow brothers in Christ "wrong."

P: I am compelled to because they have a faulty hermeneutic and exegesis, and I must stand firm for biblical truth.

C: How do you know they have a faulty method of interpretation?

P: By Scripture and linguistic study, and the consensus of scholarly commentaries.

C: But again, the others claim the same prerogative and abilities.

P: Then if they are wrong, they must be blinded by their presuppositional biases, or else by sin.

C: How do you know that?

P: Because they come to the wrong conclusions about the clearly-understood biblical data.

C: Frankly, I would say that that is circular reasoning. But, even granting your contention for the sake of argument, how does an uneducated seeker of Christian truth choose which denomination is true to the Bible?

P: The one which is most biblical...

C: Now, don't start that again [smiling]. They all claim that.

P: Well, then, the one which is apostolic and has roots in the early Church.

C: Then the Fathers must be studied in order to determine who has the early Church (apostolic) tradition?

P: Yes, I suppose so [frowning].

C: But what if it is found that the great majority of Fathers have an opinion on doctrine X contrary to yours?

P: Then they are wrong on that point.

C: How do you know that?

P: By studying Scripture.

C: So when all is said and done it is irrelevant what the early Church, or the Fathers, or the Church from 500 to 1500 believed?

P: Not totally, but I must judge their beliefs from Scripture.

C: Therefore you are—in the final analysis—the ultimate arbiter of true Christian Tradition?

P: Well, if you must put it in those blunt terms, yes.

C: Isn't that a bit arrogant?

P: Not as much as the pope and a bunch of celibate old men in red hats and dresses telling me what I should believe [scowling].

C: You make yourself the arbiter of all true Christian doctrine, down to the smallest particular, yet you object to a pope who makes an infallible pronouncement about every hundred years or so. Most remarkable and ironic! I say you are obviously a Super-Pope, then.

P: You can say that if you like. We call it the primacy of the individual conscience.

C: So you think that your own individual opinion and "conscience" is superior to the combined consensus of hundreds of years of Church history, papal pronouncements, apostolic Tradition, ecumenical councils, etc.?

P: Yes, because if a doctrine is biblical, I must denounce any tradition of men that is otherwise.

C: For that matter, how do you know what the Bible is?

P: Well, I'll quote from John Calvin: "Scripture is indeed self-authenticated; hence it is not right to subject it to proof and reasoning... Illumined by his power, we believe neither by our own nor by anyone else's judgment that Scripture is from God... We seek no proofs,... Such, then, is a conviction that requires no reasons... I speak of nothing other than what each believer experiences within himself."[1]

C: That seems intrinsically unreasonable, by Calvin's own stated criteria. Yet you've attempted to give me reasons and logic throughout this whole conversation!

P: Faith requires no reasons. The Holy Spirit makes it clear.

C: Well, that's a whole 'nother ball of wax. But I would say that you would not know what New Testament Scripture was for sure, if not for the Catholic Church. Calvin's criteria is essentially no different than the Mormons' "burning in the bosom" as a justification for their beliefs. Besides, on what grounds do you trust Calvin, when he contradicts earlier Church Tradition? Scripture is not self-authenticating, in the sense of its determining the extent and parameters of itself. This is clearly shown in the divergences in the early Church on the question of the New Testament Canon.

P: There was a broad consensus among the Fathers.

C: I'll grant you that... very broad. But there is more than enough difference to require an authoritative decree by the Church to put the matter to rest.

P: But God guided those Christians specifically because His Word was at stake.

C: Oh? First of all, I'm glad to hear that you acknowledge the 4th century Church as "Christians." Many Calvinists and other Protestants think the Church was already off the rails by then!

P: Well, that's silly, because Chalcedon was a good Council, and that was held in 451. So was Ephesus in 431.

C: Good. So you agree that God guided the early Church. But not in all matters?

P: No, not when they talked about the papacy, Mary, bishops, the Real Presence, communion of saints, penance, purgatory, infused justification, baptismal regeneration, confession, absolution, apostolic Tradition, apostolic succession, and many other erroneous doctrines.

---

[1] *Institutes of the Christian Religion*, Book I, chapter 7, section 5.

C: How do you know that?

P: Because those doctrines clearly aren't biblical.

C: According to which "clear" denominational tradition?

P: Ours...

C: [smacks forehead, then throws hands up and gazes toward the heavens, wincing in despair]

And so on and so forth...

The Real Presence of Christ in the Holy Eucharist

Thomas (Protestant): Hey Joe, how can you Catholics believe that the communion wafer actually turns into the Body and Blood of Christ? Do you expect me to accept that?!

Joe (Catholic): Because in this case, we are the ones who insist on taking the Bible literally. There is much to suggest the miracle we call Transubstantiation. For instance, in John 6:51-56, Jesus states five times that *whoever eats My flesh and drinks My blood has eternal life* (6:54).

Thomas: That's obviously symbolism. Jesus usually taught in parables, and He was often misunderstood, like when He said He would rebuild the Temple in three days (John 2:18-21).

Joe: Yes, Thomas, but when the Jews (John 6:52) and "many" of His disciples (6:60) objected, Christ merely restated His words forcefully, rather than assure them He wasn't speaking literally. He was so firm that many left Him (6:66). He could have easily prevented their confusion.

Thomas: One exception to the rule doesn't prove much.

Joe: It's not an exception. Jesus took great care to correct wrong impressions, when the hearers were open to receiving His words, such as in John 3:1-15, where Nicodemus didn't comprehend being "born again," and Matthew 16:5-12, concerning the "leaven of the Pharisees."

Dave Armstrong

Thomas: Hmmm. That's interesting. Do you know of any other examples where Jesus simply repeated an unpopular teaching?

Joe: Sure, like when Jesus talked about His power to forgive sins (Matthew 9:2-7), and His eternal existence (John 8:56-58). These are cases where He was talking with hostile listeners such as the Pharisees. Since Jesus knew everything, He knew who would reject His words and who would accept them, and acted accordingly. In John 6, then, it looks like the hearers understood full well what He was saying, but didn't want to accept it, rather than accepting it while misunderstanding that it was symbolic, as Protestants maintain.

Thomas: But why should we just accept something without explanation? Isn't that expecting too much? Why does the Catholic Church make people believe stuff without giving the reasons for them—often things that seem unreasonable in the first place? I don't want to be gullible.

Joe: You and many other former Catholics may have had some bad and ineffective teaching along the way, but this doesn't prove that the doctrines of the Catholic Church are false. Reasons have been given for all its doctrines, and theologians have worked on and developed these for centuries. With a little effort, you could have found books on this subject and others which would have provided you with very good reasoning. I've talked to many people like you who have never read a single book defending Catholicism. But on the other hand reason can only go so far. After all, there is a thing called faith, too. You need to stop doubting, Thomas [John 20:24-31]! Jesus performed enough miracles to be trusted for the difficult things He said, such as *This is My body* (Luke 22:19). The Real Presence is no less believable than the Resurrection, Virgin Birth, walking on water, or the Second Coming—all supernatural physical events.

Thomas: You make some good points, but what about Paul? He doesn't talk about trans... sub... What is it?

Joe: *Transubstantiation*. That's a 50 cent word which means, simply, "change of substance." I have to disagree about St. Paul. He sure seems to refer to some sort of Real Presence in 1 Corinthians 10:16 and 11:27, where he states that those taking communion... *unworthily, shall be guilty of the body and blood of the Lord*. Is a man guilty of someone's "body and blood" if he desecrates a photograph (symbol) of them? The early Church concurred. All the Fathers, such as St. Ignatius (d.c.110), St. Justin Martyr (d.c.150), and St. Irenaeus (d.c.202), strongly affirm the Real Presence.

In fact, Protestantism in the 16th century was the first Christian group of any historical and lasting importance to think differently. Even Martin Luther believed in the Real Presence and read others who differed with him on this out of the Church. It was Zwingli, primarily, who introduced this doctrine into Protestantism and "mainstream" Christianity. Many Protestants today, however, such as Lutherans and Anglicans, still uphold the Real Presence.

Thomas: But a piece of bread is really Christ!? What sense does that make? Isn't that going a little bit too far!

Joe: We believe the substance of the bread has changed, while the appearance ("accidents") of bread remains. There are some partial parallels: That glass in your hand has H2O in two forms or accidents—ice and water, but both have the same substance. The food we're eating changes both in terms of substance and accidents when it is digested. Transubstantiation is hard to imagine, but nothing is impossible with God.

Thomas: Well, I guess I do need to read and study further. I'm not yet convinced, but if so many Christians, as you say, have believed this way, I can't simply dismiss it as nonsense. That would be kind of arrogant. I'll have to think about it—you've really challenged me. See ya later, Joe!

Penance

Calvin (Protestant): You know, Joe, you Catholics ought to get rid of penance—punishing yourself to please God. Don't you know God has already forgiven you?

Joe (Catholic): We would, Calvin, if the Bible allowed us to, but it teaches that there is a penalty to pay for sin in this life, too. For instance, David had to suffer terribly even though God had forgiven his sin (2 Samuel 12:13-14).

Calvin: That's in the Old Testament, so it doesn't apply anymore. God is only merciful now.

Joe: That's just wishful thinking. In Malachi 3:3 God purifies His people "as gold and silver" to make them righteous. He hasn't changed His mind. In Hebrews 12:6-8 He still "chastens" and "scourges" his "sons." Jesus commands us to "take up a cross" if we want to follow Him (Matthew 10:38, 16:24), and St. Paul wants us to compassionately suffer with fellow Christians (1 Corinthians 12:26).

Calvin: Well, God can discipline us since that is His prerogative, but the Catholic Church acts like it can give out penalties. Isn't that an abuse of love and Scripture?

Joe: No, not at all, since the Lord Himself gave St. Peter and the disciples the power and authority to "bind and loose" (Matthew 16:19, 18:17-18). St. Paul imposes a penance for the well-being of a straying Christian (1 Corinthians 5:3-5). Later on, he issues an indulgence by lessening the temporal penance for sin of this same brother (2 Corinthians 2:6-11). This is all that the word "indulgence" means, despite all the rhetoric against it from Luther and Protestants ever since, absurdly implying that it winks at, or "indulges" sin!

Calvin: But Jesus suffered for us so we wouldn't have to, as it says in Isaiah 53:4-5.

Joe: He took away the penalty of eternal hellfire for those who obey His will and accept His work as our Redeemer, but not all suffering. That's a candy-coated gospel. In fact, in a sense, we even participate in this Redemption, by our intercessory prayers and penitential acts and suffering. St. Paul repeatedly speaks of suffering with Christ, almost in a literal fashion (Romans 8:17, 2 Corinthians 4:10, Philippians 3:10, and especially Colossians 1:24; cf. 1 Peter 4:1,13). He even considers himself an "offering" (2 Timothy 4:6; cf. Exodus 32:30-32).

Calvin: Man, you sure quote Scripture like a "Bible-thumping" Protestant! I've never seen a Catholic do that! I thought that all your doctrines were gullibly accepted on unquestioned authority and blind faith alone, from the nuns!

Joe: Well, I've gotten to know the biblical evidences for my beliefs because I've studied the Bible, Catholic catechisms and Catholic apologetic works, which give a biblical defense of Catholic doctrine, along with logical reasons and the history of Christian teaching on any given doctrine. Unfortunately, many Catholics settle for their childhood instruction in the faith and never progress or grow any further by reading and pursuing theological truth on their own.

Calvin: That's for sure, and many Protestants do the same. But on our subject, I still don't understand the purpose of penance. Why can't God just forgive and be done with it?

Joe: He could, but penance is for our benefit, due to our stubbornness and rebelliousness. Sin causes a disorder in the universe, and Justice requires that it be punished. You know, Calvin, even your own life is an illustration of this spiritual principle. You're in this jail, and have a broken arm and suspended driver's license due to the sin of drunk driving. This is your "penance," in a legal, secular sense.

Calvin: But I'm very sorry and the judge believes I'm sincere and will reform my behavior.

Joe: That's the whole point. You have "repented," but still a penalty must be paid for your own good and society's. Even though the judge likes you, he is bound by law to jail you for a time. That's how it is with God and sin, since He is perfectly holy. Purgatory continues the process after death, until finally we enter into Heaven, for which all our sufferings have prepared us (Romans 8:18, Hebrew 12:14, Revelation 21:4).

Calvin: I still have trouble with this whole idea because it seems to me to be perverting the grace of God and making us do works in order to be saved (Ephesians 2:8-9). That's a losing battle because none of us can be good enough (Psalms 53:3).

Joe: You're constructing a false dichotomy: Because God is perfectly good, therefore we cannot be good at all. But the Bible teaches that we can cooperate with God in our salvation, even though all grace and good always comes from Him (Ephesians 2:10, 1 Corinthians 3:9, Philippians 2:13). Grace is entirely God's work, but that doesn't make us mere puppets or robots. The Council of Trent declared that:

> Neither is this satisfaction so our own as not to be through Jesus Christ. For we can do nothing of ourselves; He cooperating strengthens us (Philippians 4:13)... No Catholic ever thought that, by this kind of satisfactions on our parts, the efficacy of the merit and of the satisfaction of our Lord Jesus Christ is either obscured or in any way lessened.[2]

---

[2] *On the Sacrament of Penance*, chapter 8, session 14, November 25, 1551.

Chapter Three

Is Catholicism Half-Pagan?

It is often stated that the Catholic church mingles pagan (pre-Christian Roman, Babylonian, Persian) practices and feasts into its worship and ways. First of all, one would have to define *pagan*. All of God's creation is good. For example, even one of God's greatest gifts, sexual intercourse, can be utterly immoral outside of marriage (fornication or adultery), but entirely sacred and righteous within marriage.

The same physical act (or "practice") can be good or evil depending on the circumstances and meaning given to it. Likewise with many pagan practices, if they are not objectively or inherently immoral in and of themselves (e.g., cannibalism would be wrong in any event).

Critics of the Catholic Church will claim that in the 4th century or so, many pagan rituals were incorporated into the Christian faith, such as genuflection, incense, and candles. But this is a case in point. There is nothing intrinsically wrong with candles (one had to have light at night somehow prior to electric light bulbs), incense (which represented prayer in Old Testament temple worship), or the submissive, venerating gesture of genuflection (after all, we make similar gestures to earthly kings and judges—even the innocent and quaint curtsey is a form of this, as is the oriental bow).

It matters not that some pagans may have used them in a sense foreign to Christianity. We can adopt them, give them a new meaning, and so "reclaim" them for God and the Church, because the key to true worship and religion is the *inner attitude* and disposition; the *heart* (see, e.g., Mark 7:6-8, among many other passages). The outward gestures merely represent whatever meaning we choose to give them (except for the sacraments, which work and dispense grace in and of themselves).

It is pointed out that the feasts of Christmas and Epiphany were intentionally derived from the pagan celebrations on those days. In a certain sense, this is true. The quickest way to get rid of an old pagan religious belief and festival is to incorporate its outward aspects, while not compromising any Christian belief in so doing.

Thus, the Church placed the feast day of Christmas on December 25th precisely because that was the date of the Roman feast of the Unconquered Sun, or *Sol Invictus* (it is now thought by many scholars that Jesus was actually born in October). Result?: *Sol Invictus* eventually went the way of the dinosaur. The Roman Feast of *Saturnalia*, which was held from December 1-23 also disappeared, having been superseded by Advent.

In this fashion paganism was historically defeated. And if some remaining customs have a similarity to pagan practices, it is not a matter of concern or compromise. No one even remembers the meaning of the old customs; the inner meaning is primary (or the application of the practice to Christmas, the Christ-child, etc.).

The pagans of northern Europe (like the ancient enemies of the Hebrews) perhaps used trees as idols; but *we* use the evergreen Christmas tree as a symbol of *everlasting life*: life in the dead of winter—just as Christ brought life to the deadness of humanity and the Fall and original sin. The tree itself is a neutral (and, I might add, beautiful) object: a part of God's good creation. To think otherwise is pure superstition.

Critics of the Catholic Church—when levying these charges—seem to neglect the crucial role of inner meaning and the heart. They view a crucifix or statue or Rosary beads as a talisman or a charm. We view them simply as aids to devotion to our Lord Jesus (an entirely different concept), just as Passover was a means of remembrance to the Jews for God's deliverance of them (Exodus 12:13-14). Many other similar biblical analogies could be brought forth also.

To some early Calvinists, church organs and stained glass windows—indeed statues of Christ Himself—were "clearly" idolatrous, so they smashed them. This is the ancient heresy known as *iconoclasm* (some historians have traced it back to the influence of Islam). Much of this thought (knowingly or not) stems from a quasi-Gnostic suspicion of God's creation as evil.

Even well-known Protestant Church historian Philip Schaff—no friend of the Catholic Church, and often a severe critic of it—, while deeply ambivalent about some of these "pagan customs," nevertheless sees the essential utility and "Christianness" of the Catholic Church's traditional approach to such things:

> This connection [to pagan Roman festivals] accounts for many customs of the Christmas season,... and gives them a Christian import; while it also betrays the origin of the many excesses in which the unbelieving world indulges in this season, in wanton perversion of the true Christmas mirth, but which, of course, no more forbid right use, than the abuses of the Bible or any other gift of God... Besides, there lurked in those pagan festivals themselves, in spite of all their sensual abuses, a deep meaning and an adaptation to a real want; they might be called unconscious prophecies of the Christmas feast. Finally, the church fathers themselves confirm the symbolical reference of the feast of the birth of Christ, the Sun of righteousness, the Light of the world, to the birth-festival of the unconquered sun, which on the 25th of December,

after the winter solstice, breaks the growing power of darkness, and begins anew his heroic career.[1]

The origin of Easter is similarly questioned. The etymological derivation of *Easter* is said to be uncertain. The Venerable Bede (c.673-735) thought it was connected to the Anglo-Saxon spring goddess *Eostre*.

If that is true, this is once again an incorporation of an old custom into Christianity ("Christianizing" or "baptizing" human custom) in order to supersede the old paganism and to give the rituals an entirely new meaning. A word is not evil in and of itself. Even sacred words usually have secular origins (e.g., the Greek *Christ* simply meant *anointed one*).

We observe the Apostle Paul "incorporating paganism" in a sense when he dialogues with the Greek intellectuals and philosophers on Mars Hill in Athens (Acts 17). He compliments their religiosity (17:22), and comments on a pagan *altar with the inscription, 'To an unknown god.'* (17:23). He then goes on to preach that this "unknown god" is indeed Yahweh, the God of the Old Testament and of the Jews (17:23-24).

Continuing his exposition, St. Paul expands upon the understanding of the true God as opposed to "shrines made by human hands" (17:24-25), and God as the Sovereign and Sustaining Creator (17:26-28). In doing so he cites two pagan poets and/or philosophers: Epimenides of Crete (whom he also cites in Titus 1:12) and Aratus of Cilicia (17:28) and expands upon their understanding as well (17:29).

This is basically the same thing that the Church does with regard to pagan feasts and customs: it takes whatever is not sinful and Christianizes it. This exhibits a great practical wisdom and a profound understanding of human nature.

The frequent critical assumption that this is a wholesale adoption of paganism per se, and an evil and diabolical mixture of idolatry and paganism with Christianity, is way off the mark. If that were true, the Apostle Paul is also clearly guilty of mixing paganism and Christianity. After all, it was Paul who stated,

> *To the weak I became weak, that I might win the weak. I have become all things to all men, that I might by all means save some.* (1 Corinthians 9:22; RSV—read the context of 9:19-21).

---

[1] *History of the Christian Church*, volume 3: *Nicene and Post-Nicene Christianity: A.D. 311-600*, Grand Rapids, MI: Eerdmans, 1974; reprint of the revised 5th edition of 1910, 396-397.

In my opinion, the Church's practice concerning Easter, Christmas, All Souls Day, All Saints Day, and other feasts, is a straightforward application of Paul's own "evangelistic strategy." That puts all this in quite a different light, and backed up explicitly from Scripture.

The early Church merely followed Paul's lead. Furthermore, skeptics of Christianity trace the Trinity itself to Babylonian three-headed gods and suchlike, and the resurrection of Christ to Mithraism or other pagan religious beliefs, but that doesn't stop the non-Catholic Christians who make the sort of complaints we have been examining from believing in the Triune God or the resurrection. So this whole critique eventually backfires on those who utilize it.

Chapter Four

Sin and Sinners in the Catholic Church: Disproof of its Ecclesiastical Authority?

Catholics believe in a visible, apostolic, institutional Church, as well as a Mystical Body. God already predicted that there would be *wheat* and *tares* in His Church, so that should not be surprising to anyone. Sin, even at high levels in the Church occasionally, should not surprise anyone, either. One would be foolish to expect otherwise in any human institution. What is indeed striking is how God has used the Catholic Church despite the corruption that has tended to come and go in cycles.

This brings to mind the wry comment about the non-Catholic man who went to Rome. His Catholic friend was worried to death about what he would find there—corrupt, immoral clergy, etc. But the man came back saying he was convinced of the truth of the Catholic Church. His Catholic friend was dumbfounded, and asked, "how could that be?" And the man answered, "God must be behind the Catholic Church, seeing the type of people who run it. Otherwise it would have died off hundreds of years ago."

The above story illustrates the Catholic attitude and approach very well. People will fail, but the Church will prevail, not because Catholics are better than anyone else (God knows that's no more true than it was true that the Jews were at all "superior' to their surrounding cultures), but because it is God's will that *the gates of hell shall not prevail against the Church* (Matthew 16:18).

Fortunately, today we have widespread literacy, communications, and now even the Internet, so there is less excuse for ignorance, disobedience, and heterodoxy than ever. It was also wrong to blindly depend on Fr. Doe without doing any study on one's own. This was the tendency in the years before the Second Vatican Council.

We are all ultimately responsible for our own spiritual development and walk with God—including proper instruction. God gave us minds and the ability to reason and separate the wheat from the chaff, doctrinally speaking. And He gave us the Holy Spirit. If anyone desires to know true Catholic teaching, he can obtain the new *Catechism*, or the Documents of Vatican II, or hit the worldwide web, or watch EWTN. There are any number of ways to do that. Anyone who can read can easily determine what the Catholic Church teaches.

The big mistake is to think that the present crisis in the Church disproves that the Catholic Church is what it claims to be. God only has us sinful, rebellious humans to work with. He has His work cut out for Him! Many bishops and priests have been lax in their duty (to put it very mildly). They will stand accountable before God. The Bible says, *let not many teach...* (James 3:1).

I have argued that one can never judge a communion (and its claimed "unity") by the actual views of its members, by polls and sociological surveys (as with American partisan politics today), because they will always fall short. If this is the proper method, certainly there is no Church on the earth, and none of us want to pessimistically conclude that. One will always find "heterodoxy" (as internally or externally defined) among the masses, so to speak, or the people in the pews, in any and every Christian group.

Jesus assumed this would always be the case, and spoke of it frequently (Matthew 13:24-30, cf. 3:12, Matthew 13:47-50, 22:1-14, 24:1-13, 25:14-30). St. Paul concurs (Acts 20:17,28,30, 2 Timothy 2:15-20). As usual, the biblical writers anticipate what would be a problem and a stumbling-block throughout Church history. Even Judas was regarded as a true apostle (Matthew 10:1,4, Mark 3:14, John 6:70-71, Acts 1:17).

Sinners (and dissenters) are in the Church, in the true Church. This is the biblical and apostolic teaching. The attainment of perfect moral purity is ultimately irrelevant with regard to the determination of which Church is divinely-established by Christ, even though dissent and corruption are, of course, troubling and scandalous of their own accord.

The Corinthian church did not cease to be part of the true universal Church, in St. Paul's mind (1 Corinthians 1:2, 2 Corinthians 1:1, 11:2), even when he was rebuking it for exceedingly serious and widespread sins (1 Corinthians 3:1-4, 5:1-2, 6:1-8, 11:17-22, 2 Corinthians 11:3-4). Nor was it said that there was no institutional Church because of the early controversy over the Judaizers, spoken of in the Book of Acts (see, e.g., Acts 15:5, which refers to believers who were Pharisees).

Such problems are always with us, and cannot be avoided, given original sin. Therefore, one can only go by the official teaching of any group (i.e., hopefully the passed-down equivalent of Paul's *gospel* or *tradition*: 1 Corinthians 11:2, 15:1-2, Galatians 1:9,12, 1 Thessalonians 2:13, 2 Thessalonians 2:15, 3:6, 1 Timothy 3:15, 2 Timothy 1:13-14, 2 Timothy 2:2, 2 Peter 2:21, Jude 3) and whether or not it institutionalizes and sanctions division and schism (not to mention various moral and doctrinal errors). The Catholic Church is inconsistently often criticized on the basis of dissent in *practice* within its ranks rather than by what it actually *teaches*, and has taught consistently, through the ages.

The biblical support for the concept of a Church containing sinners (even very many sinners) within it, yet remaining a true Church, is abundant (New Revised Standard Version):

1) The parable of the wheat and tares (Matthew 13:24-30, 36-43) reads as if the tares (weeds) are at least equal in number to the wheat. A moment's reflection on the proliferation of uncontrolled weeds (13:30) in any lawn will bring this point home! This is also apparent in the similar pronouncements about wheat and chaff (Matthew 3:12, Luke 3:17): a parable of the saved and the damned.

Since every wheat plant has chaff, too (the worthless part of it), then it would seem that we are talking about a 50/50 proposition. I wouldn't push the analogy too far, as the proportion is not the essential aspect of it, but it does lend itself to an interpretation that the non-believers and dissenters mixed in with the elect and orthodox will be many, not few.

2) Matthew 24:10 states that *many will fall away*. We are not given percentages.
3) Matthew 7:21-23 seems to imply that there are many counterfeit believers, since even some of those who *prophesy, cast out demons,* and *do many deeds of power* in Jesus' name will be cast from Jesus' presence at the Judgment, and He will say to them, *I never knew you; go away from me, you evildoers*. Since most of us are doing far less than acts of this magnitude (which outwardly suggest a commitment to Christ), it stands to reason that there are many people who go to Mass, etc., who will not be saved, and hence are *tares*. Cf. Luke 13:25-28.
4) Jesus also said, *when the Son of Man comes, will he find faith on earth?* (Luke 18:8). This doesn't present a very rosey picture about great numbers of faithful, or elect.
5) *Jesus said many are called, but few are chosen* (Matthew 22:14).
6) *For the gate is narrow and the road is hard that leads to life, and there are few who find it.* (Matthew 7:14).
7) *... The harvest is plentiful, but the laborers are few.* (Matthew 9:37).
8) *Someone asked him, 'Lord, will only a few be saved?' He said to them, 'Strive to enter through the narrow door; for many, I tell you, will try to enter and will not be able.'* (Luke 13:23-24)
9) A straightforward reading of Paul's chastisement of the Corinthians lends itself to the view that these problems were massive: definitely a majority of the believers there, if not a near-unanimity. This church had some heavy-duty problems!:

   a) His rebuke concerning their divisiveness (1 Corinthians 3:1-4) seems to be directed at the group as a whole, not just a few.

b) The incest spoken of in 5:1-2 was of one man, yet the whole body is rebuked for not having *mourned* that, and for failing to *remove* the incorrigible sinner.
c) Likewise concerning bringing lawsuits into the secular arena. Paul writes,... *Can it be that there is no one among you wise enough to decide between one believer and another...?* (1 Corinthians 6:5).
d) Likewise with divisions and abuses of the Lord's Supper (... *each of you...*—1 Corinthians 11:21). This is a general rebuke, directed towards practically all the members, not a dissenting minority.
e) Finally, in 2 Corinthians 11:4, Paul speaks of the church as a whole being prone to chasing after false teachers. This leads him into his famous "boasting" discourse. He is touting his own qualifications as an apostle so that they won't go running after false apostles and deceivers, and will keep to the true path (2 Corinthians 12:20-21).

So we see that in each example with regard to the Corinthians, Paul's rebukes are very broad and give no hint that such problems are only affecting a tiny minority.

10) Jesus Himself rebukes six of the seven churches of Asia He addresses. Most scholars think that the Book of Revelation was written no later than 100 A.D. Yet look at all the serious problems we already observe in these apostolic churches, before the last apostle (John) died:

a) The church at *Ephesus abandoned the love* [they] *had at first* (Rev 2:4), and is urged (corporately) to repent, lest its *lampstand* be removed (2:5).
b) Pergamum was accused of idolatry and fornication: *the teaching of Balaam* (2:14) and for allowing some of their ranks to adopt the Nicolaitan heresy (2:15). *Nicolas* is the Greek equivalent of *Balaam*.
c) Thyatira is also accused of idolatry and fornication (2:20-23).
d) Sardis is rebuked as spiritually dead (3:1-3), but Jesus says *yet you have still a few persons in Sardis who have not soiled their clothes; they will walk with me, dressed in white, for they are worthy.* (3:4). Even so, Jesus calls this group *the church in Sardis* (3:1), just as He refers to all seven as *churches*.
e) Philadelphia had *but little power* (3:8).
f) Laodicea *was lukewarm,... wretched, pitiable, poor, blind, and naked* (3:15-18).

This is not a pretty picture at all. Only Smyrna escapes a stern, sweeping rebuke of Jesus. But this is what God has to work with. The Church then, as now, was riddled with problems: hypocrisy, lukewarmness, heterodoxy, fornication, idolatry; much was "pitiable." Nothing has changed. Sinners are in the Church because we all are prone to sin, as fallen creatures. This should surprise no one.

11) The Apostle Paul has very stern words for the Galatian church as well. None of these congregations "had it all together" spiritually (not even close), as many today seem to arrogantly believe about their own particular fellowships. Again, nothing has changed. The Puritan notion of a "pure" church or denomination is a myth if ever there was one. And it is unbiblical, if the examples of apostolic churches prove anything.

   a) *I am astonished that you are so quickly deserting the one who called you in the grace of Christ and are turning to a different gospel.* (Galatians 1:6)
   b) *You foolish Galatians! Who has bewitched you?... Are you so foolish? Having started with the Spirit, are you now ending with the flesh? Did you experience so much for nothing?...* (3:1,3-4)
   c) *Now... that you have come to know God, or rather to be known by God, how can you turn back again to the weak and beggarly elemental spirits? How can you want to be enslaved to them again?... I am afraid that my work for you may have been wasted.* (4:9,11)
   d) *Have I now become your enemy by telling you the truth?... I am perplexed about you.* (4:16,20)
   e) *For freedom Christ has set us free. Stand firm, therefore, and do not submit again to a yoke of slavery. Listen! I, Paul, am telling you that if you let yourselves be circumcised, Christ will be of no benefit to you... You who want to be justified by the law have cut yourselves off from Christ; you have fallen away from grace.* (5:1-2,4)
   f) *You were running well; who prevented you from obeying the truth?* (5:7)

The above view is anchored in reality: Scripture, Church history, and reason (as well as original sin and the resultant fallenness of human beings). God used Balaam's ass to convey His truth, and a murderer and adulterer to make an eternal covenant with (David) and another murderer to be the foremost apostle (Paul), and a wavering wimp to lead His Church (Peter). Of course it is preferable for the Catholic Church and all its members to be perfectly holy, but this is the real world.

Sin does not rule out the possibility of a true Church. And no one needs to drive a wedge between Jesus and His ordained structure of the Church. The truth is to be believed even if one person in the world believes it. And sometimes the reality gets close to that (*Athanasius contra mundum*).

The good things in Protestantism still can be (and are) affirmed by the Catholic Church. It's not an *either/or* proposition when it comes down to individual beneficial spiritual acts and beliefs. But when one discusses what the one "Church" is, we must draw the line and state that it is the Catholic Church, because of apostolic succession, and because it is the only plausible choice which possesses the four marks of the Church (from the Nicene Creed) in their undiluted fullness.

Chapter Five

Denominationalism and Sectarianism

Jesus' prayer of unity in John 17 refers to a unity both of love and of doctrine. Love is the primary thrust. But we must not discount the implicit doctrinal oneness which our Lord also commands. In John 17:22 Jesus prays that the disciples would be *one, as we are one*. And in 17:23, He prays that Christians (like the Father and the Son) would be *completely one* (NRSV). KJV, NKJV: *perfect in one*. RSV, NEB, REB: *perfectly one*. NIV: *complete unity*. NASB: *perfected in unity*.

Now, it is pretty difficult to maintain that this entails no **doctrinal** agreement (and "perfect" agreement at that). And, reflecting on John 17:22, obviously the Father and the Son do not differ on how one is saved, on the true nature of the Eucharist or the Church, etc. They don't disagree about *anything*.

Likewise, St. Paul commands: *mark them which cause divisions and offences contrary to the **doctrine** [Gk., didache] ye have learned; and avoid them*. (Romans 16:17). In 1 Corinthians 1:10, he desires *no divisions*, and that Christians should be *perfectly joined together in the same mind*. No one can say this is simply a "warm fuzzy" love and mutual recognition.

Paul goes on to condemn even mere *contentions* in 1:11, and asks in 1:13: *Is Christ divided?* In 1 Corinthians 3:3, Paul says that a group experiencing *strife and divisions* is *carnal, and walk as men*. In 1 Corinthians 11:18-19 he seems to equate *divisions* and *heresies*. He calls for *no schism* in 1 Corinthians 12:25, etc., etc. (cf. Romans 13:13, 2 Corinthians 12:20, Philippians 2:2, Titus 3:9, James 3:16, 1 Timothy 6:3-5, 2 Peter 2:1).

In an online discussion, a Protestant friend stated that "heresy in the modern sense of the word is absolutely foreign to the context of 1 Corinthians 11:18-19." That passage reads:

> *For, in the first place, when you assemble as a church, I hear that there are divisions among you; and I partly believe it, for there must be factions among you in order that those who are genuine among you may be recognized.* (RSV)

Renowned Protestant Greek scholar Marvin Vincent, in his famous work, *Word Studies in the New Testament*, disagrees with that assessment, in commenting on this biblical text. He sends the reader to his comment on 2 Peter 2:1, which even my dialogue partner admitted was referring to "dogma." There he writes:

A heresy is, strictly, the choice of an opinion contrary to that usually received; thence transferred to the body of those who profess such opinions, and therefore a 'sect.'... commonly in this sense in the NT (Acts 5:17; 15:5; 28:22)... See Acts 24:14; 1 Corinthians 1:19; Galatians 5:20. The rendering 'heretical doctrines' seems to agree better with the context; false teachers bringing in 'sects' is awkward.[1]

H. Richard Niebuhr, a prominent Lutheran scholar and author, lamented that "Denominationalism... represents the accommodation of Christianity to the caste-system of human society."[2]

I readily grant that there is (very broadly speaking) a "mere Christianity" type of unity in Protestantism, but why should anyone accept this "lowest common denominator" unity? We should seek after all the truth and nothing but the truth. Jesus in His prayer at the Last Supper, in John 17, demands nothing less.

Why should any Christian tolerate error? We know that it *must* be present, by logical necessity, wherever one or more groups contradict one another in their doctrinal teaching. *Where* the falsehoods are located might be argued about, but *that* they are present where contradiction exists is inescapable.

Both Martin Luther and John Calvin fully recognized the scandalous nature of sectarianism. The latter wrote in a letter to Luther's cohort and successor Philip Melanchthon:

> ... But it greatly concerns us to cherish faithfully and constantly to the end the friendship which God has sanctified by the authority of his own name, seeing that herein is involved either great advantage or great loss even to the whole Church. For you see how the eyes of many are turned upon us, so that the wicked take occasion from our dissensions to speak evil, and the weak are only perplexed by our unintelligible disputations. **Nor in truth, is it of little importance to *prevent the suspicion* of any difference having arisen between us from being handed down in any way to posterity; for it is worse than absurd that parties should be found disagreeing on the very principles, after we have been compelled to make our departure from the world.** I

---

[1] Grand Rapids, MI: Eerdmans Publishing Co., 1946 reprint of the 1886 set by Charles Scribner's Sons, vol.1, 689.
[2] *The Social Sources of Denominationalism*, New York: Meridian Books, 1929, 6, 21. See also, Donald Bloesch, *The Future of Evangelical Christianity*, Garden City, NY: Doubleday, 1983, 56-57, 65.

know and confess, moreover, that we occupy widely different positions; still, because I am not ignorant of the place in his theatre to which God has elevated, there is no reason for my concealing that our friendship could not be interrupted without great injury to the Church...

And surely it is indicative of a marvellous and monstrous insensibility, that we so readily set at nought that sacred unanimity, by which we ought to be bringing back into the world the angels of heaven. Meanwhile, Satan is busy scattering here and there the seeds of discord, and our folly is made to supply much material. At length he has discovered fans of his own, for fanning into a flame the fires of discord. I shall refer to what happened to us in this Church, causing extreme pain to all the godly; and now a whole year has elapsed since we were engaged in these conflicts...[3]

Melanchthon replied: "All the waters of the Elbe would not yield me tears sufficient to weep for the miseries caused by the Reformation."[4] He also wrote elsewhere: "I am unable to suggest anything that could heal this anarchy."[5] And:

I am extremely afflicted by the universal trouble of the Church. Had Christ not promised to be with us until the end of the world, I should fear lest religion be totally destroyed by these dissensions."[6]

Luther complained with dripping disdain: "There are nowadays almost as many sects and creeds as there are heads."[7]

---

[3] Letter CCCV (305), written to Philip Melanchthon on 28 November 1552. From: *Selected Works of John Calvin: Tracts and Letters: Letters, Part 2, 1545-1553*, vol. 5 of 7; edited by Jules Bonnet, translated by David Constable; Grand Rapids: Baker Book House (a Protestant publisher), 1983, 375-381; reproduction of *Letters of John Calvin*, vol. 2 (Philadelphia: Presbyterian Board of Publication, 1858). Emphasis and italics added.

[4] in Stoddard, John L., *Rebuilding a Lost Faith*, New York: P.J. Kenedy & Sons, 1922, 88 / Epistles, Book 4, Ep. 100.

[5] Bretschneider, ed., *Corpus Reformation*, Halle, 1846, vol. 8, 504 / Letter to Hardenburg, c.1558. In Janssen, Johannes, *History of the German People From the Close of the Middle Ages*, 16 vols., tr. A.M. Christie, St. Louis: B. Herder, 1910 (originally 1891), vol. 7, 140.

[6] In Daniel-Rops, Henri, *The Protestant Reformation*, vol. 2, tr. Audrey Butler, Garden City, NY: Doubleday Image, 1961, 86.

[7] In Durant, Will, *The Reformation*, (vol. 6 of 10-volume *The Story of Civilization*, 1967), New York: Simon & Schuster, 1957, 441.

The founders of Protestantism, therefore, were quite aware of the scandalous nature of denominationalism and sectarianism. But—sadly—this awareness seems to have been lost among many (but not all) of their legatees today.

Rather than seek doctrinal unity, many non-Catholic Christians today take the view that divisions and disagreements in "secondary matters"—as opposed to "central" doctrines—are not only *permissible* but *healthy* and to be *expected* (whereas the early Protestants were willing to *fight* and *die* for their particular theological points of view). Such a quasi-relativistic view is utterly unbiblical, as demonstrated above.

Chapter Six

Catholicism is Neither Pelagian Nor Semi-Pelagian (The Nature and Extent of Human Effort in Salvation)

The Second Council of Orange (529 A.D.), accepted as dogma by the Catholic Church, stated in its Canon 7:

> If anyone asserts that we can, by our natural powers, think as we ought, or choose any good pertaining to the salvation of eternal life... without the illumination and inspiration of the Holy Spirit... he is misled by a heretical spirit... [the canon later cites John 15:5, 2 Corinthians 3:5]

Likewise, the ecumenical Council of Trent (1545-63): Chapter 5, *Decree on Justification*:

> ... Man... is not able, by his own free-will, without the grace of God, to move himself unto justice in His sight.

Canon I on Justification:

> If anyone saith that man may be justified before God by his own works, whether done through the teaching of human nature or that of the law, without the grace of God through Jesus Christ; let him be anathema.

There is no disagreement (as some Protestants maintain) between the two councils whatsoever. Orange was reacting against Pelagianism and Semi-Pelagianism, and so emphasized God's enabling and totally necessary preceding grace for salvation. Trent had to deal with the Protestant utter rejection of human free will and cooperation with God for the sake of salvation, and so emphasized the validity and necessity of free will and cooperative works, yet wholly derived from grace.

Councils are always opposing the prevalent heresy in the age immediately preceding them. Nicaea defined the Trinity over against the Arians, Ephesus the title *Theotokos* (*Mother of God*) in opposition to Nestorius, Constantinople I the Divinity of the Holy Spirit, in rejection of Macedonianism, Chalcedon the Two Natures of Christ, contrary to the Monophysites, etc.

Semi-Pelagianism is defined by the non-Catholic *Oxford Dictionary of the Christian Church*[1] as follows:

> [Semi-Pelagianism], while not denying the necessity of Grace for salvation, maintained that the first steps towards the Christian life were ordinarily taken by the human will and that Grace supervened only later.

The *Encyclopedia Britannica*[2] states:

> The result of Semi-Pelagianism, however, was the denial of the necessity of God's unmerited, supernatural, gracious empowering of man's will for saving action... From [529]... Semi-Pelagianism was recognized as a heresy in the Roman Catholic Church.

It is impossible to harmonize the two canons from Trent above with the definition of Semi-Pelagianism from these two non-Catholic sources (assuming the definitions are correct). The existence of a measure of human free will in order for man to cooperate with God's grace does not reduce inevitably and necessarily to Semi-Pelagianism, as Luther, Calvin, and present-day Calvinists wrongly charge.

The Catholic view is a third way. Our "meritorious actions" are always necessarily *preceded* and *caused* and *crowned* and *bathed* in God's enabling grace. Yet this doesn't wipe out our cooperation, which is not intrinsically meritorious in the sense that it derives from us and not God. In order to fully understand this, we must briefly examine the Catholic notion of merit:

Second Orange again:

> The reward given for good works is not won by reason of actions which precede grace, but grace, which is unmerited, precedes actions in order that they may be accomplished meritoriously.

This is not Semi-Pelagianism, and Protestants admit that Orange was not a Semi-Pelagian council by placing it in alleged opposition to Trent. Yet this is the identical teaching of Trent, and not contrary at all to the notion of God-originated grace.

St. Augustine wrote:

---

[1] edited by F.L. Cross, Oxford Univ. Press, revised edition of 1983, 1258.
[2] 1985 edition, vol. 10, 625.

What merit of man is there before grace by which he can achieve grace, as only grace works every one of our good merits in us, and as God, when He crowns our merits, crowns nothing else but His own gifts?[3]

And again:

The Lord has made Himself a debtor, not by receiving, but by promising. Man cannot say to Him, "Give back what thou hast received" but only "Give what thou hast promised." [4]

The concept of merit and its corollary reward is well-supported in Scripture: Matthew 5:12, 19:17,21,29, 25:21, 25:34 ff., Luke 6:38, Romans 2:6, 1 Corinthians 3:8, 9:17, Colossians 3:24, Hebrews 6:10, 10:35, 11:6, 2 Timothy 4:8, Ephesians 6:8.

Trent must be understood in this light, and nothing in it contradicts the Second Council of Orange, Scripture, or the doctrine of all grace as originating from God, not man. Thus, neither the Council of Trent nor Catholicism are Pelagian or Semi-Pelagian.

The "central point" in the definition of Pelagianism or Semi-Pelagianism is human free will (or ability) over against or separate from the utter causal primacy of divine grace for all good human actions. Catholics and Orthodox (and Arminian Protestants) think the primacy of grace and human free will can work together harmoniously without contradiction and without implying a "first step" on man's part at all.

Calvinists, on the other hand, apparently believe that even cooperation is anathema in a certain sense, but nevertheless, speak of "free agency." As pertains human will and action, this is largely a distinction without a difference.

In other words, the two systems work out the same in this respect, for all practical purposes. When all is said and done, all Christians must make a profession of faith in Jesus, and His work on the Cross for us. We must follow Him, and live morally upright lives, including works, which we are commanded to do.

Many Protestants separate the works from justification and classify them under "sanctification." We make no such distinction. But both sides agree in the sense that these works are absolutely necessary, whether they are meritorious, or flow from gratefulness to God, or both. Theology ought to always be related to some practical application, which is the more biblical approach to things.

---

[3] Ep. 194,5,19.
[4] Enarr. in Ps 83,16.

One must also make a distinction between Total Depravity and Total Inability. Calvinists accept the former and believe man acquired a "sin nature" after the Fall. The rest of us (I'm not sure about *all* Arminians) do not take the view that man was rendered absolutely, essentially evil at the Fall (at least not after baptism, at any rate).

But cooperating with God by virtue of preceding grace is not Semi-Pelagianism. If so, then Arminian Protestants are Semi-Pelagians, as well as Catholics and Orthodox. There is no need to go to the extreme lengths of asserting that man can do absolutely nothing with regard to his salvation. After all, God has "implanted" His image in us.

Arminianism derives, classically, from the Remonstrance of 1610, a codification of the teachings of Jacob Arminius (1559-1609). Here are the 3rd and 4th articles of five (emphasis added):

III. That man **has not saving grace of himself**, nor of the working of his own free-will, inasmuch **as in his state of apostasy and sin he can for himself and by himself think nothing that is good**—nothing, that is, truly good, such as saving faith is, above all else. But that **it is necessary that by God, in Christ and through his Holy Spirit he be born again** and renewed in understanding, affections and will and in all his faculties, that he may be able to understand, think, will, and perform what is truly good, according to the Word of God [John 15:5].

IV. **That this grace of God is the beginning, the progress and the end of all good; so that even the regenerate man can neither think, will nor effect any good, nor withstand any temptation to evil, without grace precedent (or prevenient), awakening, following and co-operating.** So that all good deeds and all movements towards good that can be conceived in through must be ascribed to the grace of God in Christ. But with respect to the mode of operation, grace is not irresistible; for it is written of many that they resisted the Holy Spirit [Acts 7 and elsewhere passim].

Much more documentation from the many Arminian denominations could easily be produced. But two shall suffice at this point. John Wesley and the Methodists have long been a target of Calvinist theological suspicion. Wesley's *Twenty-Five Articles of Religion* (1784), considered normative for Methodists, states in its Article VIII ("Of Free Will" - virtually the same as Article X of the Anglican *Thirty-Nine Articles*); emphasis added:

> The condition of man after the fall of Adam is such that **he can not turn and prepare himself, by his own natural strength and works, to faith and calling upon God;** wherefore we have no power to do good works, pleasant and acceptable to God, without the grace of God by Christ preventing us, that we may have a good will, and working with us, when we have that good will. [5]

Likewise, in the Lutheran *Formula of Concord* (1580), the distinction between Melanchthonian Arminianism and semi-Pelagianism could not have been more clearly stated (emphasis added):

> **We also reject the error of the Semi-Pelagians** who teach that man by virtue of his own powers could make a beginning of his conversion but could not complete it without the grace of the Holy Spirit. [6]

All of these non-Calvinist viewpoints, pertaining to the relationship of grace and free will, whether classic Protestant Arminian or Catholic, are quite essentially different from Semi-Pelagianism. The often-stated contrary charge is, therefore, groundless.

---

[5] In *Creeds of the Churches*, ed. John H. Leith, Garden City: NY: Doubleday Anchor, 1963, 356.
[6] Part I: Epitome, Article II: *Free Will, Antitheses: Contrary False Doctrine*, section 3; cf. Solid Declaration, Article II: *Free Will*, error #2: "coarse Pelagians."

Chapter Seven

"Is This God?": Biblical and Philosophical Reflections on the Blessed Eucharist [1]

I held aloft with both my hands the golden chalice, gazing upwards at it, performing one of the central liturgical rituals of the Mass, in which the consecration of the wine takes place. My attitude, however, was not one of reverence or solemnity. I possessed neither the eyes of faith, nor the traditional Christian understanding of the Blessed Eucharist.

I was not standing at an altar, let alone in a church. My friend and frequent evangelistic partner, nearby, was neither kneeling, nor bowing his head, nor crossing himself. He was chuckling, and I myself had a mocking, sarcastic scowl, as I wore a makeshift priestly robe, looking as ridiculous as the cowardly lion in The Wizard of Oz, in his "king's robe."

For I was not a priest, or ordained clergyman of any sort. I was a non-denominational evangelical Protestant lay missionary, and my former Catholic friend and I were making light of the gestures and rituals of a priest as he performs the Mass. This was in the late 1980s, several years away from my own surprising conversion to Catholicism, in 1990.

I still have the shameful photograph of this mock liturgy—taken by my friend. It remains an absurd testament to my former rather dim comprehension of liturgy and sacramentalism—as well as a certain adolescent silliness when it came to Things Catholic.

The interesting thing to ponder in retrospect is the question of how I—a serious evangelical Christian, who had a well above average knowledge of, and appreciation for, Church history—could have had such an insufficient understanding of the Holy Eucharist: the central focus of Christian worship for 1500 years up to the advent of Protestantism?

How is it that I could somehow manage to regard liturgy itself as a stale, boring, non-essential "extra" which was by no means necessary to Christian communal fellowship?

Despite this (which makes it fascinating to think about now), I actually had a fairly high respect—relatively speaking—for the Lord's Supper, or Holy Communion, or Holy Eucharist. My belief was somewhat akin to John Calvin's "mystical presence," which was a "step higher" than the purely symbolic view

---

[1] A version of this essay was published as the cover story in *Envoy Magazine*, Jan/Feb 2000 issue.

which many Protestants today hold. Nor did I for a moment believe that what was taking place at the Last Supper was *merely* empty ritual, or its re-creation a bare "remembrance."

Furthermore, I wasn't "anti-Catholic" in the sense that I would ever have denied that the Catholic Church was Christian, or that it had commendably preserved the Bible and what I then called "central Christian doctrine" throughout all the centuries prior to the 16th.

To understand how such an odd state of affairs could happen at all requires one to delve a bit into past Church history, especially the course of Protestant doctrinal history. My friend and I—as is characteristic of so many non-Catholics—thought, in the final analysis, that the Eucharist was an accretion, an optional part of the Church service, because we were simply being good evangelical low-church Protestants (albeit without much reflection on this particular point).

Most Protestant denominations have elevated the sermon to the primary position and climax of the Sunday service. Everything builds up to it. For many attendees (including, formerly, myself—very much so), the sermon was the thing to look forward to, and the drawing card (especially if one's particular pastor was especially skilled at oratory and homiletics). It was the means by which one got "fired up," exhorted, and charged to go out and make a difference in the world, as a Christian disciple (things which aren't bad, in and of themselves).

I should stress that I still appreciate a good sermon (including many non-Catholic ones), and I wish more stirring preaching could be had in the Catholic Church. But much of Protestantism has transformed church almost exclusively into a prolonged liturgy of the Word—that is, the first half of the Catholic Mass—, with usually far less actual Bible reading, and a sermon many times longer than the average ten-minute Catholic homily. I speak mainly of low-church evangelicalism, but it is not too far-fetched to apply this observation to Protestantism as a whole.

Behind this sort of thinking lies an antipathy to sacramentalism itself, in which it is held that matter can convey grace. Accordingly, Protestants who place less emphasis on the Eucharist tend to also regard baptism as basically a symbolic ritual also, without the regenerating power which Catholics believe it inherently possesses. And we must ask ourselves why this is; how vast portions of Christianity can today deny what was accepted without question by virtually all Christians right up to the time of Martin Luther (who also retained the doctrine of the Real Presence in slightly-diluted form, and baptismal regeneration as well)?

The first Christian leader of any consequence and lasting historical importance and influence to deny the Real Presence was Huldreich Zwingli (1484-1531), the Swiss Protestant "Reformer." He dissented from not only received Catholic doctrine, but also from the Lutheran doctrine of consubstantiation, which gained him Martin Luther's considerable hostility and inveterate opposition (the Founder of Protestantism regarded him as "damned" and "out of the Church" for precisely this reason).

We shall briefly examine some of the rationale Zwingli gives for adopting this novel, radical position, which set the tone for all subsequent Protestant symbolic viewpoints:

> A sacrament is the sign of a holy thing. When I say: The sacrament of the Lord's body, I am simply referring to that bread which is the symbol of the body of Christ who was put to death for our sakes. The papists all know perfectly well that the word sacrament means a sign and nothing more, for this is the sense in which it has always been used by Christian doctors... the sign and the thing signified cannot be one and the same. Therefore the sacrament of the body of Christ cannot be the body itself. [2]

First of all, it is simply untrue that Christian doctors "always" denied the "reality" aspect of the sacraments, particularly concerning the Eucharist. This matter is so well-documented as to seriously bring into question Zwingli's credibility as a student of Christian doctrinal history. Literally hundreds of counter-examples could be brought forth, but suffice it to say that the evidence for the Real Presence in the Eucharist in the Church Fathers is among the most compelling of any of the doctrines or dogmas which Protestants now dispute. As proof of this, I shall cite just one standard Protestant reference work, *The Oxford Dictionary of the Christian Church* [3]:

> That the Eucharist conveyed to the believer the Body and Blood of Christ was universally accepted from the first, and language was very commonly used which referred to the Eucharistic elements as themselves the Body and Blood... From the fourth century, the language about the transformation of the elements began to become general... The first controversies on the nature of the Eucharistic Presence date from the earlier Middle Ages.

---

[2] *On the Lord's Supper*, 1526, translated by G.W. Bromiley; in *Zwingli and Bullinger*, edited, with introductions and notes, by G.W. Bromiley, Philadelphia: Westminster Press, 1953, 176-238; this excerpt is from p. 188.

[3] Second edition, edited by F.L. Cross and E.A. Livingstone, Oxford University Press, 1983, 475-476: "Eucharist".

Secondly, "sign" and "reality" need not be opposed to each other. Later in his essay Zwingli attempts to enlist St. Augustine as espousing his views, by exploiting this false dichotomy. But Augustine accepted the Real Presence as well as a conception of the Eucharist in which it is also a "sign" (just as the Catholic Church does today). In popular terms, this argument doesn't fly!

The Bible itself confirms this. For example, Jesus refers to the *sign of Jonah*, comparing Jonah's time in the belly of the fish to His own burial (Matthew 12:38-40). In other words, both events, although described as "signs," were literally real events. Jesus also uses the same terminology in connection with His Second Coming (Matthew 24:30-31), which is, of course, believed by all Christians to be a literal, not a symbolic occurrence. [4]

Zwingli gets down to brass tacks in the following blast against Catholic eucharistic doctrine, and it is here where I believe we begin to clearly see the philosophical and skeptical roots of his false belief:

> The manna which came down from heaven was of the same size and shape as coriander seed, but its taste was quite different. Here the case is otherwise, for what we see and what we taste are exactly the same, bread and wine. And how can we say that it is flesh when we do not perceive it to be such? If the body were there miraculously, the bread would not be bread, but we should perceive it to be flesh. Since, however, we see and perceive bread, it is evident that we are ascribing to God a miracle which he himself neither wills nor approves: for he does not work miracles which cannot be perceived. [5]

I answer Zwingli as follows:

The Eucharist was intended by God as a different kind of miracle from the outset, requiring more profound faith, as opposed to the "proof" of tangible, empirical miracles. But in this it was certainly not unique among Christian doctrines and traditional beliefs—many fully shared by our Protestant brethren. The Virgin Birth, for example, cannot be observed or proven, and is the utter

---

[4] J.N.D. Kelly, a highly-respected Protestant scholar of early Church doctrine and development, writing about patristic views in the fourth and fifth centuries, concurs with this judgment, in his *Early Christian Doctrines*, revised edition, 1978, San Francisco: Harper Collins, p. 442, and about St. Augustine in particular: pp. 446-447. See also, Cross, *ibid.*, 475, and my online paper, *History of the Doctrine of the Eucharist: Nine Protestant Scholarly Sources*, located on my website at: http://ic.net/~erasmus/RAZ459.HTM.

[5] In Bromiley, *ibid.*, 196.

opposite of a demonstrable miracle, yet it is indeed a miracle of the most extraordinary sort.

Likewise, in the Atonement of Jesus the world sees a wretch of a beaten and tortured man being put to death on a cross. The Christian, on the other hand, sees there the great miracle of Redemption and the means of the salvation of mankind—an unspeakably sublime miracle, yet who but those with the eyes of faith can see or believe it? In fact, the disciples (with the possible exception of St. John, the only one present) didn't even know what was happening at the time.

Baptism, according to most Christians, imparts real grace of some sort to those who receive it. But this is rarely evident or tangible, especially in infants. Lastly, the Incarnation itself was not able to be perceived as an outward miracle, though it might be considered the most incredible miracle ever. Jesus appeared as a man like any other man. He ate, drank, slept, had to wash, experienced emotion, suffered, etc. He performed miracles and foretold the future, and ultimately raised Himself from the dead, and ascended into heaven in full view, but the Incarnation—strictly viewed in and of itself—, was not visible or manifest in the tangible, concrete way to which Herr Zwingli seems to foolishly think God would or must restrict Himself.

To summarize, Jesus looked, felt, and sounded like a man; no one but those possessing faith would know (from simply observing Him) that He was also God, an uncreated Person who had made everything upon which He stood, who was the Sovereign and Judge of every man with whom He came in contact (and also of those He never met). Therefore, Zwingli's argument proves too much and must be rejected. If the Eucharist is abolished by this supposed "biblical reasoning," then the Incarnation (and by implication, the Trinity) must be discarded along with it.

Besides all that, did not Jesus habitually call us on to a more sublime faith? For instance, in Matthew 12:38-39, Jesus had one of His frequent run-ins with the Pharisees, who requested of Him:

> *Teacher, we wish to see a sign from you.' But he answered them, 'An evil and adulterous generation asks for a sign, but no sign will be given to it except the sign of the prophet Jonah.'*

(cf. Matthew 16:1-4, Luke 11:29-30, John 2:18-22; NRSV)

Note that He does implicitly appeal to the sign of His Resurrection, but look how He regards the seeking of signs! (see also Mark 8:11-12). In fact, in the eucharistic passage of John 6 our Lord Jesus seems to emphasize the same point by the thrust of His dialogue. He mentions "signs" in 6:26 in reference to the feeding of the five thousand the previous day, but then when they ask Him for a "sign" (6:30), He spurs them on to the more profound faith required with regard to the eucharistic miracle.

Furthermore, we have the example of Doubting Thomas (John 20:24-29). Jesus appeared to Thomas, after His Resurrection, apparently for the express purpose of demonstrating graphically to him that He was raised from the dead. But then what does He say?:

Have you believed because you have seen me? Blessed are those who have not seen and yet have come to believe.

Signs, wonders, and miracles (that is, in the empirical, outward sense which Zwingli demands for the Eucharist) do not suffice for many hard-hearted people anyway:

... If they do not listen to Moses and the prophets, neither will they be convinced even if someone rises from the dead.

(Luke 16:31)

For Jews demand signs and Greeks desire wisdom, but we proclaim Christ crucified, a stumbling block to Jews and foolishness to Gentiles... For God's foolishness is wiser than human wisdom, and God's weakness is stronger than human strength.

(1 Corinthians 1:22-23,25)

Likewise, when He was explaining the Eucharist, Jesus said:

Does this offend you?... among you there are some who do not believe...

(John 6:61,64)

This is why Jesus merely reiterated His teaching in John 6 in ever-more forceful terms, rather than explain it in a different way, or reveal the meaning of the alleged symbolic language, as many Protestants would have it. He repeated it because He knew that the problem was flat-out unbelief, not lack of comprehension. The Eucharist is no less "foolish" than Christ crucified. People will disbelieve both because they are difficult to grasp with the natural mind, whereas the mind of faith can see and believe them. Romano Guardini, the great Catholic writer, stated about John 6:

Should they have understood? Hardly. It is inconceivable that at any time anyone could have grasped intellectually the meaning of these words. But they should have believed. They should have clung to Christ blindly, wherever he led them... and simply said: we do not understand; show us what you mean. Instead they judge, and everything closes to them. [6]

Jesus could walk through walls after His Resurrection (John 20:26), and even a mere man, Philip, could be "caught away" and transported to another place by God (Acts 8:39-40). So Zwingli, and Protestants who follow his reasoning, think God "couldn't" or "wouldn't" have performed the miracle of the Real Presence and Transubstantiation (which means, literally, "change of substance")?

I don't find this line of thought convincing in the least, and no one should rashly attempt to "tie" God's hands by such arguments of alleged implausibility. The fact remains that God clearly can perform any miracle He so chooses.

Many Christian beliefs require a great deal of faith, even relatively "blind" faith. Protestants manage to believe in a number of such doctrines (such as the Trinity, God's eternal existence, omnipotence, angels, the power of prayer, instantaneous justification, the Second Coming, etc.). Why should the Real Presence be singled out for excessive skepticism and unchecked rationalism?

I contend that it is due to a preconceived bias against both sacramentalism and matter as a conveyor of grace, which hearkens back to the heresies of Docetism and even Gnosticism, which looked down upon matter, and regarded spirit as inherently superior to matter (following Greek philosophy, particularly Platonism).

The ancient heresy of Docetism held that the sufferings of Christ were apparent rather than real. Many think[7] that St. John wrote his Gospel with his Gnostic/Docetic opponent, one Cerinthus (fl. 100 A.D.), in mind, thus accounting for his strong emphasis on Jesus' "flesh" and "blood"—as in John 6. Many Protestants believe that the Eucharist is apparent and not real. But the Eucharist is an extension of the Incarnation of Christ, just as the Church is (most obviously seen in Paul's title of the *Body of Christ*—see 1 Corinthians 12:27, Ephesians 1:22-3, 5:30). A denial of the Real Presence might, therefore, be regarded as an anti-incarnational strain of thought.

The prior Catholic assumption of sacramentalism (which lies behind the Real Presence) has a sound biblical basis. The Incarnation, which made the Atonement

---

[6] *The Lord*, Chicago: Henry Regnery, 1954, 206.
[7] Based on St. Irenaeus: *Against Heresies*, 3,11,1, and Eusebius: *Church History*, 3,28,6).

possible, raised matter to previously unknown heights. God took on human flesh! All created matter was "good" in God's opinion from the start (Genesis 1:25).

This pervasive anti-eucharistic bias smacks of an analogy to the Jewish and Muslim belief that the Incarnation as an unthinkable (impossible?) task for God to undertake. They view the Incarnation in the same way as the majority of Protestants regard the Eucharist. For them God wouldn't or couldn't or shouldn't become a man. For evangelicals God wouldn't or couldn't or shouldn't become substantially, sacramentally present under the outward forms of bread and wine.

I think the dynamic is the same. "Coulda woulda shoulda" theology is not biblical theology. Every Christian exercises faith in things which are very difficult to grasp with the natural mind, because they are revealed to be true by God in the Bible. I have attempted to show why I think Protestants inconsistently require a higher criterion of "proof" where the Holy Eucharist is concerned.

No a priori biblical or logical case can be made against a literal Eucharist on the grounds that matter is inferior to spirit and/or indicative of a stunted, primitive, "pagan" spirituality or some such similar negative judgment. If Christ could become Man, He can surely will to become actually and truly present in every sense in what continues to appear as bread and wine, once consecrated. If Protestants wish to argue against the Real Presence, they must do it on scriptural, exegetical grounds, not Docetic, philosophical ones.

The classic biblical texts which Catholics utilize in support of their position are John 6:47-66, Luke 22:19-20 (cf. Matthew 26:26-28, Mark 14:22-24), 1 Corinthians 10:16, and 1 Corinthians 11:23-30. Zwingli attacks each of these in turn, but with invalid and insubstantial reasoning such as that seen above, spawned from the same false premises and unbiblical philosophical assumptions. I shall now briefly explain why I believe that the standard Protestant objections (following Zwingli) to all these proof texts fail.

As for John 6 and Jesus repeatedly commanding the hearers to *eat my flesh and drink my blood*, it is known that such metaphors were synonymous with doing someone grievous injury, in the Jewish mind at that time (see, e.g., Job 19:22, Psalms 27:2, Ecclesiastes 4:5, Isaiah 9:20, 49:26, Micah 3:1-3, Revelation 16:6).

Therefore, it isn't plausible to assert that Jesus was speaking metaphorically, according to the standard Protestant hermeneutic of interpreting Scripture in light of the contemporary usages and customs and idioms.

We Catholics are often accused of reading our own prior beliefs into the biblical texts,—of special pleading, as it were. With regard to the present question, I submit that non-sacramental Protestants are the ones committing that error.

When His hearers didn't understand what He was saying, the Lord always explained it more fully (e.g., Matthew 19:24-26, John 11:11-14, 8:32-34; cf.

4:31-34, 8:21-23). But when they refused to accept some teaching, He merely repeated it with more emphasis (e.g., Matthew 9:2-7, John 8:56-58). By analogy, then, we conclude that John 6 was an instance of willful rejection (see John 6:63-65; cf. Matthew 13:10-23).

Only here in the New Testament do we see followers of Christ abandoning Him for theological reasons (John 6:66). Surely, if their exodus was due to a simple misunderstanding, Jesus would have rectified their miscomprehension. But He did no such thing. Quite the contrary; He continually repeated the same teaching, using even stronger terms (as indicated by different terms in the Greek New Testament). All of this squares with the Catholic interpretation, and is inconsistent with a symbolic exegesis.

Furthermore, Protestants often (ironically) interpret John 6:63 literally, when in fact it was intended metaphorically:

It is the spirit that gives life, the flesh is of no avail; the words that I have spoken to you are spirit and life. (RSV)

Protestants claim that this establishes the symbolic and metaphorical nature of the whole discourse. What they fail to realize is that when the words "flesh" and "spirit" are opposed to each other in the New Testament, it is always a figurative use, in the sense of sinful human nature ("flesh") contrasted with humanity enriched by God's grace ("spirit").

This can be clearly seen in passages such as Matthew 26:41, Romans 7:5-6,25, 8:1-14, 1 Corinthians 5:5, 2 Corinthians 7:1, Galatians 3:3, 4:29, 5:13-26, and 1 Peter 3:18, 4:6. In other words, Jesus is saying that His words can only be received by men endowed with supernatural grace. Those who interpret them in a wooden, carnal way (equating His teaching here with a sort of gross cannibalism) are way off the mark.

Likewise, in the Last Supper passages (Luke 22:19-20; cf. Matthew 26:26-28, Mark 14:22-24), nothing in the actual text supports a metaphorical interpretation. When the word "is" is meant to be figurative, it is readily apparent (Matthew 13:38, John 10:7, 15:1, 1 Corinthians 10:4), whereas here it is not. The Last Supper was the Jewish feast of Passover, which involved a sacrificial lamb.

The disciples could hardly have missed the significance of what Jesus was saying. Before and after this passage, He spoke of His imminent suffering (Luke 22:15-16,18,21-22). John the Baptist had already referred to Him as the "Lamb of God" (John 1:29).

The two Pauline eucharistic passages (1 Corinthians 10:16 and 11:23-30) are also on their faceintended quite literally. How can one be guilty of profaning the "body and blood of the Lord" by engaging in a merely symbolic act (1 Corinthians 11:27)? Furthermore, the whole thrust of the contextual passage of 1

Corinthians 10: 14-22 is to contrast Christian eucharistic sacrifice with pagan sacrifice. St. Paul writes in 10:18:

Consider the people of Israel; are not those who eat the sacrifices partners in the altar?

He had stated just two verses earlier,

The cup of blessing which we bless, is it not a participation in the blood of Christ? The bread which we break, is it not a participation in the body of Christ?

As the Jewish sacrifices were literal and not symbolic, so is the Christian Sacrifice of the Mass—this is the entire thrust of Paul's argument. Following this line of analogical thought, Paul contrasts the pagan "sacrifice" to the Christian one (10:19-20), and the pagan "table of demons" to the *table* [i.e., altar] *of the Lord* (10:21). It is inescapable. The Catholic literal interpretation requires no twisting of the text into preconceived notions (which is called "eisegesis").

The Eucharist requires faith, and that causes many to stumble, because it is a miracle of a very sophisticated nature, not amenable to empirical or scientific "proof." But in a sense, it is no more difficult to believe than the changing of water to ice, in which the accidents change, while the substance (molecular structure) doesn't. The Eucharist merely involves the opposite scenario: the substance changes while the accidents don't.

Can anyone reasonably contend that one process is any more intrinsically implausible than the other, where an omnipotent God—particularly One who took on human flesh and became Man—is concerned?

Jesus, after His Resurrection, could walk through walls while remaining in His physical (glorified) body (John 20:26-27). How, then, can the Real Presence be regarded as impossible or implausible by many Protestants (even before Catholic proof texts are considered), who accept numerous other supernatural and mysterious events in Christian theology?

Many non-Catholics often argue that Jesus was not referring to the Eucharist at all in John 6. The word *Eucharist* comes from the Greek words *eucharistia*, *eucharisteo*, and *eucharistos*.[8] Together these occur 54 times in the New Testament, so obviously *Eucharist* is an eminently biblical word. Its meaning is *thanks*, *thankfulness*, or *thanksgiving*. But how is that related to the Last Supper, or Lord's Supper, or Communion? It's very simple (all verses: RSV):

---

[8] Words #2168, #2169, and #2170 in *Strong's Concordance*.

Matthew 26:27-28: *And he took a cup, and when he had given **thanks**, he gave it to them, saying, 'Drink of it, all of you; for this is my blood of the covenant,...'*

(cf. Mark 14:23, Luke 22:17,19)

There is a fascinating parallel between this language and that with regard to the feeding of the 4000 and 5000. Scripture records that Jesus "gave thanks" on those occasions, and then "broke" the fish and the loaves and "gave them to the disciples, and the disciples gave them to the crowds" {Matthew 15:36; cf. Mark 8:6}. Likewise, we see the same progression in the accounts of the Last Supper:

Luke 22:19: *And he took bread, and when he had given **thanks** he broke it, and gave it to them, saying, 'This is my body which is given for you. Do this in remembrance of me.'*

(cf. Matthew 26:26, 1 Corinthians 10:16, 11:23-24, Acts 2:42, 20:7)

So we have already established a parallel between the Last Supper and the ritual initiated by Jesus there (which is the central essence of the Mass), and the miraculous feeding of the crowds with bread and fish. In John 6, the same miracle occurs, except that this time the biblical writer records that Jesus ties the two together explicitly. First, we have the narrative concerning the feeding:

John 6:11: *Jesus then took the loaves, and when he had given **thanks** [eucharisteo], he distributed them to those who were seated...*

(cf. 6:23)

John 6:22 informs us that the rest of the story took place on the following day. But Jesus had a rebuke for the people who sought Him out on this occasion:

John 6:26-27: *'... you seek me, not because you saw signs, but because you ate your fill of the loaves. Do not labor for the food which perishes, but for the food which endures to eternal life, which the Son of Man will give to you...'*

In other words, Jesus is contrasting the utility of physical food with eucharistic, sacramental food (His own Body). He continues, getting more and more explicit as He goes along:

John 6:35:...' *I am the bread of life; he who comes to me shall not hunger...'*

(cf. 6:33)

John 6:51: *'I am the living bread which came down from heaven; if any one eats of this bread, he will live for ever; and the bread which I shall give for the life of the world is my flesh.'*

(cf. 6:48-50)

John continues:

John 6:52: *The Jews then disputed among themselves, saying, 'How can this man give us his flesh to eat?'*

Does Jesus then say, "look guys, settle down; you misunderstood Me! I was just talking symbolically; don't be so literal!" No, not at all. Rather, He reiterates His point in the strongest (and most literal) language:

John 6:53-58:...*'unless you eat the flesh of the Son of man and drink his blood, you have no life in you; he who eats my flesh and drinks my blood has eternal life,... For my flesh is food indeed, and my blood is drink indeed. He who eats my flesh and drinks my blood abides in me, and I in him... he who eats me will live because of me. This is the bread which came down from heaven, not such as the fathers ate and died; he who eats this bread will live forever.'*

When Jesus told parables, He always explained them, lest their meaning be lost on the hearers (and us readers of the Bible). Here he does no such thing, even though many of these people forsook Him as a result of His difficult teaching (6:60-61,64, 66-67). The symbolic interpretation makes no sense at all.

I think it is quite obvious that Jesus is referring to the Eucharist in John 6, for these reasons:

1) The parallelism between the miraculous mass feedings and the Last Supper.
2) The use of *eucharisteo* in the descriptions of both instances, in the same fashion.
3) The repeated reference in John 6 to His Body (i.e., eucharistically; sacramentally) giving eternal life to the recipients (John 6:27,33, 50-

51,54,58). This is clearly not merely referring to belief, since if that were the case, explicit references to His Body and Blood would be entirely superfluous. He could have just spoken in terms of "belief" rather than eating and drinking His flesh and blood (which He did in many other instances: e.g., John 12:44-46, 14:10-12).

4) The equation of (what appeared to be) bread and His Body in both John 6 and the Last Supper (Matthew 26:26, Mark 14:22, Luke 22:19, 1 Corinthians 10:16-17, 11:23-24,27,29, John 6:33,48,50-51,53-58).

5) The equation of (what appeared to be) wine and His Blood in both John 6 and the Last Supper (Matthew 26:27-28, Mark 14:23-24, Luke 22:20, 1 Corinthians 10:16, 11:25,27, John 6:53-56).

Another very fascinating passage has often been interpreted as related to the Eucharist (by, for example, St. Augustine), for reasons which are already made clear by the above biblical data. At the end of the post-Resurrection appearance of Jesus to the two disciples on the road to Emmaus, we are given this account:

Luke 24:30-31: *When he was at table with them, he took the bread and blessed, and broke it, and gave it to them. And their eyes were opened and they recognized him; and he vanished out of their sight.*

Cross-referencing biblical texts with a willingness to go wherever the texts lead can cause one to arrive at many interesting (sometimes surprising) conclusions, such as a belief that the doctrines of the Catholic Church are not without much biblical sanction and support.

Chapter Eight

Why the Catholic Mass is Not Idolatry

Sometimes the claim is made that the Catholic Sacrifice of the Mass is idolatry, or, in particular, the same in essence and purpose as the sinful, idolatrous worship of the Golden Calf by the wandering Israelites (while Moses was on Mt. Sinai receiving the Ten Commandments).

But the Israelites in this instance (unlike Catholics) were guilty of true idolatry. God (and Moses) know idolatry when they see it. In Exodus 32:1, the NRSV reads,

> *... Come, make gods for us, who shall go before us...* (cf. 32:23)

Exodus 32:4-5 informs us:

> *He took the gold from them, formed it in a mold, and cast an image of a calf; and they said, "These are your gods, O Israel, who brought you up out of the land of Egypt!" When Aaron saw this, he built an altar before it; and Aaron made proclamation and said, "tomorrow shall be a festival to the LORD."*

It is, therefore, clear that this is idolatry and otherwise sinful, on many counts:

1) It represents not even the one God, but "gods," so that it falls under the absolute prohibition of polytheism which was known to any observant Hebrew (see, e.g., Psalms 106:19-23; cf. Habakkuk 2:18).
2) Nowhere are the Jews permitted to build a calf as an "image" of God. This was an outright violation of the injunctions against "molten images" (Exodus 34:17, Leviticus 19:4, Numbers 33:52, Deuteronomy 27:15—all condemn such idols, using the same Hebrew word which appears in Exodus 32:4,8,17: *massekah*).
3) Aaron built an altar before what the people regarded as "gods," thus blaspheming the true God.
4) Lies were told and believed about "gods," not God, liberating the Hebrews from Egyptian slavery.
5) Aaron used "orthodox" God-language, too. But does that release him from his responsibility? No. Obviously Aaron was a "progressive," in his dishonest, equivocating use of language.

6) NASB and NKJV read "god" at Exodus 32:4 (not even capitalized), so that is clearly not intended as a reference to the one true God, YHWH, according to the accepted practice of all Bible translations. NRSV, KJV, RSV, NIV, NEB, and REB have "gods." In either case, the view is not monotheistic, nor is it at all analogous to the belief and practice of those Christians who accept the Real Presence.

In the latter instance, Christians are merely following Christ's instructions at the Last Supper, as to a "memorial" of Him (which idea doesn't necessarily exclude the Real Presence, as is often wrongly assumed). We find many explicit indications in Scripture that what He intended was a literal, miraculous, physical presence.

Furthermore, in Catholic, Orthodox, Lutheran and High Church Anglican belief, the Real Presence is not brought about by a "work of magic" on the part of the priest or pastor, nor the "work of men's hands," as is the case with the golden calf. Rather, it is a supernatural transformation wrought by God, in which the priest merely stands in as an *alter Christus*.

Any Bible student knows that the lower-case "g" in the word "god" is a reference to false gods, which are no gods at all, in the monotheistic conception. Accordingly, all of the Hebrew scholars who produced all these translations have made a previous judgment as to which sort of "god" is being spoken of here, and they have concluded that it is not YHVH, the true God.

But context also proves to be conclusive in favor of my interpretation:

1) Exodus 32:1 (cf. 32:23), quoted above, is revealing as to the state of mind of these idolaters. They ask Aaron to "make" them "gods." Obviously, they could not have YHVH in mind at that point, since I imagine they at least knew that He is not "made by hands" and is eternal. Then they say these gods "shall go before us." In my opinion, the most straightforward interpretation of that is the golden calf being carried before them. How could they think (even in their debased state of mind) that YHVH Himself could be compelled to "go before them?" Therefore, they must have regarded the calf as a pure idol of their own making, not as a mere representation of the true God, because these contextual verses make clear that they didn't have YHVH in mind.
2) Exodus 32:23 is another indication of their state of mind, which was a lack of faith in God's designs and purposes and impatience in waiting for Moses to come down from Mt. Sinai (cf. 32:1a). It is yet again a disbelief in and distrust of YHVH (what else is new?). They "don't know what has become" of Moses, and ungratefully attribute to him the feat of bringing

them "out of the land of Egypt," whereas the credit should have gone to YHVH (cf. 32:11).

Both of these factors mitigate against a "calf-symbolic-of-God" scenario and tend towards the notion of a pagan idol not representative of the true God. Otherwise, a state of affairs ensued whereby they were mad at God and Moses, so as a result they proceeded to worship God as a Golden Calf, which makes little sense.

3) If the above data isn't sufficient, surely Psalms 106:19-21 nails down my case (NRSV):

They made a calf at Horeb and worshiped a cast image. They exchanged the glory of God for the image of an ox that eats grass. They forgot God, their Savior, who had done great things in Egypt.

Obviously, they could not "forget" the true God, whose glory they "exchanged" for the idolatrous image, while at the same time, supposedly worship YHVH under the form of the golden calf.

4) Therefore, the attempted analogy to the Real Presence in the Eucharist completely fails. Also, the state of mind of the Catholic at Mass is important (since idolatry involves states of mind). The devout, orthodox Catholic is certainly not angry, distrustful, or "forgetting" God during the consecration, but rather, worshiping Him and giving him all the glory, and "remembering" Him, too, just as Jesus explicitly commanded. This is a separate issue from whether or not a supernatural change occurs or not.
5) To conclude my analysis of Exodus 32, I shall cite a highly-reputable Protestant archaeologist in favor of my interpretation. William F. Albright (the dean of biblical archaeologists), wrote:[1]

In spite of the unanimous testimony of Israelite tradition, scholars have made repeated efforts to prove the existence of representations of deity in early Israel. Every effort of this kind has been based on subjective arguments and on arbitrary assumptions which have won only

---

[1] *From the Stone Age to Christianity*, Garden City, NY: Doubleday, 2nd ed., 1957, 264-266. See also: Merrill F. Unger, *Archaeology and the Old Testament*, Grand Rapids, MI: Zondervan, 1954, 236-237, and J.D. Douglas, ed., *The New Bible Dictionary*, Grand Rapids, MI: Eerdmans, 1962, 180.

the most limited acceptance even in friendly circles... The testimony of our written sources, plus the completely negative results of excavation, should be evidence enough to prove that Yahwism was essentially aniconic and that material representations were foreign to its spirit from the beginning.

Catholics, Orthodox, Anglicans and Lutherans do not "reduce" God at all in believing in a literal Eucharist. The analogy fails, pure and simple. Bread and wine are legitimate elements as determined by the commands of Jesus Himself, vastly unlike the Golden Calf. The Real Presence is established—we think—by Scripture, so worship follows as a matter of course. And men don't bring about the change of transubstantiation—God does. [2] So again, there is no analogy at all, and to deny this involves a gross representation of the views of those Christians who accept the Real Presence, just as the Church Fathers did, with virtual unanimity.

The charge of idolatry in this instance is absolutely wrongheaded to begin with. To be an idolater is fundamentally to put something in place of God. An animist who is truly worshiping a statue of wood or stone or amulet as God in and of itself (i.e., over against the true, one Creator God) is a true idolater. The Catholic (or Lutheran, or Anglican, or Orthodox, broadly speaking) is doing no such thing, for they believe that the one true Creator God is really, truly, substantially present under the appearances of bread and wine.

Thus, they are consciously worshiping the eternal God, as far as they are concerned, not a piece of bread (this is especially true for Catholics, who maintain that the bread and wine are no longer even *there*, but only the appearance or "accidents"). Nor is the Lutheran worshiping the bread and wine which he still believes is present after consecration, but God, who is now present "in, with, and under" the elements of bread and wine (consubstantiation).

Now, one may wish to quibble with the belief in the Real Presence and/or transubstantiation (a development of same), but it is a very incoherent argument to claim that one is committing idolatry when in fact they are consciously worshiping God Himself in the consecrated Host That is the very opposite of idolatry.

---

[2] See, e.g., the *Catechism of the Catholic Church*, #1375, which cites St. John Chrysostom and St. Ambrose.

Chapter Nine

The Old Testament, the Ancient Jews, and *Sola Scriptura*

A Baptist man whom I met on the Internet, wrote a thought-provoking and well-researched essay, seeking to establish an analogy between the faith and religious authority structure amongst the Jews, as evidenced in the Old Testament, and the Protestant principle of *sola Scriptura* (Bible Alone as the final authority in Christianity).

I disagree with his assessment of the exclusive and final status of the written word of God over against the patriarchal, prophetic, and priestly proclamations of it, and its oral, traditional (and talmudic) aspects. I contend that he reached his conclusions with far too little and insubstantial evidence, whether biblical or historical.

There are many highly relevant factors which prove, in my opinion, that the Old Testament analogy is much more in line with both the early Church and present-day Catholicism (which developed from that early Church) and its notions of Church authority and Tradition, than with the *Protestant sola Scriptura* rule of faith. I shall summarize these, each in turn:

1) THE JEWISH LAW, OR *TORAH*, WAS NOT EXCLUSIVELY WRITTEN DOWN

According to the reputable Protestant reference, *Eerdmans Bible Dictionary*[1], oral communication and traditions in ancient Middle Eastern societies were much more common and standard than in our own time. The oral Torah was regarded as equal in authority to the written Hebrew Scriptures, and was believed to have been given to Moses on Mt. Sinai.

This vast collection of oral teaching was in due course codified in the Mishnah. Further interpretation of this text led to the Palestinian and Babylonian Talmuds. Halakhah, or legal teaching, is predominant in the Talmud (as in the written Torah). The task of the rabbis was to interpret the law of Moses, and to aply broad ordinances to individual cases.

The better (more biblically-oriented) strains of Jewish tradition perfectly understood that the Law dealt with the heart, not just outward and/or ritualistic conformity. Jesus introduced nothing radically new in this respect, contrary to the

---

[1] Edited by Allen C. Myers, Grand Rapids, MI: Eerdmans Pub. Co., 1987 (from *Bijbelse Encyclopedie*, ed. W.H. Gispen, Kampen, Netherlands, 1975), 1014.

jaded views of Judaism held by many Christians of all types. Jeremiah talked explicitly about the New Covenant.

It seems fairly certain from Holy Scripture itself that various writings and oral traditions were compiled and canonized at a later date (the time of Ezra and Nehemiah) and put into the form with which we are familiar (just as the New Testament itself was). I don't think this implies either a denial of Mosaic authorship or of biblical infallibility.

Whether or not the Pentateuch was not codified until a later date is a different proposition from the question of Mosaic authorship. If later compilation was the case (as many conservative biblical scholars believe, I think), this no more means that such a process is illegitimate or untrustworthy than the late canonization of the New Testament brings into question Pauline authorship of his Epistles. It is all merely development, not change in essence.

All these facts being true, and agreed upon by Protestant and Catholic biblical and historical scholars, it is hardly possible to make an analogy between the ancient Jewish authority structure and Protestantism. The oral tradition was central from the beginning, and flourished even more after the Canon of the Old Testament was finalized. At that point, the (mostly oral) methods and traditions which later crystallized into the written Talmud, intensified and continued on unabated for another six or so centuries. And then after that Judaism continued to discuss and comment on the Talmud itself, to this day. So the analogy is much more to Catholicism:

a) Oral Law in Judaism corresponds to Oral Tradition in the New Testament (e.g., 2 Timothy 1:13-14, 2:2) and Catholic Tradition.
b) In its interpretive and developmental aspects, Jewish Oral Law is similar to Catholic development of dogma and historical growth of conciliar and magisterial understanding of Christian teaching.
c) The Jews believed that the "oral Torah" went back to Moses on Mt. Sinai and ultimately to God, and was received simultaneously with the written Torah. Likewise, Catholics believe that Catholic Tradition was received simultaneously from the Apostles—who received it from Jesus—with the "gospel," which itself was eventually formulated into the New Testament.

The analogy to *sola Scriptura*, then, is impossible to maintain, since the Jews accepted the oral Torah as equally authoritative, the Canon of the Old Testament was only gradually formed (even the Pentateuch alone was authoritatively collected 500 years after David!), and authoritative and binding talmudic speculation and interpretation flourished even after the Old Testament had been completed and organized.

We believe that the authoritative Church is placed by God in the position as Arbiter of doctrinal disputes and Guardian of the Apostolic Deposit. Just as it verified the New Testament Canon, so it acknowledges Apostolic Traditions and distinguishes them from corrupt, merely human ones.

Several tenets of Jewish religious belief developed subsequent to the finalization of the Old Testament Canon, such as eschatology and angelology in particular—adopted virtually wholesale by the early Christians. The Sadducees were the *Sola Scripturists* (and liberals) of that time.

2) JEWISH ORAL TRADITION WAS ACCEPTED BY JESUS AND THE APOSTLES

a) Matthew 2:23: the reference to "... He shall be called a Nazarene" cannot be found in the Old Testament, yet it was passed down "by the prophets." Thus, a prophecy, which is considered to be "God's Word" was passed down orally, rather than through Scripture.

b) Matthew 23:2-3: Jesus teaches that the scribes and Pharisees have a legitimate, binding authority, based on *Moses' seat*, which phrase (or idea) cannot be found anywhere in the Old Testament. It is found in the (originally oral) Mishna, where a sort of "teaching succession" from Moses on down is taught. Thus, "apostolic succession," whereby the Catholic Church, in its priests and bishops and popes, claims to be merely the Custodian of an inherited apostolic Tradition, is also prefigured by Jewish oral tradition, as approved (at least partially) by Jesus Himself.

c) In 1 Corinthians 10:4, St. Paul refers to a rock which "followed" the Jews through the Sinai wilderness. The Old Testament says nothing about such miraculous movement, in the related passages about Moses striking the rock to produce water (Exodus 17:1-7; Numbers 20:2-13). Rabbinic tradition, however, does.

d) 1 Peter 3:19: St. Peter, in describing Christ's journey to Sheol/Hades ("he went and preached to the spirits in prison... "), draws directly from the Jewish apocalyptic book 1 Enoch (12-16).

e) Jude 9: about a dispute between Michael the archangel and Satan over Moses' body, cannot be paralleled in the Old Testament, and appears to be a recounting of an oral Jewish tradition.

f) Jude 14-15 directly quotes from 1 Enoch 1:9, even saying that Enoch prophesied.

g) 2 Timothy 3:8: Jannes and Jambres cannot be found in the related Old Testament passage (Exodus 7:8 ff.).

h) James 5:17: the reference to a lack of rain for three years is likewise absent from the relevant Old Testament passage in 1 Kings 17.

Since Jesus and the Apostles acknowledge authoritative Jewish oral tradition (even in so doing raising some of it literally to the level of written Revelation), we are hardly at liberty to assert that it is altogether illegitimate. That being the case, the alleged analogy of the Old Testament to *sola Scriptura* is again found wanting and massively incoherent.

Jesus attacked corrupt traditions only, not tradition per se, and not all Oral Tradition. The simple fact that there exists such an entity as legitimate Oral Tradition, supports the Catholic "both/and" view by analogy, whereas in a *strict sola Scriptura* viewpoint, this would be inadmissible, it seems to me. It is obvious that there can be false oral traditions just as there are false written traditions which some heretics elevated to "Scripture" (e.g., the *Gospel of Thomas*).

This is precisely why we need the Church as Guardian and Custodian of all these traditions, and to determine (by the guidance of the Holy Spirit) which are Apostolic and which not, just as the Church placed its authoritative approval on the New Testament Canon. Holy Scripture is absolutely central and primary in the Catholic viewpoint, just as in Protestantism. No legitimate Oral Tradition can ever contradict Scripture, just as no true fact of science can ever contradict it.

Jesus is clear to distinguish what is called *the tradition of the elders* (Mark 7:3,5) from the legitimate Tradition, by saying,

> *You leave the commandment of God, and hold fast the tradition of men.* (Mark 7:8—RSV; cf. 7:9)

I would argue that neither *commandment* nor *tradition* per se are restricted to the written. Jesus contrasts human tradition with the *word of God* in 7:13, but *that word of God* is not only not restricted to the written Bible, but even *identical* to Divine Tradition, once one does some straightforward comparative exegesis.

Protestants wish to make a dichotomy, based on this passage, between oral and written Tradition, whereas Jesus, I think, is clearly contrasting human (false) tradition and Divine Tradition, whether oral or written. I think the notion that any of this proves *sola Scriptura* is eisegesis at best and special pleading at worst.

There were also many false books parading as Scripture in the early Christian period. If falsity alongside truth is a disproof of that truth (and its medium), then the Protestant *Scripture Alone* view is just as fatally flawed as the Catholic view. Protestants needed the authoritative Church to proclaim the Canon of the New Testament, just as we need it to determine true Apostolic Tradition.

3) JEWISH "ECCLESIOLOGY" INCLUDED AUTHORITATIVE INTERPRETATION

The Jews did not have a "me, the Bible, and the Holy Ghost" mindset. Protestants have, of course, teachers, commentators, and interpreters of the Bible (and excellent ones at that—often surpassing Catholics in many respects). They are, however, strictly optional and non-binding when it comes down to the individual and his choice of what he chooses to believe. This is the Protestant notion *of private judgment* and the nearly-absolute primacy of individual conscience (Luther's "plowboy").

In Catholicism, on the other hand, there is a parameter where doctrinal speculation must end: the Magisterium, dogmas, papal and conciliar pronouncements, catechisms—in a word (well, two words): Catholic Tradition. Some things are considered to be settled issues. Others are still undergoing development.

All binding dogmas are believed to be derived from Jesus and the Apostles. Now, who did the Jews resemble more closely in this regard? Did they need authoritative interpretation of their Torah, and eventually, the Old Testament as a whole? The Old Testament itself has much to "tell" us (RSV):

a) Exodus 18:20: Moses was to *teach* the Jews the *statutes and the decisions*—not just *read* it to them. Since he was the Lawgiver and author of the Torah, it stands to reason that his interpretation and teaching would be of a highly authoritative nature.

b) Leviticus 10:11: Aaron, Moses' brother, is also commanded by God to *teach*.

c) Deuteronomy 17:8-13: The Levitical priests had binding authority in legal matters (derived from the Torah itself). They interpreted the biblical injunctions (17:11). The penalty for disobedience was death (17:12), since the offender didn't obey *the priest who stands to minister there before the LORD your God*. Cf. Deuteronomy 19:16-17, 2 Chronicles 19:8-10.

d) Deuteronomy 24:8: Levitical priests had the final say and authority (in this instance, in the case of leprosy). This was a matter of Jewish law.

e) Deuteronomy 33:10: Levite priests are to teach Israel the *ordinances* and *law*. (cf. 2 Chronicles 15:3, Malachi 2:6-8—the latter calls them *messenger of the LORD of hosts*).

f) Ezra 7:6,10: Ezra, a priest and scribe, studied the Jewish law and taught it to Israel, and his authority was binding, under pain of imprisonment, banishment, loss of goods, and even death (7:25-26).

g) Nehemiah 8:1-8: Ezra reads the law of Moses to the people in Jerusalem (8:3). In 8:7 we find thirteen Levites who assisted Ezra, and *who helped the people to understand the law*. Much earlier, in King Jehoshaphat's reign, we find Levites exercising the same function (2 Chronicles 17:8-9). There is no *sola Scriptura*, with its associated idea "perspicuity" (evident clearness in the main) here. In Nehemiah 8:8:... *they read from the book, from the law of God, clearly* [footnote, *"or with interpretation"*], *and they gave the sense, so that the people understood the reading.*

So the people did indeed understand the law (8:12), but not without much assistance—not merely upon hearing. Likewise, the Bible is not altogether clear in and of itself, but requires the aid of teachers who are more familiar with biblical styles and Hebrew idiom, background, context, exegesis and cross-reference, hermeneutical principles, original languages, etc.

h) I think all Christians agree that prophets, too, exercised a high degree of authority, so I need not establish that.

The Catholic Church continues to offer authoritative teaching and a way to decide doctrinal and ecclesiastical disputes, and believes that its popes and priests have the power to "bind and loose," just as the New Testament describes. Protestantism has no such system.

The Old Testament and Jewish history attest to a fact which Catholics constantly assert, over against *sola Scriptura* and Protestantism: that Holy Scripture requires an authoritative interpreter, a Church, and a binding Tradition, as passed down from Jesus and the Apostles.

4) PROPHETS' SPOKEN WORDS CONSTITUTED THE WORD OF GOD

Protestant arguments in favor of *sola Scriptura* frequently contain the gratuitous assumption that *word of the Lord, word of God*, etc. is always or usually a reference to the written word (i.e., Holy Scripture). This simply is not the case. In fact, the exact opposite is true, as a good Concordance ("word") will quickly confirm. In the very verse my Baptist correspondent was trying to use as an example of the written Word (Daniel 9:6), one can readily observe this. It reads:

> *We have not listened to thy servants the prophets, who spoke in thy name to our kings, our princes, and our fathers, and to all the people of the land.*

It seems to me that the most straightforward primary meaning of this passage is as a reference to oral proclamation. The Old Testament "Church" and its Torah perpetuated itself—roughly up to the time of Ezra (5th century B.C.) primarily by oral and liturgical (Temple, priestly) Tradition. Just as in Catholicism, Scripture for the Jews (to the extent that it was recognized as such—which was a process) was *central* but not the be-all and end-all of faith, or the sole rule of faith for atomistic individuals.

Like any other book, it needed (and needs) an interpreter, and when differences of interpretation arise, there is the need of a binding authority to settle the matter, so that chaos and relativism may not reign amongst God's covenant people.

A prophet's inspired utterance was indeed *the word of the Lord*, but it obviously was not written as it was spoken! Most if not all prophecy was first oral proclamation, but it was just as binding and inspired as oral revelation, as it was in later written form (i.e., those prophecies which were finally recorded—surely there were more). In this sense truly inspired prophecies are precisely analogous to the proclamation of the gospel, or *kerygma*, by the apostles.

Both the gospel and virtually the entire New Testament (excepting perhaps Revelation) began as oral preaching (notably, Jesus Himself wrote nothing), and was increasingly recognized by the early Church as inspired and hence Scripture. But it was just as binding before it was finally proclaimed Scripture in 397 A.D. It didn't *become* Scripture because the Church said so; rather, the Church authoritatively proclaimed, in effect, that *these particular books are inherently Scripture and divinely-inspired.*

Sola Scriptura couldn't possibly be the formal authoritative model for Jews often without a written Scripture, nor for the early Church up to 397 AD! This is obviously the Catholic model of authority. Just as the Catholic Church verified the extent of New Testament Scripture, so it has the burden of orthodox interpretation of that Scripture, in order to maintain true Apostolic Doctrine. *Sola Scriptura* is historically (and logically and biblically) self-defeating.

Like its Jewish predecessor, this state of affairs (the process of canonization) is not *sola Scriptura*: it is Tradition and binding Church authority which has the prerogative of determining the parameters of what is of its own essence Scripture.

The Church doesn't *create* Scripture (which is "God-breathed"), but merely *recognizes* it. It *has* to recognize it. That is the whole point. It is *practically* necessary. Tradition and binding Church authority also claim possession of the apostolic deposit and final say as to what are true Christian doctrines, and which are to be rejected as false.

When Peter interpreted Old Testament Scripture messianically and "Christianly," in the Upper Room (as recorded in Acts 2), his word was just as authoritative and inspired as when it was set down in writing later. Throughout the book of Acts we see St. Peter and St. Paul exercising apostolic authority and preaching, not handing out Bibles.

Prophets were the Old Testament equivalent of apostles. Apostles passed on their office and authority (albeit in less spectacular and "inspired" form, no doubt) to bishops. And so the early Church had the notion of apostolic succession and apostolic Tradition, which was the bottom line in doctrinal disputes—not simple recourse to Holy Scripture, as if there were no differences of opinion on it, and as if it were "perspicuous."

Virtually all the heretics of the early Church period based themselves on *Scripture Alone*, but a skewed interpretation of the Scripture (and Tradition). This was particularly true, I believe, of the Marcionites, Arians, and Nestorians.

5) PHARISEES, SADDUCEES AND THE NATURE OF TRUE JEWISH TRADITION

Many people do not realize that Christianity was derived in many ways from the Pharisaical tradition of Judaism. It was really the only viable option in the Judaism of that era. Since Jesus often excoriated the Pharisees for hypocrisy and excessive legalism, some assume that He was condemning the whole ball of wax. But this is throwing the baby out with the bath water. Likewise, the Apostle Paul, when referring to his Pharisaical background doesn't condemn Pharisaism per se.

The Sadducees, on the other hand, were much more "heretical." They rejected the future resurrection and the soul, the afterlife, rewards and retribution, demons and angels, and predestinarianism. Christian Pharisees are referred to in Acts 15:5 and Philippians 3:5, but never Christian Sadducees. The Sadducees' following was found mainly in the upper classes, and was almost non-existent among the common people.

The Sadducees also rejected all 'oral Torah,'—the traditional interpretation of the written that was of central importance in rabbinic Judaism. So we can summarize as follows:

a) The Sadducees were obviously the elitist "liberals" and "heterodox" amongst the Jews of their time.
b) But the Sadducees were also the *sola Scripturists* of their time.
c) Christianity adopted wholesale the very "postbiblical" doctrines which the Sadducees rejected and which the Pharisees accepted: resurrection, belief in angels and spirits, the soul, the afterlife, eternal reward or damnation, and the belief in angels and demons.

d) But these doctrines were notable for their marked development after the biblical Old Testament Canon was complete, especially in Jewish apocalyptic literature, part of Jewish codified oral tradition.
e) We've seen how—if a choice is to be made—both Jesus and Paul were squarely in the "Pharisaical camp," over against the Sadducees.
f) We also saw earlier how Jesus and the New Testament writers cite approvingly many tenets of Jewish oral (later talmudic and rabbinic) tradition, according to the Pharisaic outlook.

Ergo) The above facts constitute one more "nail in the coffin" of the theory that either the Old Testament Jews or the early Church were guided by the principle *of sola Scriptura*. The only party which believed thusly were the Sadducees, who were heterodox according to traditional Judaism, despised by the common people, and restricted to the privileged classes only.

The Pharisees (despite their corruptions and excesses) were the mainstream, and the early Church adopted their outlook with regard to eschatology, anthropology, and angelology, and the necessity and benefit of binding oral tradition and ongoing ecclesiastical authority for the purpose (especially) of interpreting Holy Scripture.

Chapter Ten

Was the Catholic Church an Avowed Enemy of Holy Scripture in the Middle Ages or at any Other Time?

Many critics of the Catholic Church claim that it has traditionally and perpetually feared the reading of the Bible, and deliberately tried to suppress it and keep it from the people, in order to preserve its own despotic power. It is blamed for obscuring the Bible, keeping it in a language not understood by the masses (Latin), opposing translations, so that those who spoke various languages could understand it, and hence learn its *true* (i.e., contra-Catholic) teachings, and so forth.

This is classic polemical rhetoric, repeated endlessly ever since the 16th century and very difficult to dislodge from the minds of those who accept it uncritically. But it is an outrageously selective and thus ultimately profoundly misinformed presentation.

I shall treat this subject of the Catholic Church's reverence for, and attiude towards Scripture at some length, since it is supremely important and so vastly misunderstood, even by Protestant and secularist scholars, who ought to know better.

Catholic author and former Protestant Henry G. Graham observes:

> The common and received opinion about the matter among non-Catholics in Britain, for the most part, has been that Rome hates the Bible... If she cannot altogether prevent its publication or its perusal, at least she renders it as nearly useless as possible by sealing it up in a dead language which the majority of people can neither read nor understand... The Protestant account of pre-reformation Catholicism has been largely a falsification of history... She has been painted as all black and hideous, and no beauty could be seen in her. Consequently people came to believe the tradition as a matter of course, and accepted it as history.[1]

Protestant scholars concur with this opinion. For example, Robert McAfee Brown wrote that "Catholicism has a high regard for Scripture" which "would satisfy the most rigorous Protestant fundamentalist."[2] Peter Toon comments that during the Middle Ages the Bible was considered "infallible and inerrant," and

---

[1] *Where We Got the Bible*, St. Louis: B. Herder, rev. 1939, 1,4.
[2] *The Spirit of Protestantism*, Oxford: Oxford Univ. Press, 1961, 172-173.

granted "the highest honour."[3] And Harold Lindsell, former editor of *Christianity Today* and well-known evangelical scholar, asserted that the Catholic Church holds to an exalted view of the Bible "no different from that held by the Reformers."[4]

Convert from Lutheranism Louis Bouyer further expands:

> In the same way that Popes, Councils, theologians, always resorted to the scriptural argument as the really fundamental one, the practice of the great spiritual writers of every epoch attests the fully traditional character of a devotion based on the Bible... The same is true of the great teachers of the Middle Ages... Not only did they know the Bible and make abundant use of it, but they moved in it as in a spiritual world that formed the habitual universe of all their thoughts and sentiments. For them, it was not simply one source among others, but the source par excellence, in a sense the only one... What in fact was for so many monks the most important of their religious practices, the one which virtually contained all the others? It was what the Benedictine rule, which only codified in this the practice of the sixth century, called the 'lectio divina.' This 'lectio,'... was nourished exclusively on the Bible... Not only with the approval of the hierarchy but by the positive and emphatic insistence of the Pope himself, there has come about a general return to the close study of Scripture, which has been restored, not only as the base, but as the source, of all teaching of theology.[5]

Many more similar quotes could be produced. The reader desiring further evidence is urged to peruse the Vatican II document *Divine Revelation*, and the papal encyclicals of Leo XIII (1878-1903): *On the Study of Holy Scripture (Providentissimus Deus*—1893), and Pius XII (1939-58): *Promotion of Biblical Studies (Divino afflante Spiritu*—1943). These are sometimes found in the beginning of Catholic Bibles, and can be easily located online. The Jesuit Hartmann Grisar, author of a six-volume biography of Martin Luther, noted that:

> It would be to perpetuate a prejudice... founded on Luther's often false or at least exaggerated statements, were one to fail to recognise how widely the Bible was known even before Luther's day and to what extent it was studied among educated people. Modern research, not seldom

---

[3] *Protestants and Catholics*, Ann Arbor, MI: Servant Books, 1983, 39.
[4] *The Battle For the Bible*, Grand Rapids, MI: Zondervan, 1976, 54-56.
[5] *The Spirit and Forms of Protestantism*, tr. A.V. Littledale, London: Harvill Press, 1956, 164-165.

carried out by open-minded Protestants, has furnished some surprising results in this respect.[6]

Documents from before the 15th century and historiography back up these observations:

The publisher of the Cologne Bible [1480] writes...:

All Christians should read the Bible with piety and reverence, praying the Holy Ghost, who is the inspirer of the Scriptures, to enable them to understand... The learned should make use of the Latin translation of St. Jerome; but the unlearned and simple folk, whether laymen or clergy... should read the German translations now supplied, and thus arm themselves against the enemy of our salvation.

The rapidity with which the different editions followed each other and the testimony of contemporary writers point to a wide distribution of German Bibles among the people.[7]

It says at the end of a Koberger Vulgate of 1477:

The Holy Scriptures excel all the learning of the world... All believers should watch zealously and exert themselves unremittingly to understand the contents of these most useful and exalted writings, and to retain them in the memory. Holy Scripture is that beautiful garden of Paradise in which the leaves of the commandments grow green, the branches of evangelical counsel sprout...

These words admirably describe the attitude which the Church in the Middle Ages held with regard to Holy Scripture. That the Bible at that time was a book lying under a bank is an unhistorical assertion... First and foremost the study of the Bible was urgently enjoined on the priests... The Breviary and the Missal... are for the most part made up of words from Holy Scripture... Thomas a Kempis, in agreement with the Fathers, compares the Word of Christ with the Eucharist, the body of

---

[6] *Luther*, tr. E.M. Lamond, ed. Luigi Cappadelta, 6 vols., London: Kegan Paul, Trench, Trubner & Co., 1917, v. 5, 536.
[7] Johannes Janssen, *History of the German People From the Close of the Middle Ages*, 16 vols., tr. A.M. Christie, St. Louis: B. Herder, 1910 (originally 1891), vol. 1, 58-60.

Christ, and declares that without the Eucharist and the Holy Scriptures, his food and his light, life would be unbearable to him.[8]

In Catholic countries the walls of churches and monasteries and convents, and even cemeteries, are covered with pictures representing Scriptural scenes... Stained glass windows may be mentioned in the same category... The simple truth is that the Catholic Church adopted every means at her disposal in these old days to bring a knowledge of God's Word to those who could not read, as well as to those who could. Bibles were not printed because there was no printing press; but whose fault was that? Is the Church to blame for not inventing printing sooner?[9]

The Canon of the Bible... was framed in the fourth century. In that same century Pope Damascus commanded a new and complete translation of the Scriptures to be made into the Latin language, which was then the living tongue not only of Rome and Italy, but of the civilized world. If the Popes were afraid that the Bible should see the light, this was a singular way of manifesting their fear. The task of preparing a new edition of the Scriptures was assigned to St. Jerome, the most learned Hebrew scholar of his time. This new translation was disseminated throughout Christendom, and on that account was called the Vulgate, or popular edition. In the 6th and 7th centuries the modern languages of Europe began to spring up like so many shoots from the parent Latin stock. The Scriptures, also, soon found their way into these languages.[10]

There were just two classes of people then: those who could read, and those who could not read. Now, those who did read could read Latin, and, therefore, were perfectly content with the Scriptures in Latin. Those who could not read Latin could not read at all... The whole mistake in peoples' minds arises, of course, from the supposition they make that Latin was then a dead language, whereas it was really a living one in every sense of the term, being read and spoken and written universally in Europe.[11]

---

[8] Janssen, *ibid.*, vol. 14, 381-383.
[9] Graham, *ibid.*, 85-86.
[10] James Cardinal Gibbons, *The Faith of Our Fathers*, New York: P.J. Kenedy & Sons, rev. ed., 1917, 74.
[11] Graham, *ibid.*, 89, 91.

The Bible and other books were chained in the libraries and churches in the Middle Ages to preserve them from theft, and especially to make them accessible to students... The Reformers adopted this custom of having chained Bibles in their churches, and the practice lasted for over 300 years. There were chained libraries at Grantham (1598), Bolton (1651) and Wimborne (1686), England, and chained Bibles in most of the English churches... The Oxford Colleges of Eton, Brasenose and Merton did not remove the chains until the 18th century, while some libraries removed them only in the 19th (Manchester, Cirencester, Llanbadarn). At the present time we have records of over 5000 chained books in eleven Protestant and two Catholic libraries.[12]

The desire to possess the Holy Scriptures in the mother tongue is already met with on German soil in the time of Charlemagne [742-814]; and, strange to say, it is just the earliest translators of the Middle Ages who have come nearest to perfection in this task.[13]

The number of translations... of the complete Bible, was indeed very great... Between this period [1466] and the separation of the Churches at least fourteen complete editions of the Bible were published in High German, and five in the low German dialect. The first High German edition was brought out in 1466 by Johann Mendel, of Strasburg...[14]

Raban Maur, born in Mainz in 776, translated the Old and New Testament into the Teutonic, or old German, tongue. Some time later, Valafrid Strabon made a new translation of the whole Bible. Huges of Fleury also translated the Scriptures into German, and the monk Ottfried of Wissemburg rendered it into verse...

Hallam, the non-Catholic historian, in his work on the Middle Ages, chap. 9, part 2, says:

---

[12] Bertrand Conway, *The Question Box*, New York: Paulist Press, 1929, p. 86. Sources: Lenhart, *Chained Bibles*, Savage, *Old English Librarie*.
[13] Janssen, *ibid.*, vol. 14, 384.
[14] Janssen, *ibid.*, vol. 1, 56-57; In vol. 14, 388. A catalogue of such translations is presented: Other editions in High German: Strasburg: 1470,1485 / Basel, Switzerland: 1474 / Augsburg: 1473 (2),1477 (2),1480,1487,1490,1507,1518 / Nuremburg: 1483]. Bible Translations in Low German: Cologne: 1480 (2) / Lubeck: 1494 / Halberstadt: 1522 / Delf: before 1522.

> In the 8th and 9th centuries, when the Vulgate ceased to be generally intelligible... translations were freely made into the vernacular languages, and, perhaps, read in churches.[15]

The well-known Anglican writer, Dr. Blunt, in *his History of the Reformation* (Vol. I. pp. 501-502), tells us that:

> There has been much wild and foolish writing about the scarcity of the Bible in the ages preceding the Reformation... that the Holy Scripture was almost a sealed book until it was printed in English by Tyndale and Coverdale, and that the only source of knowledge respecting it before them was the translation made by Wyckliffe. The facts are... that all laymen who could read were, as a rule, provided with their Gospels, their Psalter, or other devotional portions of the Bible. Men did, in fact, take a vast amount of personal trouble with respect to the productions of the Holy Scriptures... The clergy studied the Word of God and made it known to the laity; and those few among the laity who could read had abundant opportunity of reading the Bible either in Latin or English, up to the Reformation period.[16]

> We shall... refute once more the common fallacy that John Wycliff was the first to place an English translation of the Scriptures in the hands of the English people in 1382. To anyone that has investigated the real facts of the case, this fondly-cherished notion must seem truly ridiculous; it is not only absolutely false, but stupidly so, inasmuch as it admits of such easy disproof...
>
> To begin far back, we have a copy of the work of Caedmon, a monk of Whitby, in the end of the 7th century, consisting of great portions of the Bible in the common tongue. In the next century we have the well-known translations of the Venerable Bede, a monk of Jarrow... In the same (8th) century we have the copies of Eadhelm... of Guthlac,... and of Egbert... these were all in Saxon, the language understood and spoken by the Christians of that time. Coming down a little later, we have the free translations of King Alfred the Great... and of Aelfric, Archbishop of Canterbury... After the Norman conquest of 1066, Anglo-Norman or

---

[15] Patrick F. O'Hare, *The Facts About Luther*, Rockford, IL: TAN Books, rev. ed., 1987 (originally, Cincinnati, 1916), 183,185.
[16] O'Hare, *ibid.*, 185-186.

Middle-English became the language of England, and consequently the next translations of the Bible we meet with are in that tongue... such as the paraphrase of Orm (about 1150) and the Salus Animae (1250), the translations of William Shoreham and Richard Rolle... (d.1349)...

The translators of the Authorised Version, in their 'Preface,' refer to previous translations...:

> Much about that time [1360], even our King Richard the Second's days, John Trevisa translated them into English, and many English Bibles in written hand are yet to be seen that divers translated, as it is very probable, in that age... So that, to have the Scriptures in the mother tongue is not a quaint conceit lately taken up... but hath been... put in practice of old, even from the first times of the conversion of any nation.[17]

From 1450 to 1520 [there were] many translations of the whole Bible... seventeen German, eleven Italian, ten French, two Bohemian, one Belgian,... and one Russian edition.[18]

Says another Protestant scholar,...:

> It can no longer be said that the Vulgate alone was in use and that the laity consequently were ignorant of Scripture... We must admit that the Middle Ages possessed a quite surprising and extremely praiseworthy knowledge of the Bible, such as might in many respects put our own age to shame.[19]

We know from history that there were popular translations of the Bible and Gospels in Spanish, Italian, Danish, French, Norwegian, Polish, Bohemian and Hungarian for the Catholics of those lands before the days of printing...

In Italy there were more than 40 editions of the Bible before the first Protestant version appeared, beginning at Venice in 1471; and 25 of

---

[17] Graham, *ibid.*, 98-101.
[18] Grisar, *ibid.*, vol. 5, 536. Data from Franz Falk, *The Bible in the Middle Ages*, Cologne: 1905, 24, 91 ff.
[19] Grisar, *ibid.*, vol. 5, 537. Citation of E. v. Dobschutz, *Deutsche Rundschau*, 101, 1900, 61 ff.

these were in the Italian language before 1500, with the express permission of Rome. In France there were 18 editions before 1547, the first appearing in 1478. Spain began to publish editions in the same year, and issued Bibles with the full approval of the Spanish Inquisition (of course one can hardly expect Protestants to believe this). In Hungary by the year 1456, in Bohemia by the year 1478, in Flanders before 1500, and in other lands groaning under the yoke of Rome, we know that editions of the Sacred Scriptures had been given to the people. In all... 626 editions of the Bible, in which 198 were in the language of the laity, had issued from the press, with the sanction and at the instance of the Church, in the countries where she reigned supreme, before the first Protestant version of the Scriptures was sent forth into the world... What, then, becomes of the pathetic delusion... that an acquaintance with the open Bible in our own tongue must necessarily prove fatal to Catholicism?...

Many senseless charges are laid at the door of the Catholic Church; but surely the accusation that, during the centuries preceding the 16th, she was the enemy of the Bible and of Bible reading must, to any one who does not wilfully shut his eyes to facts, appear of all accusations the most ludicrous...

We may examine and investigate the action of the Church in various countries and in various centuries as to her legislation in regard to Bible reading among the people; and wherever we find some apparently severe or unaccountable prohibition of it, we shall on enquiry find that it was necessitated by the foolish or sinful conduct on the part either of some of her own people, or of bitter and aggressive enemies who literally forced her to forbid what in ordinary circumstances she would not only have allowed but have approved and encouraged.[20]

---

[20] Graham, *ibid.*, 98,105-106,108,120. See also the excellent *Catholic Encyclopedia* article on *Scripture*, by A.J. Maas, section VI: "Attitude of the Church Towards the Reading of the Bible in the Vernacular" online: http://www.newadvent.org/cathen/13635b.htm; original: edited by Charles B. Herbermann et al, New York: The Encyclopedia Press, 1913, vol. XIII, 640.

Chapter Eleven

Insurmountable Practical Problems of *Sola Scriptura*

The Protestant notion of *sola Scriptura* takes into account other factors besides Scripture (Church history, commentaries, sermon material, creeds and confessions, etc.). But the ultimate determinant of any given doctrinal conclusion is the individual, because he is "condemned to choose (the proper interpretation and exegesis)," so to speak. That principle of *sola Scriptura* is unassailable, or else the system collapses into merely a variant of Tradition.

The Scripture is the "sole" authority for the Protestant in the sense that nothing else is binding (or so it is said, anyway. I would maintain to the contrary: that there are many subconscious or unconscious implicit and unacknowledged traditions mixed into the process of interpretation).

Again, other factors may be taken into account, but they are never *binding*. The individual is the final authority (claiming that he is standing on Scripture Alone—when in fact he is almost always not).

Protestant apologists, in trying to explain how differential interpretations and doctrines within Protestantism come about, will often blame faulty hermeneutical procedures, rather than the principle of *sola Scriptura* itself. Indeed, this may often be the case for *any* interpreter of Holy Scripture, yet it must be asked in return:

> Who had the faulty hermeneutical procedure, Martin Luther or John Calvin, when they disagreed on the nature of baptism and Holy Communion? How is this to be judged? Why should I believe either party when both appeal to Scripture?

This is the sort of conundrum *sola Scriptura* inevitably reduces to: a sort of theological relativism, even though that is not the intended result at all for the adherents of this theological system, who sincerely believe that it is the only way to resolve the matter of authority for the Christian.

But given the divisions in Protestantism, it is reasonable and plausible to suspect a flaw in *the underlying premise*, rather than question the ability to interpret of every person who happens to come down on the other side of a given theological dispute (although that is clearly a possibility, too in individual instances: just not an all-encompassing one).

Every Protestant is operating under certain premises, which he has inherited from whatever Protestant tradition he is in: whether or not he is aware of them. A Protestant may believe in *sola Scriptura* or *sola fide* (*faith alone*) or instantaneous salvation, or double predestination, or any number of Protestant distinctives. These came from somewhere, and they can be traced historically. It can be surmised, for example, whether they were believed by the Church Fathers or not.

In any event, it is usually an illusion for a lone person to think that their interpretation of Scripture came right from the Holy Spirit to them (with the aid of pure, unadulterated reason), without the influence of churches, pastors, books, professors, Bible studies, spiritual experiences, one's own biases and personal preferences, denominational traditions and/or creeds (even things like hymns), etc., etc.

So *sola Scriptura* inherently and unavoidably involves a hidden premise which is false (viz., that the individual somehow rises above all traditions—completely or at least substantially—in his ascertaining of biblical truth). The individual must judge in the end.

That is inescapable. It necessarily follows once authoritative Tradition is discarded. Protestants need to demonstrate that the Protestant individual is not the final determinant of doctrine—that he is not his own theologian or his own pope, as we like to rhetorically point out.

The Protestant may consult a commentary, as Protestants certainly do (and commendably, and much more often than Catholics do). But the whole point (assuming he applies *sola Scriptura* consistently) is that he ultimately judges that commentary and any other ones, in order to arrive at his own conclusion. That is the root of the problem, and why relativism (hence necessarily error somewhere) reigns.

The final authority rests with the individual and his interpretation of Scripture, not actually "Scripture Alone"—which is a mere pipe dream and fantasy. The Protestant inquirer could read every commentary in the Library of Congress or at Wheaton College or Westminster Seminary, or Calvin's and Luther's complete works, but that would not change this foundational principle in the slightest, if he remains the final arbiter.

Is every Christian in the world is able to find enough time, and become educated enough and familiar enough with Scripture to be his own theologian? And if he consults other ones, wise enough to always get it right when he chooses?

How does the Protestant decide which view is correct when far greater minds than he (Luther, Calvin, Wesley, Kuyper, Strong, Hodge, et al) contradict each other? How can the very concept "correct doctrine" (i.e., "orthodox") have any meaning when one is unable to reasonably ascertain this true belief? The only final test of orthodoxy under these premises consistently applied is one's own belief. "Orthodoxy" then (logically) boils down to "whatever my belief is."

It is often stated that Scripture is "perspicuous" (clear) and able to be understood in the main by the committed, regenerate layman, and that by comparing Bible passage with Bible passage, the truth can always be found.

But the rub is that there are different *ways* of harmonizing the Scripture. There is the Calvinist way and the Arminian way and the Baptist way, the Lutheran, Anglican, Nazarene, Presbyterian, Methodist, Plymouth Brethren, 7th-Day Adventist, Mennonite, Church of God, Church of Christ ways, etc., etc. ad infinitum. Simply invoking the principle does not solve the problem in the least.

More sophisticated Protestants—of course—consult commentaries and a respectable Protestant tradition of some sort, but they still decide themselves which. It is inescapable, given the underlying assumptions of *sola Scriptura*.

For the Catholic, on the other hand, truth is determined by its accord with apostolic Tradition, which can be traced back historically to the Apostles, and which is most fully preserved in the Catholic Church—itself in full accord with biblical teaching. This was the patristic method, the biblical method, and the Catholic method, now and always. Catholics have the pope, the Councils, catechisms, apostolic succession (i.e., an authoritative Church).

The logical result of Protestantism is that the congregant (or layman) is the judge of the pastor (and pastors will even state this as a principle, from the pulpit). In reality, the congregant more often than not simply takes in what the pastor says and accepts it as gospel truth, without doing his own research (out of laziness, inability, or apathy).

On the other hand, when one contends vigorously (but respectfully) against a pastor (as I myself did on one occasion before my conversion), they are more often than not ostracized and denounced (as I was). One quickly discovers that this vaunted ability (and "duty") to judge the pastor with Scripture is not all that that respected after all, when the rubber meets the road.

The Bible does not interpret itself. It is a book, and a book must be read by a human being and interpreted, just like any other book (but hopefully, with prayer and the willingness to follow what God is teaching in Holy Scripture). Theoretically, even if Scripture were perspicuous (clearly understood), it would still require a human being to determine precisely what these teachings are which are so clear and self-evident in Scripture—contrary to the oft-expressed quasi-Islamic notion of "Scripture without human beings."

Likewise, the U.S. Constitution might be regarded as true and wonderful and sufficient, etc. But the fact remains that this abstract belief only lasts undisturbed as long as the first instance of case law in which two parties claim divergent interpretations of the Constitution. It's the same with Protestants. Merely invoking "Bible Alone" doesn't change the fact that there is a "Lutheran Bible" and a "Presbyterian Bible" and a "Baptist Bible" etc., etc.

Besides, the Bible itself teaches that the Church and Tradition are also authoritative, so if one wants to invoke "Bible Alone" they are already assuming the Catholic tripartate view of Church + Scripture + Tradition. Furthermore, the very Canon of Scripture was also a matter of Church and Tradition.

On the other hand, *sola Scriptura* as a principle and rule of faith never ever appears in Scripture. Why would that be? If it is so important, so fundamental, so supposedly self-evident, why didn't God simply express this in one indisputable verse, and thus settle the matter once and for all?

Protestants believe everything has to be spelled out in the Bible. Therefore, since *sola Scriptura* isn't, it is a self-defeating proposition; therefore false, and obviously so, if indeed (as I strongly contend) no Scripture can be found to support it.

How does a person using the method of *sola Scriptura* arrive at belief in any particular doctrine? Do they simply take some teacher's word for what is true? If so, then they have let a man decide their belief (to some extent), and not Scripture Alone. They decided who to believe for the true interpretation of Scripture. If—on the other hand—they decide completely on their own, with Bible in hand, then they have proven what I am claiming.

The Catholic knows which Traditions are true by tracing them back historically, and because such historical, apostolic beliefs are consistent with Holy Scripture (as the infallible standard of true Christian belief). And he knows (by faith) because great Councils and popes decided that they were true Christian beliefs, based on the preceding two criteria.

How do we know that the Traditions handed down to us are the same ones believed in by the Apostles? We determine that by reading their writings (the Bible), reading the Fathers, and following the unbroken line back to the apostles. This is apostolic succession. Most Protestants also claim that their beliefs were those of the early Church, so virtually every Christian acknowledges the historic aspect of "orthodoxy" to some extent.

It is a truism for all conservative Christians (or should be, anyway) that the Bible is true, God's Word, infallible, inspired, revelation, etc. That is not in dispute at all. So we need not debate that Now—that being the case—our task is to determine what this true and trustworthy Bible *teaches*.

The Bible is a book, like other books in the respect that it must be interpreted. Whether it is obscure or not is a separate issue. Catholics don't think it is so much "obscure" as it is prone to distorted interpretations because of, e.g., false theological presuppositions applied to it, selective proof texting, neglect of context, unbridled private judgment, wanton disregard for exegetical and doctrinal precedent, etc.

Protestant apologists tend to maintain that "either we interpret a clear Bible individually, or else an authoritative Church simply tells you how to interpret an obscure, mysterious Bible." There are, of course, many intermediate positions between those two extreme antinomies. The Bible is God's written Revelation, but that doesn't at all prove that it is therefore *self-interpreting* and isolated from Church and Tradition. Nor is it *all-encompassing* (see, e.g., John 20:30; 21:25; Acts 1:2-3).

The authoritative Bible must be synthesized with Christian Apostolic Tradition, which is itself most fully preserved within the Catholic Church. Catholics have no problem with the theoretical clearness of Scripture in the main. What we regard as the fundamental problem, rather, is the relativizing of biblical interpretation by means of contradicting denominational traditions, rather than synthesizing Scripture with the one Apostolic Tradition passed down from the apostles and preserved in unbroken succession.

If a person had a Bible on a deserted island, and knew not the slightest thing about Christianity, the Church or Christian history, then surely they could attain eschatological salvation by means of the Bible alone. But that is not the usual situation we find ourselves in.

Reality is generally not that simple. There are competing denominations and churches out there, which make truth claims. The idea of a "Church" (Big "C") is very biblical. Protestants also routinely speak of "**the** Church" when referring to the early Church.

But somehow, after the 16th century, this notion was more and more lost among Protestants in general, save for (I generalize) a vague, ethereal concept of an invisible church, whose membership is ultimately known by God alone. Yet they usually don't refer to the early Church in those terms.

The basic salvation message in the Bible (notwithstanding Protestant-Catholic disputes as to its finepoints) is *not* difficult to understand, but we find that in the *application* of these biblical words to the Christian life and theology, Christians start to disagree.

For example, Jesus also said that if one doesn't eat His flesh and drink His blood, they have no life in them (let alone eternal life: John 8:53). If someone does do that, Jesus says they have eternal life (Jn 8:54). So we see that now sacraments and the nature of Holy Communion are brought to bear on the topic.

We must synthesize Scripture and incorporate cross-references and comparative exegesis. The same applies to baptism, since there are several explicit verses connecting it, too, with salvation. But these are some of the very issues Christians are most divided on.

Protestants believe that God can and does protect His Bible from error (and that He uses sinful and fallible men to write it). So do we. We then merely extend that principle to His visible, apostolic Church, as an aspect of His omnipotence and the function of the Holy Spirit to "lead us into all truth." This is all quite biblical (and plausible).

But one of the fallacies of the Protestant view is that even the Canon of Scripture was determined by sinful, fallible men in Church councils. So Protestants are forced to accept the validity of infallible Church Tradition in at least that one instance. But if God did that then, why not at all times? So we merely consistently apply a notion that Protestants are forced to apply in one instance, even against their own formal principle. There is no end to the logical, biblical, and historical incoherence and inconsistency of *sola Scriptura*.

The verdict is in with regard to *sola Scriptura*—we have seen the tragic and destructive fruit of these false and unbiblical notions. Truths will work in the real world (what I have referred to as the *reverse pragmatic argument*: "something isn't true because it works, but it works because—or when—it is true").

Conservative, evangelical, "orthodox" Protestants must ask themselves: why do Luther and Calvin disagree? Which one was the supposedly ignorant and/or sinful interpreter? And why should I believe any individual Protestant when he makes such a judgment?

Such alleged "clearness" has not in fact brought about unanimity of belief, as Luther naively assumed it would. One has to speculate as to why this is. The usual reason given is "sin and ignorance." I agree that those things are definite factors, but I also take it further and assert that the root problem lies in the premise, the foundation: *sola Scriptura*. Protestants are understandably reluctant to do that, because to do so would mean questioning Protestantism itself—knocking down (or chipping away at) one of its two pillars (the other being *faith alone*).

My Protestant friend in one of my online dialogues, oblivious to the above considerations, asserted, "if more Protestants read the Scriptures, there wouldn't be the vast divisions that there are." This is the theory, and I understand full well the viewpoint (having once held it myself), but I think it is utterly simplistic and naive, since it breaks down as soon as two or more brilliant and scholarly Protestant commentators or theologians apply rigorous standards of Protestant hermeneutics, yet come to different conclusions. The reality of Protestant history and current-day division is far too complex and troublesome to allow for this explanation.

Doctrinal history is one crucial component which helps to determine correct exegesis and hermeneutics ("how have the Fathers understood this passage?").

What's to stop a Protestant from *highly regarding* the authority of Scripture and yet coming up with false teaching? Nothing! No council, no pope, not even a denomination (if "pure" *sola Scriptura* is to be upheld) can bind the individual over against his private judgment and conscience. This is what Luther brought about, and Protestants have to face up to the logical outcome of their own stated position.

I conclude, then, that the Bible is apparently not so clear on these matters, and that therefore, a key element of *sola Scriptura* is brought into question. But the *sola Scriptura* advocate just turns around and says, "but the other guy got it wrong; he didn't study hard enough. I got it right!" This is special pleading.

Catholics, on the other hand, conform their biblical interpretation to that of the Church, where the two differ, and the Catholic Church sees what the sinfulness of man can do to the Scriptures, if left unchecked (in terms of having no binding authority over them).

I believe that the Scriptures are very clear on many issues. My own research has constantly reinforced that conclusion. Yet (pious, scholarly, theologically conservative) people disagree. It is that disagreement (and consequent necessary error) which the Catholic system tries to prevent. Unless they have some binding corporate church authority, the individual is ultimately on his own.

Protestant apologists often say that the definition Catholic apologists use for *sola Scriptura* (I derive my working definition from Protestant theologians R.C. Sproul, G.C. Berkouwer, and Bernard Ramm: two Reformed and the latter a Baptist) doesn't represent the real definition, and is therefore the construction of a "straw man." But then they are immediately faced with the following dilemmas:

Who speaks authoritatively for Protestantism (and by what authority?), in order to define *sola Scriptura* in the first place? The best answer, I believe, is some sort of Protestant creed or confession, but then one immediately faces the problem of accounting for non-creedal Protestants (such as Baptists or Church of Christ), who consider themselves not bound to any Creed, but the Bible Alone. So—as usual—there is no final resolution to this; thus all "ironclad" Protestant definitions of *sola Scriptura* are inadequate and questionable to some extent—due to the very nature and essence of the outlook.

Thus this futile yet common counter-tactic of claiming that Catholic apologists (many of whom—like myself - were formerly evangelical Protestants) don't know the definition is somewhat analogous (since we *do* know it—insofar as it is possible to ascertain) to the old "slippery fish" polemical tactic.

As soon as the Catholic critiques one thing or other in Protestantism, the Protestant who uses this tactic says, "oh, but that's not **me!** Those **other** guys believe that! You can't pin that on me!" Or, "I don't care what Luther and Calvin taught! I go by the **Bible**, which is clear." It's sort of like trying to shoot the moving ducks at a carnival, whereas the "target" of the Catholic Church is like the giant ferris wheel at the carnival: a very easy and convenient target.

The Catholic Church holds that Scripture and Tradition are two sides of the same coin. They are of a piece, and never to be separated. Unless a Protestant grasps this notion, they can never hope to understand our view. This does not mean that the Church and/or Tradition is *above* Scripture. It is *higher*, so to speak, only in a *practical* (not essential) sense of unity of authoritative interpretation. Church and Tradition are not at all superior to Scripture, yet they are authoritative interpreters of same (and I would maintain further that this is precisely the view of the Fathers).

Martin Luther declared in his "Here I stand" plea at the Diet of Worms in 1521: "unless I am convinced by Scripture and plain reason..." He was willing to "veto" the entirety of Church history where he disagreed with it, as a matter of conscience, and place himself in the position of "final arbiter." This is private judgment, the Protestant principle. It follows inexorably from the rejection of binding Church authority.

For the Church Fathers, Scripture was the "measuring rod," so to speak, but—most importantly—seen through the "lens" of received Apostolic Tradition. The Tradition was actually the final determinant in the Fathers' eyes (because—like today—all the heretics cited Scripture in support of their views).

Apostolic Tradition is a separate entity, which provides an independent "verifying mechanism." It is closely related to Church and Scripture, but it is still separate, and is subject to historiographical scrutiny, thus making it a means whereby to "test" Catholic claims, and eliminating the common charge of "circularity" with regard to Catholic claims of Church authority. The Bible is also a separate entity in this sense, and one can test Catholic claims by that "standard." But *sola Scriptura* certainly is a circular claim.

Protestants, on the other hand, all appeal to Scripture (using—ultimately—their own interpretations), but since they have no overall authority and too often care little (often not at all) about historical precedent (pre-1517), they have no way of resolving their myriad disputes.

Catholics appeal to the unbroken Apostolic Tradition, which has developed, but never changed in any essential way since the time of the apostles, from whom the Church received the "deposit."

As for a "self-validating system," secularists make the same charge of Protestants, since some (i.e., those with poor apologetics skills, or a disdain of reason) claim the Bible as their source, and go on to claim that the Bible is true because it claims to be God's Word, etc.

They see circularity all over Protestant views (usually falsely), just as Protestants think they see it in ours. But both views (to more or less degrees) can be theoretically verified on historical grounds. The Resurrection of Jesus Christ is a prime example of historically-verifiable evidence for both Scripture and Christianity itself.

Once history can test the veracity of a system, then the "problem" of alleged circularity is solved, regardless of disputes within historiography. To paraphrase C.S. Lewis: "the rules of chess create chess problems." All fields of scholarly inquiry, whether science, or philosophy, or whatever else, have "problems" to be resolved. All one can do in this case is consult the Fathers themselves, or rely on other scholars who study them.

We can consult history as given by patristic, ancient, and mediæval historians, of whatever creed (as long as they are good scholars). Catholics can go to Philip Schaff and Jaroslav Pelikan and Kenneth Scott Latourette and J.N.D. Kelly and other Protestant or Orthodox church historians and verify Catholic historical claims. The particular reasons for why we think the Church is the "Guardian" of the apostolic deposit is another discussion. But we also know it from the Bible and from patristic views.

There is, assuredly, a place for submission and faith, of course. I don't mean to deny that for a second (this is not just a matter of reason, but also one of revelation and grace), but my present point is that Catholic ecclesiological reasoning and authority is not logically circular, as is so often charged, and Catholic claims about history are relatively easily verifiable from non-Catholic sources.

Nor does the Catholic Church deny that the Holy Spirit guides individuals, in biblical interpretation and all other matters. But one must make sure such guidance is verified by the teaching of the Catholic Church, just as is the case with an "informed conscience" and with regard to spiritual experiences within Protestantism.

Protestantism in its better forms seeks to verify peoples' experiences by the Bible, or the Bible and a Creed or Confession (such as in Presbyterianism or Anglicanism). Catholics do it by the Bible and the dogmatic teaching of the Catholic Church, and the appeal to Sacred Tradition, if need be.

There is not much difference between the two methods, in a certain sense. If a Protestant (say, a Baptist) claims that the Holy Spirit told him that the Trinity was a false doctrine, his pastor will in all likelihood tell him this was not the Holy Spirit speaking to him. We merely extend that principle further and make it more all-encompassing. But all Christian groups have their boundaries of orthodoxy.

One (as a Protestant inquirer) determines from Scripture the nature of the Church, the nature of Church government, etc., whether apostolic succession is true, patristic beliefs, and other such things. Then one looks around for a Christian body which best "fits the bill." Orthodoxy offers some plausibility (and we regard it as a "sister Church").

But I assert that the Catholic Church and it alone fills all the requirements for an authoritative, historically-continuous and consistent Christian Church (in the *visible* sense, which is the biblical view). It takes much faith, of course, but we can verify this by history and the Bible. We believe that Jesus Christ our Lord and Savior established a Church with real authority, and that there is One

Church, not many, or an invisible society where no one knows for sure who is in it, or even where it starts and ends.

We believe that Jesus and/or the Apostles:

1) established a visible, concrete Church (not a quasi-secret, esoteric, nebulous, invisible society of fellow believers) to propagate the teachings of Jesus and Christianity;
2) established a papacy as well, to lead that Church (Matthew 16);
3) passed down a definite and identifiable "deposit of faith" which St. Paul refers to as having been "received" or "delivered."

The Church Fathers had a strong overriding sense of "preserving" this same deposit of faith which they received from the Apostles, and they taught that there was really only one choice of a Church which respected and maintained all of these biblical and historic Christian elements, and functioned as the "Guardian" of apostolic Tradition.

This was all brought together for me personally by Cardinal Newman and his *Essay on the Development of Christian Doctrine* (though it was a process). I found the "Catholic case" as a whole (particularly Newman's historical argument for it) consistent with (in no particular order): 1) Church history, 2) reason, 3) the Bible, 4) the moral theology I had developed as an evangelical, 5) my own spiritual experience(s), and 6) even things like aesthetics and philosophy. One can hardly be on more firm ground than that in matters of theology (or any field of thought). Faith (and the emotionally scary step of actual commitment) are still required, of course, as in any Christian view.

With regard to apostolic succession, some doctrines were more developed early on than others, but none are virtually entirely absent, as in the case of, e.g., *sola Scriptura*, *sola fide*, symbolic baptism, and symbolic Eucharist (and many other Protestant distinctives).

It is argued that the Fathers looked to Scripture for proof of their doctrine in the face of heresy. But these are almost always examples of simply citing Scripture, which proves nothing in and of itself. The Protestant then superimposes his own presupposition of *sola Scriptura* onto the Father and contend that he agrees with the Protestant outlook. This is anachronistic interpretation.

I refuted a clear example of this one time on an Internet list. A Church Father was cited to the effect that he believed in *sola Scriptura*. I promptly posted another explicit and unambiguous quote from the same Father showing that he clearly accepted a binding Tradition and apostolic authority. So one quote can be misleading (just as biblical proof texts taken in isolation can be).

Protestants must see what the Fathers also said about Tradition and apostolic succession as the litmus test of orthodoxy. We can easily synthesize both views within our Rule of Faith.

Catholicism is very Scripture-centered. I maintain that we take all Scripture into account, whereas Protestantism ignores large parts of it which don't fit into its theology. One only needs to read the Vatican II documents or any papal encyclical to see that. As soon as any mention of Church and Tradition are brought in, many Protestants automatically assumes that Scripture is necessarily "demoted" or "denigrated." But that is neither logically necessary, nor is it in fact true within Catholicism.

Protestants often do the same thing with God: if man is not totally depraved or if a saint is venerated, then of course they think that immediately takes away from God's glory, whereas in fact it profoundly glorifies Him through His creation, just as procreation mimics creation and glorifies God while intimately involving man in the process.

This false dichotomizing or "either/or" mentality is an unfortunately prevalent tendency in Protestant thought. Catholicism has a "both/and" outlook, which is much more Hebrew and biblical: Faith and Works; Bible and Tradition; Church and Bible' A Holy God and holy saints; Jesus as heavenly Head of the Church and the pope as the earthly head; Faith and Reason; Reason and Revelation; Old and New Testaments; The Church as a development of the Old Covenant (instead of being opposed to it, as in Dispensationalism); Law and Grace, etc., etc. These are all paradoxes and complementaries, not contradictions and false, unnessescary dichotomies.

Protestant apologists will claim that Catholic Tradition is incapable of ever being proven "false" because it is a supposedly "circular system." But—in practice—can Calvinism be proven false by Scripture? Or faith alone? Or *sola Scriptura*? It seems that, for many Protestants, *sola Scriptura* cannot be disproven. It is an indisputable fact, like gravity or the spherical earth, in his mind.

If the Protestant admits that these things are true of their belief, then we are in the same epistemological boat (though I vehemently deny the Catholic system is circular). We claim our beliefs are consistent with Holy Scripture; so do Protestants, and all Christians.

Nothing in Scripture indicates that frequently-referred-to Tradition was ever intended to cease. This is an entirely false and unbiblical assumption, based on premises which are in turn arbitrary. If something is in Scripture, it is usually considered normative for Christians, not temporary.

The same thing applies to Peter's leadership and the papacy. Why have that for 20 or 30 years, and then the office ceases and the Christian Church opts for congregationalism? It makes no sense, and has no plausibility.

Furthermore, the early Fathers take this view en masse. St. Augustine even argues for an authoritative oral Tradition alongside (but harmonious with) Scripture. Many Protestant views require a belief that the people closest in time to the apostles got it dead wrong. Somehow they went "Catholic."

Jesus allowed Doubting Thomas to feel His flesh (John 20:24-29), presented "many convincing proofs" (Acts 1:3), and reasoned extensively with the two disciples on the road to Emmaus (Luke 24:13-35). The Catholic Church highly values the mind, but in the end it does require faith to believe, just as Jesus showed mercy to Thomas in his skeptical bent of mind, yet concluded by saying, "Blessed are those who have not seen and yet have come to believe." His resurrection wasn't a "negotiable doctrine," open to skeptical, hostile inquiry.

We simply follow the Lord's model. We use our heads, but we don't ever underestimate things like prayer and grace and faith. Without grace no one can become a Christian, nor can anyone convert to Catholicism, which we believe to be the fullest expression of apostolic and biblical Christianity.

The outsider will often caricature, stereotype, paint with a broad brush, or think of this as "irrational obedience" or "blind faith" (pure existential fideism) or "autocratic dogmatism," but what else is new? The unregenerate world thinks that with regard to *all* forms of committed Christianity. They think Protestants are just as "dogmatic" (if not more so, from their vantage point) as Catholics, or only slightly less so.

The Catholic Church doesn't require blind submission in the face of honest doubt. Rather, it would have a person submit, knowing that if the Church has been right 99 times out 100 (a sort of "cumulative effect" and testimony), chances are the individual in his private judgment is wrong in the one exception and not the Church.

The person gives the assent of his will, if he wishes to be an obedient, faithful Catholic, but he will also (or should) by all means seek to understand the mind of the Church on the matter. He doesn't have to understand everything in order to submit (who does, anyway? That in itself is a fallacy). He recognizes that many minds (and holy souls) greater than he are involved, not just himself.

This is corporate Christianity. And this is Tradition, which is (in Chesterton's delightful phrase), "the democracy of the dead." This is the acknowledgment that God leads His Church, the Body of Christ—the extension of the Incarnation throughout history—in the world, as a whole, not just the Christian individual (though He certainly does that, too—that is abundantly clear in many stories of the saints).

It is not irrational to submit to an ecclesiastical authority—as if this were intrinsically opposed to the thinking process or a reasoned faith. The notion of the atomistic individual—rampant today—is a thoroughly unbiblical state of mind.

The Catholic compares any doubts that he may have with all that he has come to see as right and true about the Catholic Church. If it was still a 100-to-1 proposition, I think only a fool would opt for the one over against the 100, and that this would be an unreasonable choice to make. There must be a balance. The problem comes when a person places his own doubt above all the rest which counter-balances it (all Christian history included, if need be), and makes himself his own pope.

He condemns the papal system as autocratic and intellectually oppressive, yet ironically turns around and assumes in his own person ultimately more power—both in terms of "freedom" and of determination of his own belief—than any Catholic pope ever dreamt of. Of course Martin Luther did just that, and Protestants today follow his lead, for the most part.

It might be asked why one even needs the Holy Spirit's guidance when the Church or pope is an infallible guide. One needs the Spirit for the same reason that God gave Adam and Eve a free will and minds, yet intended them to function in obedience to God's directives. The Catholic Church doesn't desire automaton followers, just as God didn't want that. But it does want obedient and informed Catholics. The two things are by no means mutually exclusive.

One must accept the authority of the Catholic Church on its own terms, as opposed to "figuring it all out," so to speak. That is the fundamentally Catholic approach over against the Protestant one. It's like the "pearl of great price." The emphasis is all on the pearl itself, not the process by which we arrive at the discovery.

Protestantism is in many ways a perpetual search for a truth which so often is never found (at least not in totality), which is why I have compared it (in *that* regard) to philosophy, rather than a faith to be found and cherished and lived out. God never intended for us to spend our whole lives searching for **the truth**. He wanted us to **live** it, once having received it by faith, passed down from the apostles and fully preserved in the Catholic Church.

I was asked by my Baptist friend: "Where in Scripture would one find a concept like 'assent' as opposed to honest 'belief'?" I replied:

1) Mark 9:24:... *'I believe; help my unbelief!'* (NRSV)
2) The Doubting Thomas incident of John 20:24-29:
   ... *'Have you believed because you have seen me? Blessed are those who have not seen and yet have come to believe.'* (20:29; NRSV)

Note that Jesus presented to Thomas empirical proof of His resurrection (the wound in His side), yet He still implies that belief without such hard evidence ought to be sufficient.

3) We have the incident of "the bread from heaven" in John 6:35-71. Clearly, the disciples did not understand Jesus' exposition of the Real Presence (eat my flesh and drink my blood...)—see, e.g., John 6:41-43,52,60-63,66. Jesus, however, was unflinching. The disciples were required to believe what they did not understand. They refused to, and some forsook Him (6:66), the only recorded instance (apart from Judas) of disciples turning back from following the Lord. This is a crystal-clear example of required assent where one does not have a fully-developed "honest belief."

4) We see the motif of Jesus explaining to the disciples more and more explicitly that He must be killed in Jerusalem. He requires them to accept this even though it is almost incomprehensible (and understandably threatening) to them (as evidenced, e.g., by His rebuke of Peter: Matthew 16:21-23, and the similar rebuke—even post-Resurrection—of the disciples on the road to Emmaus: Luke 24:25-27).

Why should the disciples have believed Jesus? Well, because He said it! So, if His apostles and the bishops who succeeded them teach something, assent is likewise required, as St. Ignatius (d.c. 110) states in the strongest possible terms. And this is biblical:

> ... whoever receives one whom I send receives me; and whoever receives me receives him who sent me.
>
> (John 13:20; cf. Luke 9:48, Mark 9:37, Matthew 18:5—NRSV; ones "sent" refer most particularly to the apostles, and the bishops succeeded them)

For those like Thomas, Jesus was implying that his demand for empirical proof might be a bit excessive, at the least. This is similar to those who apply unnecessarily restrictive epistemological criteria in order to believe anything (usually applied with a double standard, too, if one examines it closely enough).

My point was to establish the scriptural and Christian principle that one need not have all the answers or proof or reasons for something before they can reasonably believe it and give their assent or submission. In many instances, the word of the Lord or the Church ought to be sufficient to compel assent (in faith, and by God's grace).

Chapter Twelve

Dialogue on the Alleged "Perspicuous Apostolic Message" as a Corollary of *Sola Scriptura*[1]

Protestant apologist (P): What we object to is the argument Dave has made that "*sola Scriptura* is false because it hasn't caused agreement on all the theological issues."

Catholic apologist: Dave Armstrong (C): To my recollection, I have never made such an argument. What I said was that perspicuity[2] fails as a thought-system because it presupposes possible (and actual) agreement among Protestants, at least on the so-called "central" issues, based on recourse to the Bible alone. This is clearly false, and a pipe-dream.

My point was, (paraphrasing): "what criteria of falsifiability will suffice to challenge the Protestant notion of perspicuity, given the fact of the great multiplicity of sects?" I've heard it 1000 times if I've heard it once that Protestants agree on the central issues, and that this "fact" supposedly salvages perspicuity and *sola Scriptura*.

P: Protestants, too, firmly accept what the apostles taught. And this is much of the reason why we cannot embrace the teachings of Catholicism. Indeed, maintaining the original, apostolic message is a powerful argument against the corrupt innovations and unbiblical additions of Rome over time.

---

[1] This chapter and the two following chapters are loosely based on an actual series of exchanges on Internet lists, or in personal correspondence, with Protestant apologists, two of whom are currently fairly well-known, published opponents of the Catholic Church. The arguments from my Protestant correspondents have been presented in paraphrased form, and preserve as closely as possible the original points made, without using direct citation. In other words, these are actual Protestant arguments, mostly from prominent apologists. My words are essentially the same as what I originally wrote, with minor changes. A great deal of extraneous or overly-polemical material, however (on either side), has been deleted.

[2] **Perspicuity** = the notion (a key assumption *of sola Scriptura*) that Holy Scripture is clear in the *main* and in its *central* teachings and able to be interpreted by the reasonably-educated committed Christian individual without the *necessary* assistance of an authoritative and binding teaching body.

C: Why not boldly tell us, then, precisely what "the apostles taught"? In particular, I am curious as to their teaching in those areas where Protestants can't bring themselves to agree with each other; for example:

1. TULIP
2. Baptism
3. The Eucharist
4. Church Government
5. Regeneration
6. Sanctification
7. The Place of Tradition
8. Women Clergy
9. Divorce
10. Feminism
11. Abortion
12. The Utility of Reason
13. Natural Theology
14. The Charismatic Gifts
15. Alcohol
16. Sabbatarianism
17. Whether Catholics are Christians
18. Civil Disobedience

In order to have "fidelity" to an "apostolic message" one must define what it is. And if you don't know, then you illustrate my point better than I could myself: either your case collapses due to internal inconsistency, or because Protestant sectarianism makes any such delineation of "orthodoxy" impossible according to your own first principles; or if theoretically possible, certainly unenforceable in practice. Jesus commanded His disciples to, "... [teach] *them to obey **everything** I have commanded you*" (Matthew 28:20)—not just the "central," "primary," "essential" doctrines.

P: That's easily answered, Dave. We have the New Testament, which is filled with the apostle's teaching. One such teaching is that we are justified by faith, giving us peace with God (Romans 5:1).

C: We agree in large part. But why, though, if *sola fide* is true, did "scarcely anyone" teach imputed righteousness or forensic justification from Paul to Luther, according to Protestant apologist Norman Geisler, in his latest book

Roman Catholics and Evangelicals: Agreements and Differences?[3] Very strange, and too implausible for me.

P: The apostles also taught that Jesus Christ was God (Colossians 2:9).

C: Absolutely. But we don't differ on this doctrine, so it is irrelevant to the current discussion.

P: Do you wish to contend that the Bible cannot answer these questions? That it is so unclear, confused, and ambiguous, that no one can determine its teaching on these issues by a close examination of Scripture?

C: It's ultimately irrelevant what I think, because I'm asking you. But let's assume for the sake of argument that it is clear, sufficient, and perspicuous. Okay, now, please tell me what it teaches on these issues. If we grant your perspicuity, then tell us these doctrines that are so clear! I'm saying: be true to your own principles, and don't be ashamed of them. I think you should either *demonstrate* this abstract, ethereal notion of perspicuity concretely and practically, or cease using it if it has no content.

P: Those who go by the title "Protestant" disagree on all the points above; so do Roman Catholics. So what?

C: One can only go by the official teachings of any given group. Is it a proper answer if an atheist, asked why he doesn't believe in God, says, "Well you theists can't agree whether God is a singular Being or a Trinity, so there!"? We are critiquing *your* position. Again, I'm just holding you to your own words.

P: The apostolic message is fairly narrow. They did not exhaustively address every single issue (such as cloning or computers). Does that mean, then, that the Bible is "insufficient"?

C: Are you going to seriously maintain that the apostles (in the Bible) did not address issues on my list such as: baptism, the Eucharist, church government, regeneration, sanctification, tradition, or the spiritual gifts? I'm astonished. Why don't you, then, select just five of this present list of items out of my entire list of 18 in which Protestants differ, and tell me what the apostles

---

[3] Co-author Ralph E. Mackenzie, Grand Rapids, MI: Baker Books, 1995, 502.

taught, so I can know what you know? I'm simply asking you to define what you mean by "apostolic message."

P: So you are arguing that a Christian believer with a Bible cannot find out what the apostolic message was unless Roman "tradition" informs him?

C: All the more reason for you to tell us what this mysterious "apostolic message" is. According to your logic, one can "know" what the message is, without the Catholic Church, but they can't tell *someone else* what it **is**, what it **consists** of!

P: I think, Dave, that you are fully aware that your question has been and will be answered.

C: If they have, I've missed it. If they "will" be answered, when, and by whom, I wonder? But I don't "know" one way or the other.

P: Do you claim to "know" "everything" that Jesus taught His disciples?

C: No. Do *you* wish to say this?

P: Can you defend the notion that Jesus taught His disciples the Immaculate Conception and Bodily Assumption of Mary, and papal infallibility? None of those doctrines can be found in the Fathers.

C: Answer my question, and I will be glad to deal with yours, but I would say that it would be more profitable to do that in another discussion group, so as not to cloud the issues which will take a considerable amount of time to work through as it is. I'm eagerly awaiting your response (nothing fancy required, just a laundry list) to my—as of yet—unanswered challenge.

P: What challenge was that?

C: Just a list of the true apostolic teachings on baptism, etc. At this point, I'd accept **any** interpretation. Again, I reiterate: at least Luther and Calvin had the strength of their convictions to excommunicate other Protestants for dissidence, because they truly believed in their own brand of Christianity. There is something to be said for that. Or is it the case, rather, that God doesn't care about truth when it comes to baptism, the Eucharist, ecclesiology, etc.? Is Protestantism thus reduced to an Orwellian "some doctrines are more true than others"?

P: I refuse to anathematize a brother in Christ for incorrect beliefs on baptism or Holy Communion. But I will certainly point out his error.

C: Maybe we're not that far apart after all, then. But you miss the fact that I was asking for an answer as to what the apostles believed on my 18 points. The original context of my challenge was for Protestants to define their own terms.

It occurs to me that it is exceedingly strange for Protestants to relegate the Eucharist to relativism and relative insignificance, when our Lord made it a point of division Himself. John 6:66 tells us of "many of his disciples" forsaking Him. Now, if the Eucharist were just minutiae on the grand scale of matters theological, why didn't Jesus beg and plead with these people to stay? If your view is correct, it seems reasonable that Jesus should then have said, "Hey, don't go: this isn't a matter which should divide us—we agree that I am God. Who cares about what happens in the central act of Christian worship!"

And we know also that Jesus said *unless you eat the flesh of the Son of Man and drink his blood, you have no life in you* (John 6:53). But that's "secondary" or "non-essential"? I'm sorry, but I can't give my assent to such an incoherent and unbiblical viewpoint. And of course, Scripture intimately relates baptism with both repentance and salvation (for the latter, see e.g., Acts 2:38, 1 Peter 3:21, Mark 16:16, Romans 6:3-4, Acts 22:16, 1 Corinthians 6:11, Titus 3:5). Protestantism went from one extreme to the other: baptism once meant everything; now it means virtually nothing (judging by toleration and dismissal as of little import, differing viewpoints).

P: I haven't compromised any doctrine.

C: Good, then please give me your list of my 18 points, since you're a good, "uncompromised" Protestant. That will be a wonderful start for the man on the street to ascertain apostolic and Christian truth.

P: What you don't seem to understand is that unity of belief is worthless if that belief is a falsehood!

C: I agree 100%. Thus the question boils down to (as always): is what the Catholic Church teaches true or false? (and the same for Protestantism). But you try to caricature my position as calling for a blind, absolute, clone-like unity. Of course not, as this is clearly absurd. My whole point in critiquing

Protestant disunity is that that is clearly, unarguably against the biblical injunctions to be unified, of "one mind," etc. Try as you may, neither you nor any Protestant can overcome the strength and validity of this objection to your position. That's why I asked someone "what would convince you that your view is wrong: 500,000 sects?" What does it take? How relativistic and chaotic must things become before you start to question your first principles?

P: You know what the biblical position is on these [18] topics.

C: This is the whole point! We know, but you can't figure it out. Hence your reluctance to answer (I can think of no better reason). A short answer to my question surely wouldn't put you out.

P: But you don't accept what the Bible teaches.

C: I supposedly "don't accept" what the Bible teaches on these points, but you don't have the courtesy to explain to me just what it is that it teaches on them. Such a view should cause you to blush with shame.

P: Instead of the Bible, you accept a Catholic authority that tells you differently.

C: Different than what? Again, if I don't have your answer, what do you expect me to believe? If this isn't "The Emperor's Clothes," I don't know what is.

P: Tell us again, Dave: do you claim that the Bible is insufficient to resolve these matters? That we can't learn what the Bible's position on tradition is, for instance? That a serious exegesis of texts can't give us any knowledge?

C: NO NO NO. Now, how about your equally forthright answer to me?

P: Catholics have "infallible" interpreters to explain an "infallible" authority, yet still end up with differing interpretations.

C: If a person had a Bible on a desert isle, and that's all he had, sure, he could be saved. But some Church or authority will be ordinarily necessary, so that, in the final analysis it is a moot point. I believe that all Catholic doctrines can be found in Scripture, either explicitly or implicitly or indirectly. If that is material sufficiency, then I am in that camp. But if it means that somehow the Church and Tradition are thereby taken out of the picture as not intrinsically necessary to Christianity, then I must dissent, because I don't see that in Scripture (I believe *sola Scriptura* is self-defeating, in other words).

Catholics regard Scripture as central, but not exclusive, with regard to authority and Tradition. Thus, to critique *sola Scriptura* does not at all imply a lessening of respect for the Bible, as has been implied in this group and elsewhere.

I think we need to determine what Tradition(s) were in fact believed by Christians through history, and whether these can be found to possess a scriptural basis, and I consider Church history as evidence of God's hand, working to sustain and protect His Church (however that is defined) from error. I approach these things (i.e., the *sola Scriptura* / Tradition debate) from an historical and pragmatic perspective (and of course, biblically, as do we all), rather than more philosophically. I'm all for philosophy, but since the nature of authority is a very practical matter, I think it is better to stick to a pragmatic method in this case.

P: All Christians have traditions of some sort. But they are fallible outside of Scripture. We ought to test all our traditions by Scripture.

C: Yes, but since you Protestants can't agree with the *interpretation* of Scripture, of what practical use is an infallible Bible? If the interpretation is fallible and contradictory, then—practically speaking—the Bible in effect is no more infallible than its differing interpretations. Relativism is thus smuggled in under the aegis of private judgment and so-called "tolerance."

P: The Catholic Church of 400 AD is essentially different from the present-day Roman Catholic Church.

C: There is a 1600-year difference, and living bodies grow quite a bit in that great time-span. But this does not make them different organisms. The city of Jerusalem is a lot different now than in 400, but it is still Jerusalem, is it not? I'm a lot different than I was in 1966, but I'm still me! This aspect involves development of doctrine.

P: Would you say that apart from Catholic "tradition" we can't demonstrate the divinity of Jesus Christ?

C: No. That said, I would point out, nevertheless, that, e.g., proponents of the heresies of Monophysitism (i.e., that Christ had one Nature, not two) and Monothelitism (i.e., that Christ had one will, not two) in particular, argued from Scripture alone and thought that Rome and the other orthodox churches were adding traditions of men to Scripture. So, when you get down to fine points, there is indeed a need for some authoritative pronouncements, as Church history itself clearly and unarguably affirms.

Or is it your position that the pronouncements of Nicaea, Constantinople I, Ephesus and Chalcedon on matters of the Trinity were altogether irrelevant and unnecessary? Something may indeed be quite clear (which I maintain is the case for many, many doctrines), but there will arise people who manage to distort it, and so a conciliar definition and clarification becomes necessary in a practical, very "human" sense.

P: I'm sure you have argued with Jehovah's Witnesses before. Did you end such conversations with the anathema: "you are wrong because the pope says so"?

C: Of course not. The response would be (at least in my case), if I made any appeal to Tradition, rather: "All of the predominant Christian traditions for 2000 years have agreed that Jesus is the God-Man, whereas your belief originates from a late heresy called Arianism." But historically speaking, yes, orthodoxy was—in the final analysis—determined by the Roman position, again and again and again.

I recently put together a 66-page paper on trinitarian proofs, consisting virtually entirely of Bible passages (some commentary on the Greek), and one bow to Tradition: The Athanasian Creed (which I think most Christians would acknowledge). This is my approach. But on the other hand, when it comes to doctrines such as baptism, all of a sudden the Protestant must appeal to tradition, but not universal Christian Tradition (prior to 1517). Rather, he resorts to a mere *denominational tradition*.

Thus, Baptists must appeal to a late tradition of non-regenerative adult baptism, which originated 15 centuries after Christ. My Baptist opponent freely admits that practically all the Fathers erred on this doctrine, whereas the Anabaptists and he himself got it right. And so, accordingly, he goes to the Scripture and finds his "proof texts."

So Calvin and Wesley and Luther have their proof texts for infant and/or regenerative baptism, which they believe contradict Baptist proof texts. And so on and on it goes. Protestants have five camps on baptism. So instead of "Rome saying so," now it is because Calvin, or Zwingli, or some other current-day teacher "said so." Or, of course, "The Bible says so!"

P: The Catholic, in the final analysis, says that John 20:28 says X because Rome says so.

C: You assume falsely once again that because we believe Scripture does not function as a perspicuous authority apart from some human ecclesiastical authority, therefore every individual passage is an utter "mystery, riddle, and enigma" (to borrow from Churchill's description of Russia). Of course, this doesn't follow. The hidden false assumption here is that the Protestant has no such "ultimate authority." But of course he does, and must. It is either he himself, or some aspect of a denominational tradition, which contradicts other such traditions (some of which must necessarily be man-made whenever they're contradictory).

P: Christian unity does not exist. Each person must remain true to the Word of God.

C: Theological certainty does not exist? So Christianity is indeed reduced to philosophy. That is a slap in God's face, as far as I'm concerned (although I'm sure you don't mean it in that way). The God I serve is able, through His Holy Spirit, to impart truth to us, as the Bible teaches. "True to the Word"? You seek to be; so do I. Now what do we do? "True to the Word," yet so many disagreements over that very Word of "truth." How do we resolve this dilemma? Throw up our hands in despair? Or admit that Catholics might be on to something?

P: The Roman Catholic system has just as much chaos as does Protestantism.

C: How is it, then, that even the greatest critics of Catholicism assume without question that Catholics believe certain things: e.g., (just recently), a very high regard for apostolic Tradition, apostolic succession, the Immaculate Conception, Assumption, and Perpetual Virginity of Mary, infused justification, baptismal regeneration, an *ex opere operato* notion of sacramentalism, papal infallibility, papal supremacy, etc.?

On the other hand, there is no identifiable Protestant "position" other than C.S. Lewis's "Mere Christianity," which takes in Catholic and Orthodox theology anyhow, and so is not even distinctively Protestant. About all that "orthodox" evangelical Protestants agree on is *sola Scriptura* and an agreement that Catholicism must be wrong (and even a strict *sola Scriptura* view is questionable among Anglicans and many Lutherans).

The fallacy behind Protestant presuppositional objections to Tradition is that they assume that (Catholic) Tradition is *merely* human, and therefore subject to all the foibles of that weak vessel, whereas we assert that it is guided by the Holy Spirit and hand of God, in order to preserve it from error (by means of the Magisterium of the Catholic Church).

You assert that God could produce an infallible Bible by means of fallible, sinful (mostly Jewish) men (such as David, Matthew, Peter and Paul), and confirmed in its parameters also by fallible, sinful (Jewish and Catholic) men, and translated by fallible, sinful (mostly Catholic) men, and preserved for 1500 years before Protestantism was born by fallible, sinful (mostly Catholic) men, too. We contend that God can and does likewise create and sustain an infallible Church and Tradition, which is not a whit less credible or plausible.

We are discussing Christianity (which requires faith and a belief in the supernatural, God's Providence, etc.), not epistemological philosophy. Ours is a faith position, but no more than yours (I would say less so). You argue like an atheist when you contend that our view is largely irrational blind "faith in Rome," whereas Protestantism is altogether scriptural, reasonable, and not requiring faith in any institution outside one's own radically individualistic, subjective, existential "certainty." One must examine premises, and their relative merits. That's why I like to dwell on the foundations of belief-systems, knowing that if they are found weak and crumbling, the superstructure resting upon them will necessarily collapse.

Chapter Thirteen

Dialogue on the Logic, Epistemology, and Practical Application of Catholic Infallible Authority

Protestant apologist (P): Do you concede that in order to preserve unity of belief within the Catholic Church you necessarily require an infallible interpreter of the infallible interpreter of the Pope and Magisterium?

Catholic apologist / Dave Armstrong (C): No, not at all, for one simple reason: Christianity is not a philosophy, but a religion, and faith must be exercised somewhere along the line, as I've already stated. Our faith in this instance is in God, that He will preserve His Church from error, in the sense in which infallibility has been defined, once for all (in 1870 at The First Vatican Council). This is an extension of the "incarnational principle": God became Man; thus the Body of Christ now present on earth is preserved from heresy, compromise with immorality in its ethical precepts," etc.

P: We derive our beliefs from Scripture (as did the Church Fathers), but Catholics believe what they do simply because Rome tells them to.

C: Nonsense. Notwithstanding uneducated Catholics, we are just as biblically-centered as you, historically-speaking. The difference is that for us, the Bible occupies a position of **centrality** (as in the Church Fathers), but not **exclusivity**. Yes, we believe "Rome," but we also believe that God preserves our Church from corrupting the "deposit of faith" entrusted to us, and that therefore our Church is not contrary to the Bible (rightly understood) in any way, shape, matter, or form.

P: We readily acknowledge that we have doctrinal disagreement in many areas, but you have not squarely and honestly faced that problem in your own Catholic system.

C: It is no problem. Theological liberalism or modernism or heterodoxy assuredly is, as it is in your system, but we have clear ways of defining who is in accord with our teachings, whereas you don't. You institutionalize your errors and "sanctify" them. But we will not allow for evil to be called good (e.g., contraception, abortion, homosexuality, divorce, infanticide, euthanasia, "physician"—assisted suicide, relativism, et al).

P: Most, perhaps all, of those who adhere to *sola Scriptura* are within the pale of orthodoxy, while virtually all those who accept "Scripture plus some other binding authority" are not orthodox, or if orthodox, in possession of doctrines which directly contradict the Scriptures.

C: "Orthodoxy" according to whom? I don't know what this means (well, it's "correct doctrine," but who **determines** that?). The Arians thought they were "orthodox," while the Catholics were "heretical." The Nestorians, Monophysites, Monothelites, Sabellians, etc. ad infinitum thought likewise, so this is not merely a clever, rhetorical question, but a deadly serious one.

P: You see Catholicism as an exception to all other non-*sola Scriptura* groups because you claim to be able to trace it back historically to the apostolic period. And furthermore, you start with the assumption that "Scripture plus Catholic tradition" is a legitimate principle to follow in the first place.

C: It's scarcely even an assumption; it is absolutely necessary because Scripture is part of apostolic Tradition itself, as it teaches, and because of the factor of the canon, which also necessarily involves Tradition and conciliar Catholic authority. So the unsupported assumptions here are all on your side, in my opinion. Not only are they unsubstantiated, but also self-defeating, which is all the more troublesome for your position. The assumption we all share is that Scripture is God's Revealed Word. From that starting-point we can try to determine the proper place of both Tradition and ecclesiastical authority.

Protestant sects and cults invariably result from one man or woman, who, of course, is infallible (and more often than not, an autocrat):

> Seventh-Day Adventists: Ellen White
> Jehovah's Witnesses: Charles Taze Russell
> Mormons: Joseph Smith
> Christian Science: Mary Baker Eddy
> The Way International: Victor Paul Wierwille

P: But you didn't include one, Dave. Roman Catholicism: the pope.

C: Are you serious? The short, pithy answer at this point is: which one? That expresses the fallacy of this "answer" quite well. Besides, the popes are not infallible in everything they say, nor are they autocrats.

P: If indeed *sola Scriptura* does not work, how come most Protestants separately (in denominations) came to believe in the same Trinity, deity of Christ, person of the Holy Spirit, one church, eternal bliss or punishment, the second coming of Christ, *sola Scriptura*, sola fide, priesthood of all believers, etc. If *sola Scriptura* produces "chaos," as you say, and if the Scriptures are not clearly-understood (perspicuous), then how do you explain all this extraordinary commonality of belief?

C: Because all of these doctrines are clear from Scripture (excepting the last three items). I fully agree that many (if not most) doctrines **are** clearly taught in Scripture. That is not my point in all my argumentation on this topic. **My point is:** by claiming that Scripture is the final authority, then, practically speaking, true doctrines ought to be able to be ascertained without recourse to ecclesiastical authority. But in fact this is not the case.

Therefore, some churchly authority **is** necessary because of the division that has indeed occurred (and yes, man's pride and sin definitely play into that). This is all the more necessary, biblically speaking, because disobedience to spiritual authorities, hostile division, and doctrinal relativism are all so severely condemned in Scripture.

As for the last three points, the first and third flow of necessity from the rejection of Tradition and the apostolic, visible Church. Since most Protestants reject that, ergo, *sola Scriptura* and priesthood of all believers. *Sola fide* is held in common because it was the other pillar of the "Reformation," and is the only alternative to the sacramental system and infused justification.

P: How does the pope not dominate Catholicism, like the founders of Protestant sects do in their own groups?

C: Infallible papal decisions, few as they are, deal with only one doctrine. I'm talking about the interpretation of one man entirely dominating a denomination. You simply can't assert that about any one pope. It can't be done, period. But John Calvin dominates the Reformed and the Presbyterians, Martin Luther (at least initially) the Lutherans, Menno Simons the Mennonites, etc. Our popes make infallible decrees (in the strictest sense) only every 100 years or so, whereas Luther claimed that "all" his teaching was "from God." He regarded his self-proclaimed authority as tantamount to that of a prophet: i.e., unquestionable. And *we* are accused of "authoritarianism"?

P: But aren't the councils infallible as well? And Catholic tradition?

C: Now you're making my whole point for me. First you argue that the pope as "one man" predominates. Now, you're catching on as to the true nature of Catholic authority: pope and Councils, pope and Tradition, pope and the *sensus fidelium* ("sense of the faithful"), as analogous to Peter and the other disciples, Peter and other bishops or Apostles (such as James and Paul), and Peter and the Jerusalem Council, etc.

P: None of us regards Luther as infallible, so your argument is irrelevant. I don't care what he thought of himself.

C: Your opinion on Luther is irrelevant to my argument, since it is an analogy between Protestantism and the non-trinitarian heresies. Luther had more power in his sphere than any pope ever dreamt of, and this is the whole point. You keep switching the terms of the debate, whenever you're trapped by the incoherence of your own position. All Protestants stem from Luther's dissent. Nearly all Protestants accept the departures from Catholicism which he originated (*sola Scriptura, sola fide*, tossing the "Apocrypha," communion of saints, seven sacraments, etc., etc.).

P: Catholic apologists commonly assert that Catholics have a "certainty of faith" not present in Protestantism, by means of finding the "final" answer to serious questions in "the Church." The individual Catholic deludes himself into thinking that he has not, in fact, determined by himself a number of fallible "private judgments," none of which are any more "certain" than those which Protestants make in their own search after doctrinal (and biblical) orthodoxy. This is a double standard.

C: It is not simply a reliance upon the Church in blind faith; it is, rather, the combination of Church authority, patristic consensus, and the biblical material: Church, Tradition, and Bible: the "three-legged stool." We say that this was the methodology of the Fathers themselves, in their appeal to apostolic succession or Tradition (see, e.g., St. Irenaeus). It is essentially an historical, typically Jewish argument, not a philosophical one (philosophy deriving from the Greeks).

P: All of this examination of patristic consensus, past Church rulings, and the Bible is undertaken by fallible individuals, and thus, is equally as prone to error as Protestant beliefs.

C: One could say the same about the Fathers themselves, and the Councils. The whole point is that there is an identifiable apostolic deposit which is passed down, and Catholics accept that, as clarified by their Church. We don't reinvent Christianity in each generation; we accept what has been given to us, just as the apostles and Fathers before us did. This is not a philosophical matter; it is one of faith and legal-historical grounds of ascertainable fact.

P: The Protestant's "certainty of faith" lies in the self-attesting Word of God, while the Catholic relies on the secondary testimony of the Church, a mere man-made entity, even if thought to be guided by the Holy Spirit.

C: No; everyone accepts the Scripture; that is not at issue. The alleged "self-attesting" nature of it is a real issue I have dealt with at great length. The "secondary testimony" here is that of the Luther and Calvin. If Scripture speaks of an infallible and indefectible Church, then that notion is relying on the Word of God. We rely on the apostolic Tradition passed down, verified and developed by the Fathers, Councils, great Doctors, and popes, and ultimately in the materially-sufficient Holy Scriptures.

You rely on the fallible, late-arriving distinctives of Luther and Calvin, and in effect grant them apostolic authority. They can flat-out invent doctrines and claim they are both historical and biblical. No pope would dare do that (on a few occasions when they came remotely close to that a mass uproar occurred). They are strictly dependent upon received precedent. Not so for Luther and Calvin, the "Super-Popes."

P: Catholics don't *really* have "certainty of faith" and shouldn't pretend that they do. Protestants are more honest about their epistemology.

C: I have "certainty" in the sense that believing Christians and Jews have always possessed "certainty" (I recommend Cardinal Newman's *Grammar of Assent* in this regard). It is a rational faith, backed up by eyewitness testimony and historical evidences, and the history of doctrine. No one is saying (or should say) that there is an absolute certainty in a strict philosophical sense. But there is certainty in the sense of faith.

Like any acceptance of authority: it won't work if we are blinded by a closed mind and a prideful, self-centered will (compounded by the level of individual ignorance (or prior misinformation). That is true of any teaching system, including Catholicism. But that doesn't, of course, disprove the Catholic system. It is not private judgment per se which leads one to accept Catholicism; it is precisely the opposite: it is yielding up one's private judgment in the act of recognizing the Church for what it is: the spiritual authority ordained by God. One can do this reasonably by applying historical criteria, just as Christians have always done.

When I say "private judgment" I am talking about Christian authority and ecclesiology; not philosophical epistemology. I refer to the Protestant formal system of *sola Scriptura*, which places the individual in the position as the supreme and final arbiter of his own theology and destiny. This is a formal system of Christian authority, over against the Catholic three-legged stool of "Church, Tradition, and Scripture"—all harmonious and not contradictory or competing.

So the Protestant—by the exercise of this self-granted prerogative—can stand there and judge all three legs of the stool (as Luther at Worms did), making his own conscience supreme (the corollary of private judgment). This we reject as unbiblical and against the entire previous history of the Church. And all Protestants do this—by definition. Your variant may be more subtle, nuanced, and fine-tuned, and much less ahistorical, but all the versions boil down to a rejection of the apostolic authority of the Catholic Church.

Ultimately Protestants reserve the right to interpret Scripture against the Fathers, if their views do not correspond to the theological system they espouse (e.g., a rejection of the Real Presence in the Eucharist and baptismal regeneration: both virtually unanimous views of the Fathers). So in the end, Protestantism becomes a man-centered system (Calvin, Luther, Fox et al), rather than an apostolic, patristic, traditional-centered system, where the individual yields his judgment to the historic Christian consensus of the ages: the apostolic Tradition faithfully passed down and protected from error by the Holy Spirit.

P: God's Word is the ultimate, unquestionable authority.

C: Of course; but it has to be *interpreted*, so you can't avoid human authority. Why would you assume that God cannot protect His Church from error just as He protected His written revelation from error? On what basis do you assume that? After all (I make an analogical argument, of plausibility), the gift of infallibility is far lesser in order than the gift of inspiration, by which fallible, sinful men accurately and infallibly recorded the word of God in Sacred Scripture, without error. Both gifts are supernatural and divinely-granted. It seems to me that if God could and would do one thing, then He would certainly do the other, so as to maintain a unified truth and a consistent witness to the world.

I have always maintained that the Christian notion of truth and authority is historically-based, as opposed to philosophically-based. And it requires faith. So Catholic authority is not an airtight philosophical proposition as many non-Catholics seem to think it must be in order to be adhered to. But Protestantism is not, either, and contains within itself far more problematic elements. I contend that our view is biblical, consistent, apostolic, and patristic.

Apostolic and patristic Christianity was much more analogous to Old Testament Judaism, than to, say, Greek philosophy, with its abstract "epistemology" (and I say this as a Socratic myself; one who loves philosophy). Authority flowed always from commonly-acknowledged miraculous historical events and historical criteria: a sort of "Christian mythology" (i.e., a corporately-preserved story of origins) but what C.S. Lewis would describe as "true mythology."

P: I agree. But don't you see that the selection and espousal of this "true mythology" was undertaken by fallible individuals, so that the end result could not be unquestioned? This is the Catholic difficulty of the "infallibility regress."

C: Our claim is that the Church is infallible, and that the individual yields up his private judgment to the authority of the Church, based on apostolic succession. We have faith that God will guide His Church. It is a reasonable faith, which can be backed up by many sorts of reasonable evidences (primarily historical), though it ultimately transcends them all, as all matters of faith do.

That "true (verifiable) mythology" is the following: Jesus was the incarnate God, and was a real Person. We believe Scripture is materially sufficient, but not formally sufficient without the Church as a Guide. We believe that Scripture and Tradition are "twin fonts of the same divine wellspring," as the Second Vatican Council states.

Jesus performed miracles, and many people observed these. He rose from the dead, and proved the reality of that by appearing to more than 500 people, eating fish, showing that He possessed flesh and bones, etc. This is all historical, and a matter of eyewitness testimony (so one might say it is a historical-legal approach to theological truth).

Likewise with the Church. There was one, recognized deposit of faith, passed on from our Lord Jesus to the disciples and Apostles, which Paul repeatedly refers to. Jesus established a Church, with Peter as the head (Matthew 16:13-20). This Church has definite and discernible characteristics, described in the Bible. There were apostles, and their successors were and are bishops. There were popes as well, and they exercised authority over the Church Universal.

Now, how was this Church identifiable in the early days and in the patristic period? Again, it was the historical criteria of authenticity. The Fathers always appealed to apostolic succession (a demonstrable historical lineage of orthodoxy) and Scripture, not Scripture Alone. The heretics were the ones who adopted Scripture Alone as their principle, because they knew that they couldn't produce the historical lineage (hence an early manifestation of the unChristian and unbiblical a-historicism which has been a dominant flaw of Protestantism ever since its inception).

Protestants thus adopted the heretical principle of formal authority, whereas Catholics have consistently adopted apostolic succession as the criteria of Christian truth and legitimate, divinely-ordained authority. The Catholic Church traces itself back to the beginning in an unbroken line, centered in the Roman See and the papacy.

So when someone like me (a very low-church evangelical) becomes convinced of Catholicism, it is not merely another Protestant exercise of private judgment and de facto alleged self-infallibility. It is, to the contrary, the yielding up of private judgment and the acknowledgement of something far greater than oneself: an entity which is "out there;" which has always been there since Christ established it, preserving (only by God's enabling grace and will) apostolic Christian truth in its fullness and undiluted splendor.

One can reasonably accept Catholicism, based on the historical criteria, just as one would accept the historicity of the Resurrection or the Virgin Birth, or the authority of the Bible—itself grounded in historically-verifiable elements (e.g., fulfilled prophecy, the continuance of the Jews, the astounding transformation of the early Christians, etc.). It is on the basis of history (and, of course, faith as well), as opposed to some alleged prideful, illusory, self-infallibility. Popes and ecumenical councils are just as bound to the received deposit of faith, as I am. I wanted apostolic, biblical Christianity: the Christianity which Jesus taught the disciples; not man-made variants, each containing maybe a few noble emphases left over from historical, apostolic Christianity, but always in the final analysis grossly-deficient (though also quite beneficial and good insofar as they do contain many valid Christian truths).

All of these issues are complex in and of themselves, but that is the Catholic answer: we appeal to the patristic and apostolic (Pauline) methods of determining theological and apostolic truth. The Bible is central in all this as well (absolutely!); it is just not exclusive of Church authority. How can it be? Its very parameters were authoritatively declared by this self-same Church. Before then, various Fathers disagreed somewhat on the canon. Again, it is not a matter solely of sin. Authority was truly needed to settle that issue, just as it is needed to settle theological issues. Scripture Alone will not suffice.

Besides, Scripture itself points to the teaching authority of the Church, anyway, so it is a false dichotomy from the get-go, to pit the Church against the Bible, as if there is some inherent contradiction or "competition" between them. The apostles and Fathers saw no such dichotomy. I imitate Paul, just as he imitated Christ (as he commanded me to do).

Chapter Fourteen

Dialogue on Biblical Arguments for Purgatory

Protestant apologist (P): It does seem reasonable that there are divisions in Sheol.

Catholic apologist / Dave Armstrong (C): Personally, I think Luke 16:19-31 ("parable" of Lazarus and the rich man) alone establishes that Sheol exists (as also indicated by many passages, both in the New Testament and the Old Testament), and that both righteous and unrighteous were there prior to Christ. Likewise, now the elect of God can go straight to heaven if sufficiently holy, or to purgatory as a necessary stopping-point in order to attain to the proper sanctity becoming of inhabitants of heavenly glory.

P: This theology seems fundamentally flawed to me, since Christ's blood perfectly cleanses from sin.

C: Seeing that there is plenty of sin prevalent among Christians, then if your question is in reference to this earthly life, the cleansing of us obviously isn't complete. It will be in the next life for the elect: the only difference being whether God will "zap" us *instantly* and make us perfectly holy for heaven and His Presence, or whether it will take a bit of *time*. But the *essence* of the transformation is the same in either case. We can achieve a real, actual sanctity great enough to allow us to enter heaven immediately upon death, but (in Catholic thought) not many actually achieve that level of holiness, since we have the free will to cooperate with or spurn Christ's finished work for us and His ongoing necessary enabling grace.

So, yes, Christ's blood is perfectly efficacious, but the fact remains that virtually all of us have not attained perfect sanctity. Protestants, therefore, have taken the view that we are declared perfectly righteous in a forensic or judicial sense, and separate sanctification from justification. In so doing they avoid the consequences of a lack of real, actual, infused righteousness.

P: Is sanctification real, or a 'virtual reality' type experience?

C: Yes, quite real, but since we must cooperate in the process, we mess it up enough to make purgatory necessary in most cases.

P: Purgatory, in the Catholic perspective, then, is a final purging place for sins... what element is missing? Time?

C: Yes. Protestants regard sanctification as a process in this life, and not tied to salvation. All we're doing is saying that this process often continues *after* this life, and also is not tied to salvation there (since all in purgatory are among the elect and saved), although we think it is tied to salvation in this life in the sense that one must be free of mortal sin in order to achieve eschatological salvation. On the other hand, there seems to be no explicit biblical indication that real purification and sanctification in the afterlife is *necessarily* and *only* an *instantaneous* event.

P: What purpose could purgatory serve, if Christ has cleansed us with His blood, perfectly, and finally?

C: He has completed the work and done everything necessary in Divine Providence to efficiently save everyone who will be saved, but this work is not yet actualized or appropriated in terms of true sanctity in most of us. Protestants hold that we are saved in the present, yes, but not yet perfectly holy (one of the very reasons they separate sanctification from justification).

Unfortunately it too often takes pain and suffering to "purge" us of sin and various bondages, doesn't it? Catholic thought on this simply extends God's normative disciplinary and "fatherly" dealing with us into the afterlife, and that only temporarily so. Eventually, all will be either in heaven or hell. John Henry Cardinal Newman wrote in 1838, while still Anglican:

> Now it will be answered that the merits of our Lord Jesus Christ are sufficient to wash out all sin, and that they really do wash it out. Doubtless; but the question to be decided is, whether He has promised to apply His all-sufficient merits at once on persons doing nothing more than changing their mode of living... Men in general... think that the state of grace in which they are is such as to absorb (as it were) and consume all sin as fast as it springs up in the heart;—or they think that faith has this power of obliterating and annihilating sin, so that in fact there is nothing on their conscience to repent of. They consider faith as superseding repentance... Regret, vexation, sorrow, such feelings seem to

this busy, practical, unspiritual generation as idle; as something despicable and unmanly, - just as tears may be...[1]

P: I'm inclined to believe that Christ literally descended into prison to preach to and free the captives.

C: Pretty much any Christian who adheres to the Apostles' and Nicene Creeds believes that, I think. One has to account for 1 Peter 3:19-20 and 4:6 in some fashion, and this seems to be the most reasonable way to do it. That's why I believed it both as an evangelical and now as a Catholic.

P: In that framework, I agree that it is possible that divisions in Sheol existed, or some other third place. It seems reasonably supported by Scripture. However, once Christ's work was accomplished, the need and Divine purpose for such a place as purgatory is not scriptural enough for me.

C: Yes, I understand, but I don't see why Protestants object to purgatory in principle when they already accept the urgency and requirement (if not the *necessity* for salvation) of sanctification. Why is it so unthinkable that a little or a lot more of the same process could continue after death? After all, we know that various judgments are to occur then.

For example, a noteworthy instance is described in 1 Corinthians 3:11-15, where St. Paul talks about our works being "tested" and certain people being "saved, but only as through fire." This is considered by most evangelicals to be the Judgment Seat of Christ. I fail to see how this is essentially any different than what we believe purgatory to be. After all, there is no time framework given in the passage. Once *duration* is admitted as a possibility, the non-Catholic is almost forced to concede that the Catholic view on this is every bit as plausible as the "zapped" theory. Admittedly, however, purgatory flows more straightforwardly from our view of infused justification. It isn't really consistent with forensic justification, although I can conceive a sense in which it could be (much as I've described so far).

P: "To be absent from the body is to be present with the Lord" (2 Corinthians 5:8), and since at His coming He shall resurrect our bodies, the only time we are absent from our bodies is in physical death, right?

---

[1] Sermon: "Chastisement Amid Mercy" (on Micah 7:8-9), from *Parochial and Plain Sermons*.

C: Yes, I would agree with that, prior to the general resurrection. But by the way, 2 Corinthians 5:8—if read closely—does not necessarily establish absence from the body as—ipso facto—presence with God. I could say, similarly, e.g., that "I am willing to be absent from work and to be present with my wife." It doesn't follow that whenever I am out of work I am with her. I wouldn't press this point too strongly, but at any rate I believe Paul is expressing a desire rather than a maxim or ironclad law. Nevertheless, see my next response.

P: So Christ is present in purgatory?

C: As far as I know, He is present in a sense more tangible than He is in this life, yet definitely not in terms of the Beatific Vision (perfect communion with, and vision of God), as in heaven. He is with the suffering souls during their purification at least to the degree (if not more so) that He is with us in our trials of testing on earth in a special, profound way. The suffering in purgatory is largely due to the greatly increased desire and longing to be with God in the most real sense, so then He could not be present there in the same way as He is in heaven.

P: Also, the thief on the cross was told *This day shalt thou be with me in paradise*"... and you don't think he didn't need the progressive sanctification of purgatory! (to follow your logic)?

C: "Paradise" in this verse (Luke 23:43) about the thief on the cross (if interpreted literally) is not even referring to heaven, and indeed could not, since Jesus was not yet in heaven on that day ("today..."). He was crucified on Friday and didn't rise from the dead until Sunday. In fact, He didn't ascend to heaven until forty days after that (Acts 1:3,9-11; cf. John 20:17)! Between Good Friday and Easter Sunday, He descended into Sheol, or Hades, the place of the dead (both righteous and unrighteous—see Luke 16:19-31) to preach to the "captives" (righteous dead). We know this from passages such as 1 Peter 3:19-20, 4:6, and Ephesians 4:8-10 (cf. Romans 10:7, Acts 2:27). So, then, *Paradise* in Luke 23:43 is referring to Sheol, not heaven. The conclusion is inescapable from cross-scriptural exegesis. For example, Kittel's *Theological Dictionary of the New Testament* (an impeccable and standard Protestant linguistic source) holds to this view, which is not just Catholic belief, but that of conservative Protestants as well (see also the reputable Protestant *reference New Bible Dictionary*).[2]

---

[2] Edited by J.D. Douglas, Grand Rapids, MI: Eerdmans, 1962 edition, 935.

C: Newman wrote: *"Samuel, when brought from the dead, in the witch's cavern, said Why hast thou disquieted me, to bring me up? (1 Samuel 28:15),* words which would seem quite inconsistent with his being then already in Heaven."

P: Why are they inconsistent? Because he says "up"? What in that verse would preclude Samuel being brought from Heaven?

C: Well, I would reply with the following:

1) "Down to" or, in this case, "up from," is the usual terminology with reference to Sheol, "down from" or "up to" for heaven (e.g., John 6:33,62), as Sheol was thought to be in the earth. I think you would be hard pressed to find in Scripture anyone in heaven spoken of as being "brought up" to earth.
2) Virtually all Old Testament saints are generally thought to have gone to Sheol before Christ's Death (Enoch and Elijah being the exceptions, and perhaps Moses, based on deductions from Matthew 17:1-3). Otherwise, Jesus' descent into Sheol/Hades to preach and to "release the captives" makes little sense. Further, if we are to literally regard the "Abraham" of Luke 16:23 ff. as the Old Testament patriarch, then we know that at least one righteous man went to Hades, and by logical extension, most of the others, excepting only the most extraordinary.
3) Matthew 27:52-53 speaks of saints buried in Jerusalem being resurrected at the time of Jesus' Resurrection, thus implying that they had not yet attained heavenly bliss.

Chapter Fifteen

A Biblical and Theological Primer on the Veneration of the Blessed Virgin Mary, Her Sinlessness, and Her God-Ordained Function as Mediatrix

Many people have trouble identifying with the Blessed Virgin Mary because of her Immaculate Conception. The extraordinary graces given to Mary make it difficult for us to emulate or imitate her. Many non-Catholics (indeed, also some Catholics) feel that it would actually have been more of a "miracle" for God to have chosen an ordinary, sinful woman, through whom Jesus Christ would enter the world.

All of us miserable sinners find ourselves in an awkward position when it comes to God and perfect people like the Blessed Virgin Mary. I would approach this question from several different angles:

First, we need to distinguish between *relating* to Mary and *emulating* her. Since she was indeed without sin (both original and actual), in that sense it is, of course, difficult to "walk in her shoes," so to speak. Yet, when it comes to imitation, it is a fact of life that in our better moments we all strive to emulate people who are "superior" to us, whom we admire and look up to—those who have succeeded in areas we still yearn for and dream about. That's what all the talk about "role models" is about. If we didn't have a high goal to strive for, how could we improve and become the type of people we want to be?

Second, what Catholics have most revered about Mary through the centuries (I think) is her humility and willingness to be mightily used by God as the *Theotokos* (*God-bearer*). In this sense she is like us: a mere human being who said *yes* to God, thus reversing the *no* of Eve (hence her designation as the *Second Eve* in the Fathers). This is the Mary of the Annunciation (Luke 1:38; cf. 1:48).

Now, one might counter with the objection that she *had* to say yes, being sinless, yet Catholics would not hold to that assertion, since we also believe in free will. It is true of all of us that we must *agree* to accept and cooperate with the graces that always originate from God (e.g., 1 Corinthians 3:8-9, 15:10, 2 Corinthians 6:1). We are, in a sense, "co-laborers" with God. We do not adhere to fatalism or determinism (even Calvinists deny that they hold such a view).

If we take the logic that "she had to do it, therefore it wasn't meritorious," to its logical conclusion, we would also have to say that God's voluntary good actions are not good, since He is unable—by the nature of things—to sin. So we assert that Mary did the right thing, and that she was a created human being like the rest of us, even though without sin, and that this is both her glory and her commonality with us.

Third, Mary is not *intrinsically* superior in *essence* to the rest of us. She received from God all of the grace which she possessed in abundance (Luke 1:28—*full of grace* in some translations). She was merely given more of it at one time, and earlier, than us. All human beings who are to be saved for eternity in heaven will one day be without sin, unstained, immaculate, just as Mary was from conception, and just as all of us were meant to be, but for the Fall of Adam and Eve.

Fourth, while it is appealing in a sense to ponder a sinful Mary whom God could have used as well (which is indeed not an impossible hypothetical scenario—and one I used to argue also), God chose, rather, to make her sinless since this was appropriate for the *ark of the new covenant* who carried God incarnate and shared even her own blood with Him in utero. So God chose to act in a special way to preserve Mary from sin. I don't think it is unreasonable at all to believe that He would do that, given that He will eventually cleanse totally all saved persons so that they will be fit for heaven.

If we must be clean to enter heaven and stand in God's presence (Revelation 21:27), then it seems only proper for the Mother of God to possess a commensurate righteousness for that unfathomable task, privilege, and honor. In fact, if I were her, I would much rather have been granted that special grace than to have to face that awesome situation as a sinner!

Fifth, there are plenty of other sinful, "weak" models in Scripture that we can relate to as like us in *that* sense: vacillating, overzealous Peter, perhaps proud, tempestuous Paul, stuttering Moses and his wimpy brother Aaron, blame-shifting Adam, murderous and adulterous David, doubting Thomas, deceptive Jacob, sexually-weak Samson, drunken, incestuous Noah, etc. I don't think it is implausible for God to spare one, lone human being (His earthly mother at that) from the onslaught of original sin. In fact, I wonder myself why He didn't make *more* people sinless!

Finally, getting back to the first point, I think this objection fails in the final analysis because it is unscriptural, for the following reasons: we are commanded to imitate the Apostle Paul and other saints (1 Corinthians 4:16, Philippians 3:17, 2 Thessalonians 3:7-9; cf. James 5:10-11, Hebrews 6:12 and chapter 11), which is difficult enough. Paul sinned as we do, but he also did extraordinary things that in all likelihood we will never accomplish.

He was an apostle! Yet we are called to "imitate" him. Christianity is filled with this sort of striving for what in fact is virtually unattainable in this lifetime. That's one of the many paradoxes of our faith. We may not achieve a 100% grade, but we can shoot for a 90%, or 80% (speaking of *sanctification*, not the grounds of *salvation*), as God allows, and as we are faithful in allowing Him to do His work in us. The ideals are always there to shoot for.

Now, the rub is that Paul in turn, imitates Christ, and calls for us to do that as well (1 Corinthians 11:1, 1 Thessalonians 1:6). Here we are in the same boat as with Mary, and much more so, since this is God Incarnate. Obviously we will not "imitate" Him perfectly, but we are called to do our best, and live by His example. And in our Lord Jesus we find the same humility (of course even more profound) that we find in Mary: He humbled Himself first by giving up divine prerogatives and becoming man (Philippians 2:5-7) and then dying on the cross (Philippians 2:8).

And that is the glory of the Incarnation itself: the fact that God would so humble Himself out of love for us, as to *become* one of us—like His own creatures. C.S. Lewis compared that act to a person becoming an ant. We don't say that we can't relate to Christ because He is God, but that we can relate to Him since He is a man:

For we do not have a high priest who is unable to sympathize with our weaknesses, but we have one who in every respect has been tested as we are, yet without sin. (NRSV)

(Hebrews 4:15; cf. 4:16, 5:7-8, 2:17-18, Isaiah 53:3, 2 Corinthians 5:21, 1 Peter 2:19-21)

Therefore, since we are expressly informed in Scripture that Jesus our Lord and God, who did not and could not sin, can nevertheless relate to us, "sympathize with our weaknesses," and has been tested like us "in every respect," we can relate all the more so to Mary, who is a creature as we are, yet without sin. In other words, sinlessness is not inherently opposed to human nature, as if sin and concupiscence were the "normal" state.

Rather, it is sin which is "unhuman," since it stands in the way of what God intended for the human race, and what will one day indeed be accomplished among the saved and the elect. Thus, Mary is more "human" than all of us, and therefore can help us (by example and intercession) to be what we should be: more like Jesus, her beloved Son, and less in bondage to sin. She is the example of what all of us *can* be more and more in this life, and what we assuredly will essentially be in the next if we persevere in the faith.

Catholic Christianity recognizes and venerates the Blessed Virgin Mary, the Immaculate Mother of God, as the exemplar of what redeemed humanity will one day be: the forerunner, the quintessential Christian and symbol of the Church itself, our Spiritual Mother and Queen of Heaven, who was spared by God's grace the curse of death and immediately received her glorious resurrected body after her earthly sojourn had come to an end. And that's why we and others have fulfilled the prophecy that Mary gave concerning herself:

> *... from now on all generations will call me blessed.* (Luke 1:48b)

And why is she blessed?:

> *for the Mighty One has done great things for me, and holy is his name.* (Luke 1:49)

Mary is *always* glorifying God the Father and Jesus, never herself, for this is her purpose and calling. All of the Marian doctrines are Christocentric. They were promulgated in the first place so that Jesus Christ would be glorified, not Mary. And this is why Catholics have venerated her above all creatures, and why any Christian can indeed "relate to" and "identify with" her, because she glorifies and imitates *God*, and that is what *all* serious Christians want to do (and are commanded to do) too.

> Romans 3:23:... ***all** have sinned and fall short of the glory of God.* (NRSV)

The word *all* (*pas* in Greek) can indeed have different meanings (as it does in English). It matters not if it means literally "every single one" in some places, if it can mean something less than "absolutely every" elsewhere in Scripture. As soon as this is admitted, then the Catholic exception for Mary cannot be said to be linguistically or exegetically impossible, any more than *adelphos* ("brother") meaning "sibling" in one place rules out a meaning of "cousin" or other non-sibling somewhere else.

We find examples of a non-literal intent elsewhere in Romans. In verse 1:29 the KJV reads, *being filled with all unrighteousness*, whereas NRSV adopts the more particular, specific meaning, *every kind of wickedness*. As another example in the same book, Paul writes that *all Israel will be saved,* (11:26), but we know that many will *not* be saved. And in 15:14, Paul describes members of the Roman church as *filled with all knowledge*. (cf. 1 Corinthians 1:5 in KJV), which clearly cannot be taken literally. Examples could be multiplied indefinitely, and are as accessible as the nearest *Strong's Concordance*.

Mary was freed from original sin. Granted, Jesus is of course unique, but if He proves an exception to the rule here, is it *utterly inconceivable* that Mary could as well? Adam and Eve sinned, but they are examples of immaculate human beings however short-lived it was in their case! I agree that this verse could be regarded as a "difficulty," but I don't think it is insurmountable.

A verse which *would* be irrefutable would read something like: "absolutely every human being who ever lived no exceptions—has sinned..." This would include Jesus since He is a human as we are—just that He is also God (a Divine Person), and Mary. But Romans 3:23 doesn't entail that logical conundrum.

One could also say that Mary was included in the "all" in the sense that she certainly *would* have been subject to original sin like all the rest of us *but* for God's special preventive act of grace—a "preemptive strike," so to speak. This is why she can rightly say that God was her Savior too (Luke 1:47). I don't think this is implausible at all, considering that Hebrew idiom was not at all "scientific," "philosophical" nor excessively particularistic as to literal meanings, as English in our culture seems to be today.

I myself—in my admittedly relative ignorance of technical exegesis—think that this "exception / original sin / Hebrew idiom" explanation is the most plausible. It allows one to take "all" here in its most straightforward, common sense meaning, but with the proviso that Mary was spared from inevitable sin by means of a direct, extraordinary intervention of God, and it is also in line with the thought of Luke 1:47, as interpreted by Catholic theology, in light of its acceptance of the Immaculate Conception.

That said, linguistic reference works concur with my opinion as to *pas*. According to Kittel's *Theological Dictionary of the New Testament*, *pas* has many meanings, including "great number" (see, e.g., Matthew 2:3, 3:5, 4:24, 21:10, 27:25, Mark 2:13, 9:15). Likewise, *Thayer's Greek-English Lexicon of the New Testament* gives "of every kind" as a possible meaning in some contexts. And W.E. Vine's *Expository Dictionary of New Testament Words* tells us it can mean "every kind or variety."

Nevertheless, I am inclined to go with the "exception" interpretation I described above. My point here is simply to illustrate that *pas* doesn't *necessarily* have to mean "no exceptions," so that Mary's sinlessness is not a logical impossibility based on the meaning of *pas* alone. We see Jewish idiom and hyperbole in passages of similar meaning. Jesus says:

No one is good but God alone. (Luke 18:19; cf. Matthew 19:17)

Yet He also said:

The good person brings good things out of a good treasure... (Matthew 12:35; cf. 5:45, 7:17-20, 22:10)

Furthermore, in each instance in Matthew and Luke above of the English "good" the Greek word is the same: *agatho*. Is this a contradiction? Of course not. Jesus is merely drawing a contrast between our righteousness and God's, but He doesn't deny that we can be "good" in a lesser sense. We observe the same dynamic in the Psalms:

> *The Lord looks down from heaven on humankind to see if there are any who are wise, who seek after God. They have all gone astray, they are all alike perverse; there is no one who does good* [Hebrew, *tob*] *no not one.*

(Psalms 14:2-3; cf. 53:1-3 / Paul cites these in Romans 3:10-12)

Yet in the immediately preceding Psalm, David proclaims *I trusted in your steadfast love* (13:5), which certainly is "seeking" after God! And in the very next he refers to *those who walk blamelessly, and do what is right* (15:2). Even two verses later he writes that *God is with the company of the righteous*. So obviously his lament in 14:2-3 is an indignant hyperbole and not intended as a literal utterance.

Such remarks are common to Jewish poetic idiom. The anonymous psalmist in 112:5 refers to a *good man* (Heb. *tob*), as does the book of Proverbs repeatedly (11:23, 12:2, 13:22, 14:14,19), using the same word, *tob*, which appears in Psalms 14:2-3. And references to *righteous* men are innumerable (e.g., Job 17:9, 22:19, Psalms 5:12, 32:11, 34:15, 37:16,32, Matthew 9:13, 13:17, 25:37,46, Romans 5:19, Hebrews 11:4, James 5;16, 1 Peter 3:12, 4:18, etc., etc.).

But Catholics agree with Protestants on the universality of sin, with just the one lone exception of Mary among created human beings. I don't think that is too incredible or implausible or unthinkable to imagine God doing: to make sure that one solitary created person was kept from sin. And that because she was the *Theotokos*, the *God-bearer*?

Cardinal Newman wrote that it is far less difficult to hold that Mary was freed from original and actual sin than it is to accept the proposition that *all* men are subject to *original* sin. The real mystery is why God would allow the latter to happen, not that He willed to restore His Son's earthly mother to a state which—but for original sin—would have characterized every one of us.

Another biblical argument in this regard, pointed out to me by Robert Sungenis, fellow Catholic apologist, is the consideration of 1 Corinthians 15:22: *As in Adam all die, so in Christ all will be made alive* (NIV). As far as physical death is concerned (the context of 1 Corinthians 15), not "all" people have died (e.g., Enoch: Genesis 5:24; cf. Hebrews 11:5, Elijah: 2 Kings 2:11). Likewise, "all" will not be made spiritually alive by Christ, as some will choose to suffer eternal spiritual death in hell.

Perhaps the most misunderstood Catholic Marian belief of all is the doctrine of Mary's role as Mediatrix and Co-Redemptrix. I think that the simplest way to explain it (as with many complex and deep areas of theology that no man fully understands), is by direct analogy:

1) In becoming man, God chose to involve a human being, Mary.
2) God didn't *have* to do so—He could have appeared at 30 years old to be baptized by John the Baptist if He so wished. He could have appeared as a grown man just like Adam did.
3) But God chose to involve human "mediation" in the Incarnation, by "including" Mary and human reproductive biology (i.e., in terms of a uterus and uterine development of a child, but not in terms of sexual intercourse). Mary was a real mother, not just a biological "conduit," so to speak. This is the sublime marvel of the whole thing: God could choose and use a human mother in order to come to earth and take on human flesh!
4) Now, an ancient theme in the Fathers is Mary as the "Second Eve." Eve said "no" to God and so caused (along with Adam) the Fall of Man. Mary, on the other hand, said "yes" to God at the Annunciation and so caused (along with Christ—but in an essentially lesser, and non-necessary, non-sufficient fashion) the Redemption of Man. We "get" Christ—the incarnate Man, the God-Man with a human nature—through Mary. He received His human body through Mary. He didn't *have* to, but He did. Hence we honor Mary above all other creatures as the *Theotokos*—the "God-bearer"—as well we should.
5) So Mary is *Mediatrix* in that way, but there is also a further sense, which involves the notion of *Co-Redemptrix* and the sacrifice of our Lord Jesus Christ at Calvary. As His mother, Mary offered up (with full consent of the will) Jesus on Calvary, with faith that it was all God's purpose; that this horrible event (humanly speaking) was predestined for the salvation of the human race. In doing so she did what *all* Catholics do at every Mass; we offer up Jesus (one must carefully read the eucharistic prayers) in His one sacrifice at Calvary, *re-presented* (i.e., made present, as opposed to *another* sacrifice) through the miracle of transubstantiation.
6) Mary participates objectively in the Redemption of humanity just as we participate objectively in our own individual salvation, through our free will (though it is all ultimately *caused* by God and His grace). We must willingly follow Jesus and keep His commandments, remain faithful and vigilant, and—precisely because we have free will—we may lose the graces of God which are necessary for us to obtain eschatological salvation (i.e., actual transformational salvation when we die—not the abstract "I am saved now" notion).

7) So, just as we are allowed the unfathomable privilege of participating in our own redemption, likewise God willed that the Blessed Virgin Mary, the *Theotokos*, the Immaculate one, the perpetual Virgin, the Second Eve, would play a part in the Redemption of all, by consenting to the Sacrifice on the Cross of her Son, who was God in the flesh. She doesn't (solely and sufficiently) *cause* the Redemption any more than we (solely and sufficiently) *cause* our own redemption. Her role is to freely assent and to bear the suffering in her immaculate heart that Jesus bore in His Sacred Heart (hence those two devotions in Catholic theology).
8) "Co" in Latin does not mean "equal"; it merely means "with" or "alongside." We see this even in English. If we have a "co-pay" with regard to health insurance, that doesn't mean that we always pay equally with our insurance provider! "Co-Pilot" sometimes means "equal" but usually not. Etc. But because the term *Co-Redemptrix* is so commonly misunderstood, it has fallen out of use in the last 50 years or so. Nevertheless, Pope John Paul II continues to use it on occasion.
9) This was God's marvelous plan—to involve a creature and a woman at every step of the way, so as to achieve a certain "balance"—if I may properly speak in such a way. Eve brought down the human race, acting with Adam; Mary helped to raise it, acting in concert with Jesus Christ, her Son, the second Adam (as Paul describes Him). If Satan could cause the fall of the human race through the frailty of Woman and Man, why is it not plausible that God could in turn bring about the Redemption of the human race in part through the Immaculate Mary, the Second Eve, the *Theotokos*? To me it all makes eminent sense. It is contrary neither to Scripture nor to common sense and reason.
10) There is no necessary reason—a priori—for thinking that God couldn't or *wouldn't* have done such a thing (many Protestants and Orthodox, and questioning Catholics seem to regard these notions as intrinsically impossible, excessive, idolatrous, and unbiblical). Nothing in these concepts is contrary to Scripture or Tradition.

God clearly uses human beings as mediators. We pray for each other. Paul speaks of "having saved some" in the process of his ministry. Moses interceded and "atoned" for the Jews, and God decided not to destroy them, etc. We do good works of charity and are (hopefully) vessels of God's love and the gospel, helping others to see the light which we carry as believers indwelt with the Holy Spirit. It all comes down to free will, and bearing God's image within us.

11) All that being the case, it is nothing so unbelievable or extraordinary that God chose to involve Mary in the Redemption of mankind and the

distribution of graces. God can do whatever He wants! We seem, oftentimes, to foolishly think (on an unconscious level, of course) that God can only do what we *think* He should do! It is said in the Psalms and Prophets that God could raise up a rock or a tree to sing His praises, if stubborn men refuse to do so.

God used a donkey (Balaam's ass) to speak and express His will once. He can use babies, or infants, and the most "unlikely," unexpected human beings. He appeared in a burning bush and in a cloud. He told Isaiah to walk around naked, and to describe men's actions as menstrual rags (that is the literal meaning of Isaiah 64:6). Why should *anything* He does or chooses to do surprise us? The ending of Job makes this clear enough. We should never lose the sense of wonder and initial shock when it comes to God, and presume to judge what He "shouldn't" or "wouldn't" do. His thoughts are as far above ours as the stars are above the earth (Isaiah 55:8-9).

12) So, then, what is the a priori objection to His choice to use *Mary* in such a fashion, in order to parallel Eve's disobedience with obedience; to help redeem the human race, so that a human being among us has helped raise us to where we were always meant to be? When God took on human flesh, He raised it to heights unknown since before the Fall. We were *all* meant to be sinless and immaculate. Now we are to believe that God couldn't or wouldn't raise one solitary human being to a sinless state before they get to heaven (where sin has no entrance)? Or to help redeem the human race out of that glorious bounty of sinlessness and holiness and love for all men?

13) Therefore, God chose to use Mary for the purpose of redeeming mankind. She willed the Sacrifice on Calvary just as we will that someone ought to be redeemed or to repent, through prayer. We can merit graces given to ourselves or others by means of our own sufferings and penances (another aspect of this). There is such a thing as redemptive suffering, and we all can participate in that—how much more Mary, being sinless and not heir to even original sin?

14) Mary, being immaculate and the *Theotokos*, was in a unique position to help redeem all mankind by "joining in" (in purpose and will) with Christ on Calvary. She can obtain far more than any of us from God, on the basis of the Scripture, *the prayer of the righteous man availeth much* (James 5:16). God willed it so, and Mary complied. God chose to involve both the God-Man in salvation (essentially, sufficiently) and the Woman, the Second Eve (in corroboration, as a *fellow-laborer* with God, as Paul describes disciples).

We participate in our own salvation by consent and obedience; Mary participates in the salvation of all who are saved by her consent and obedience to Calvary. In a sense, then, the difference between ourselves and the Blessed Virgin is only quantitative, not qualitative. God was pleased to do this, because it involved human beings, and He always desires for human beings to act freely in accord with His will.

15) Likewise, God chooses to distribute all graces through Mary. She is our *Advocate* and Supreme *Intercessor*, because she is so holy, and is the Mother of God. How is that in any way unbiblical? It is not! If Moses could successfully intercede on behalf of an entire sinful and disobedient group (the Jews in the wilderness), if Abraham's prayer could spare his nephew Lot (and Sodom and Gomorrah also, if enough righteous men had been found there) why is it so remarkable that God would choose to involve Mary in intercession and distribution of graces to an entire sinful and disobedient group (mankind)? If one thing can occur, so can the other.
16) The biblical evidence for all this (as Protestants will no doubt demand) is there in kernel form. It stems from Mary's Immaculate Conception (*full of grace—kecharitomene*—Luke 1:28) and the New Eve concept above all, and has been consistently developed through the centuries by the Church. Catholics believe in such a thing as the "mind of the Church." When a consensus is reached by clergy and laity, popes and Councils, liturgy and pious practice, on a certain issue, we believe this is a legitimate part of Tradition, since we believe that God continually guides His Church, en masse, by means of the Holy Spirit, Who *teaches us all things*. Catholics need not "fear" the Bible in the least. Quite the contrary.

Chapter Sixteen

Mary the Mediatrix: Biblical Rationale and Deeper Reflections and Explanations

Co-Redemptrix and *Mediatrix* are largely (but not totally) synonymous descriptions. I usually refrain from the former term (as have recent popes), in order to avoid the common and unfortunate misunderstandings (according to ecumenical directives of Vatican II and Pope Paul VI). The analogy I use to explain it, however, is the following:

In a nutshell, the Catholic doctrine (which is already well-established in Tradition and is nothing new) is that God *chose* to involve the Blessed Virgin Mary in a very profound way in the redemption, especially in terms of intercession and as the *Theotokos* ("Mother of God"). This does *not* in any way, shape, or form, make her equal to God, or the *author* and *source* of either grace or redemption. All grace and all salvation comes from God. The same holds true for the Immaculate Conception, the Assumption, or any other Marian doctrine. Mary is nothing that God did not ultimately make her—just as with all of us.

Fr. Louis Bouyer (a convert from Lutheranism) made a clever comment that the Immaculate Conception was as "Calvinist" as the most stringent Reformed notion of predestined election: Mary was chosen by God and given "immunity" from original sin at the very moment of her conception, before she could possibly have had any choice in the matter—*pure grace* and *only* grace. She did cooperate with this grace and exalted "call" when she was able to do so, and that is her glory, and why we (very biblically) call her "blessed." But she is a creature like all of us.

God uses the Blessed Virgin Mary as a vessel of His grace. He can do whatever He well pleases. Apart from the issues of whether or not the Mediatrix doctrine is explicitly indicated in Scripture (I think it is implicitly suggested), or whether or not one agrees with it, it is certainly conceivable that God could use any of His creatures for any purpose, even up to the point of interceding in *every instance of repentance*, etc., as we believe Mary is in fact involved. We must put the objection to that hypothetical concept (which I would place in the category of "unproven, hostile, and presumptuous presupposition") to rest.

I personally suspect that a lot of the fear and alarmism over the possible new dogmatic definition of *Mediatrix* (besides sheer misinformation) arises from this prior antipathy to an idea which is assumed to be impossible from the outset— somehow a usurpation of God's sole prerogatives, when in fact it is not at all. So what remains is the task of explaining our beliefs from Scripture, Tradition, and reason. There is much more biblical material about Mary than many Protestants would imagine, and it is all interrelated, like so much of Catholic doctrine.

The whole point of the Marian dogmas both in the past and now is to uphold and emphasize the divinity of Christ. The very early patristic parallelism of the Second Eve already holds within itself the essence of the notion of Mediatrix / Co-Redemptrix, as Cardinal Newman has argued so eloquently. This is the key to understanding the whole development of Mary as Mediatrix.

I myself am an "inopportunist" with regard to the definition, not because the doctrine is not solidly established in Catholic Tradition, nor because it is contrary to biblical teaching or proper Christian reflection and reason, but because obviously we have much more educating to do for a definition not to cause scandal among our non-Catholic Christian brethren. Apparently the pope is also an inopportunist, at least for the time being.

I would remind everyone, however, that the doctrine of the Assumption was similarly feared, and it has been attacked on the grounds that there is no *explicit* biblical evidence for it (which is true), and not very strong early patristic support. Yet it happened in 1950, and we have seen ecumenism proceed despite all these fears, more than ever—in the wake of Vatican II. I agree with Cardinal Newman: what greater title could Mary have than what she already has: *Theotokos* (which is accepted by all the major branches of Christianity: Luther and Calvin—even Zwingli—used it without hesitation)?

Co-Redemptrix (rightly understood) is no more shocking or unbelievable than Paul in effect calling himself a "savior" and a "steward" of God's grace:

> Ephesians 3:2: *assuming that you have heard of the stewardship of God's grace that was given to me for you...*

This is not the only passage along these lines in Paul's inspired writings:

> 1 Corinthians 9:22: *I have become all things to all men, that I might by all means save some.*

> 1 Timothy 4:16 *Take heed to yourself and to your teaching: hold to that, for by so doing you will save both yourself and your hearers.*

It is also to be noted that the *seven spirits who are before his* [God's] *throne* seem to participate in distributing God's grace as well (Revelation 1:4). If they are angels, as many commentators believe, they haven't even been saved, let alone granted the status of Apostle. Yet they, too, apparently are channels of grace. In sacramental understanding, inanimate objects are channels of grace. This shouldn't be a controversial concept at all, biblically speaking.

If Paul, Timothy, and "seven spirits" can be so used and honored, why not Mary, the Mother of God? What is the fundamental objection, other than prior antipathy to so-called "Catholic excess?" If one objectively examines the *thing itself* as at least a biblical possibility, I see no problem whatever with it.

Furthermore, the Bible explicitly states that Christians in general are God's "helpers" or "fellow workers" (Greek, *synergos*):

>2 Corinthians 6:1 *Working together with him, then, we entreat you not to accept the grace of God in vain.* (cf. Mark 16:20)

>1 Corinthians 3:9 *For we are God's fellow workers.*

Why then, is it unthinkable for Mary to be a *fellow worker* with Jesus (albeit in a much more extraordinary fashion)? No one claims that the above verses teach *our* equality with God, simply because we *work* with Him, and are His *fellow workers*. Likewise, the Blessed Virgin is in no wise equal to God in function when she is a Mediatrix or Co-Redemptrix.

When the Church uses the terms *Mediatrix of All Graces* and *Co-Redemptrix* it means "cooperation in God's plan of redemption, in a non-necessary, essentially subordinate fashion." In other words, God chose to include Mary in His saving Providence in this fashion. In no way does that make her divine. The Blessed Virgin Mary, the *Theotokos*, is a creature, and qualitatively, infinitely lesser than God. The Catholic Church always presupposes this.

We are all involved in redemption in some fashion. If we are *all* involved in this to some extent (as will be demonstrated below), why is it unthinkable that God would use Mary preeminently? There is more than enough biblical warrant to hold this view. In my first book, *A Biblical Defense of Catholicism* (in the chapter on penance), I examined the scriptural evidence for this notion of unilateral vicarious atonement and co-redemption and redemptive suffering among Christians. This is the parallel to Mary suffering with Jesus at Calvary, and "offering" Him in some fashion. Here I will simply list the relevant verses:

1) Exodus 32:30 (cf. 32:31-32, Numbers 16:46-48).
2) Romans 8:13,17 (cf. 1 Corinthians 15:31, 2 Corinthians 6:9, 1 Peter 4:1,13).
3) 1 Corinthians 11:27,30 (cf. 11:31-32, 1 Corinthians 5:5).
4) 2 Corinthians 4: (cf. 2 Corinthians 1:5-7).
5) Philippians 2:17 (cf. 2 Corinthians 6:4-10).
6) Philippians 3:10 (cf. Galatians 2:20).

7) 2 Timothy 4:6 (cf. Romans 12:1).
8) Colossians 1:24 (cf. 2 Corinthians 11:23-30, Galatians 6:17).

These titles and functions emphasize the extraordinary role of Mary, both with regard to the Incarnation, and Redemption. In other words, the fact that God would choose to utilize a creature to that extent, *does* lead to a greater appreciation of how much He loves us, and hence, of His goodness and majesty, and marvelous methods. All Mariology is intended to glorify the Son, going right back to *Theotokos*. It was *Who* she was the "mother" of which was the point, not that she was the center of attention. *Theotokos* was defined at the Council in Ephesus in 431 precisely in response to the Nestorian Christological heresy.

Likewise, with these titles under consideration for definition, it is Redemption itself which is in focus, and how God accomplishes it by means of the Cross, not that Mary was inherently worthy of such an exalted state. *It is all grace, and all God's doing and glory.* This is Catholic Mariology and Christology. If Protestants lack understanding of that, we need to educate them and increase our apologetic efforts, not retreat out of fear of caricature and stereotype. That only makes matters worse.

I agree that *Co-Redemptrix* is especially prone to misinterpretation, because "co" is taken as "equal role," rather than (what it actually is), "cooperating with, in a qualitatively inferior way." But even *Co-Redemptrix* could be properly understood by our separated brethren with a little effort. "Co"—linguistically speaking—clearly does not have to imply equality of function. And, again, anyone who has the slightest acquaintance with Catholic Mariology would know that anyway. And that gets back to the root of the problem: ignorance (and, too often: pure prejudice).

If indeed the Blessed Virgin Mary is the Second Eve, then there is a direct parallelism. Eve, along with Adam, caused the human race to fall. It was a real act of disobedience and rebellion, and a real Fall, with real consequences. Therefore, Mary as the Second Eve helps ("co-") Christ the Second Adam to redeem the human race, in a subordinate, dependent, non-essential fashion (by God's non-necessary providential choice and decree). The redemption is real and has real consequences, and Mary's "yes" at the Annunciation was a real event which had momentous consequences for the human race.

All of this flows from the Incarnation, and Mary's central and unfathomable role as the *Theotokos*, who gave the Second Person of the Trinity human flesh, and some of her own genes. Mary is involved in redemption because all of us are (or should be) involved in redemption, as I have shown with many biblical quotations. We are to strive after "divinization." The Blessed Virgin is the first fruits of that, and the "icon" or "image" or "ideal" of what the human race can be when it is exalted by God for His purposes.

She is preeminent, for obvious reasons. She is the quintessential intercessor because she is the *Theotokos* and the holiest creature who ever lived, and James tells us that *the prayer of a righteous man availeth much*. She is the leading model of faithfulness and hope and obedience and love. Jesus couldn't have faith, because He was God. Mary was the first Christian, and the model for the Church. I think all this is a very straightforward development. There is enough biblical rationale to ultimately ground all of the speculation and Tradition in biblical revelation.

The Blessed Virgin Mary's sinless holiness which flowed from her Immaculate Conception (a sheer gift of God) enabled her to carry out her extraordinary role in salvation history, and her Assumption flows from the fact that she is the *Theotokos* and without sin (therefore not subject to decay, which is the consequence of the fall and sin and death).

Our Lady is merely what *all* of us would have been (in terms of sinlessness), but for the Fall. Nothing in these doctrines contradicts the Bible—though it is true that some of the aspects are not explicitly outlined in Scripture. And they are firmly embedded in Church Tradition. It is Protestantism which has departed from apostolic Christianity on this point, not Catholicism. A development is not a corruption. Venerable John Henry Cardinal Newman wrote:

> She had a place in the economy of Redemption;... It was fitting then in God's mercy that, as the woman began the destruction of the world, so woman should also begin its recovery, and that, as Eve opened the way for the fatal deed of the first Adam, so Mary should open the way for the great achievement of the second Adam, even our Lord Jesus Christ, who came to save the world by dying on the cross for it. Hence Mary is called by the holy Fathers a second and a better Eve, as having taken that first step in the salvation of mankind which Eve took in its ruin.
>
> How, and when, did Mary take part, and the initial part, in the world's restoration? It was when the angel Gabriel came to her to announce to her the great dignity which was to be her portion... And so, as regards the Blessed Virgin, it was God's will that she should undertake willingly and with full understanding to be the Mother of our Lord, and not to be a mere passive instrument whose maternity would have no merit and no reward. The higher our gifts, the heavier our duties. It was no light lot to be so intimately near to the Redeemer of men, as she experienced afterwards when she suffered with Him.[1]

---

[1] "Mary is the *Janua Coeli*, The Gate of Heaven," in *Meditations and Devotions*, Harrison, NY: Roman Catholic Books, 1893, 125-126.

I don't deny that there is much speculation in Catholic Marian thought (who could or would?), nor that it involves much complex interplay of ideas, deduction, etc. But I do vehemently deny that this endeavor and reflection is completely disconnected from Scripture, and/or arbitrary. To find a doctrine like that, one must go to *sola Scriptura*, or the Canon of Scripture. Those are notions which have absolutely no warrant in Scripture itself (yet both are pillars of the Protestant position, ironically enough). On the other hand, there is much Marian material to draw from.

Mary freely and willingly assented to the sacrifice of her Son for the sake of the human race, and in so doing, was intimately involved in the Redemption accomplished at Calvary as no other human being was. This is what we mean by the doctrine (as well as Mary being a channel of grace from God to man). She didn't *cause* it in a direct sense (as God does), yet she was directly involved in *the event itself* and "offered up" her Son just as the entire congregation at a Mass offers up the "re-presentation" of the One Sacrifice of Christ. God allows us that great privilege.

St. Paul tells all Christians to *present your bodies as a living sacrifice, holy and acceptable to God, which is your spiritual worship* (Romans 12:1). It does not detract from His Divine prerogatives or Glory in the least; on the contrary, it magnifies them and enhances them. The artist is glorified by His masterpiece. The Blessed Virgin Mary is God's greatest created masterpiece.

The doctrine of Mediatrix of all graces holds that God so *chose* to involve Mary in a non-necessary fashion (not because of her *intrinsic, ontological* status), in the distribution of graces—basically as an intercessor for all mankind. The other aspect of Mediatrix is Mary's role in the Incarnation, Virgin Birth, wholly *secondary* cooperation (as *Theotokos* / Mother of God) with Jesus for the purpose of the redemption of mankind, etc. This is more solidly entrenched in Catholic Tradition.

But assuming Mary is profoundly involved in the process of God's giving graces to His children, it does not therefore follow that we must consciously "go through her" every time we pray. Likewise, a particularly holy person may pray for us constantly, but we wouldn't assume that whenever we wanted to pray to God that we had to contact this person and ask them to "put in a word" for us.

The two processes are entirely distinct. Mary is an intercessor like all of us, albeit an extraordinarily holy one, and our prayers are never to be directed ultimately to her as an end and final goal. Catholics are—and have always been—perfectly free to pray directly to God. All the prayers in the Mass are directed towards God alone (there are prayers which mention other saints, but they are towards God).

It can't be emphasized enough that God can do whatever He wants with His creatures; even involve them in redemption in any way He pleases, without there being the slightest necessity of them being raised to divine status. That necessity resides only in the false presuppositions of Protestants. God could say right now, "from this point on I am going to involve Charles Spurgeon and his intercession whenever I send grace to one of my children." God could do that. It is not inconceivable. Who's to say what God can or can't do? And it would not make Spurgeon part of the Godhead anymore than it would make Mary God.

Archbishop Fulton Sheen wrote:

> If it be granted with Leo XIII that, 'God willed that the grace and truth which Christ won for us should be bestowed on us in no other way than through Mary," then she, too, had to will cooperation in Redemption, as Christ willed it as the Redeemer Himself. Christ willed that she should suffer with Him, some theologians say, 'per modum unius.' If He willed His death, He willed her Dolors... But it was no imposed will; she accepted it all in her original 'Fiat' in the Annunciation.[2]

The crux of the issue is the active "willing" of Mary to concur with Christ on the Cross. Mary doesn't *cause* anything in and of herself—it was all God's Plan from all eternity. He knew she would consent to both giving birth to Jesus, and to His sacrifice on the Cross. At the same time she acted freely, without compulsion. This is the mystery and paradox of predestination, foreknowledge, and free will. Mary didn't *cause* these events—over against God—yet she made them possible in a very real sense, by her cooperation. If she hadn't wanted to cooperate, God would have simply foreseen that and chosen someone else, in His foreknowledge and Providence.

For those non-Catholics (and Catholics) who think that the proposed definitions of the Blessed Virgin Mary as *Co-Redemptrix*, *Mediatrix*, and *Advocate* are radically new in concept and advanced by only a few "ultraconservative" Catholics on the fringe of the Church, the following excerpts from the section on Mary, from *Lumen Gentium* (Dogmatic Constitution on the Church) should be most illuminating. The Second Vatican Council dealt with Mary in greater depth and length than all previous ecumenical councils combined:

II. THE FUNCTION OF THE BLESSED VIRGIN IN THE PLAN OF SALVATION

---

[2] *The World's First Love*, New York: McGraw-Hill, 1952, 214.

§55. The sacred writings of the Old and New Testaments, as well as venerable tradition, show the role of the Mother of the Saviour in the plan of salvation in an ever clearer light and call our attention to it The books of the Old Testament describe the history of salvation, by which the coming of Christ into the world was slowly prepared. The earliest documents, as they are read in the Church and are understood in the light of a further and full revelation, bring the figure of a woman, Mother of the Redeemer, into a gradually clearer light. Considered in this light, she is already prophetically foreshadowed in the promise of victory over the serpent which was given to our first parents after their fall into sin (cf. Gen 3:15)... After a long period of waiting the times are fulfilled in her, the exalted Daughter of Sion and the new plan of salvation is established, when the Son of God has taken human nature from her, that he might in the mysteries of his flesh free man from sin.

§56. The Father of mercies willed that the Incarnation should be preceded by assent on the part of the predestined mother, so that just as a woman had a share in bringing about death, so also a woman should contribute to life. This is preeminently true of the Mother of Jesus, who gave to the world the Life that renews all things, and who was enriched by God with gifts appropriate to such a role. It is no wonder then that it was customary for the Fathers to refer to the Mother of God as all holy and free from every stain of sin, as though fashioned by the Holy Spirit and formed as a new creature.[5] Enriched from the first instant of her conception with the splendour of an entirely unique holiness, the virgin of Nazareth is hailed by the heralding angel, by divine command, as "full of grace" (cf. Lk. 1:38), and to the heavenly messenger she replies: "Behold the handmaid of the Lord, be it done unto me according to thy word" (Lk. 1:38). Thus the daughter of Adam, Mary, consenting to the word of God, became the Mother of Jesus. Committing herself wholeheartedly and impeded by no sin to God's saving will, she devoted herself totally, as a handmaid of the Lord, to the person and work of her Son, under and with him, serving the mystery of redemption, by the grace of Almighty God. Rightly, therefore, the Fathers see Mary not merely as passively engaged by God, but as freely cooperating in the work of man's salvation through faith and obedience. For, as St. Irenaeus says, she "being obedient, became the cause of salvation for herself and for the whole human race."[6] Hence not a few of the early Fathers gladly assert with him in their preaching: "the knot of Eve's disobedience was united by Mary's obedience: what the virgin Eve bound through her disbelief, Mary loosened by her faith."[7] Comparing

Mary with Eve, they call her "Mother of the living,"[8] and frequently claim: "death through Eve, life through Mary."[9]

§57. This union of the mother with the Son in the work of salvation is made manifest from the time of Christ's virginal conception up to his death...

§58... the Blessed Virgin advanced in her pilgrimage of faith, and faithfully persevered in her union with her Son unto the cross, where she stood, in keeping with the divine plan, enduring with her only begotten Son the intensity of his suffering, associated herself with his sacrifice in her mother's heart, and lovingly consenting to the immolation of this victim which was born of her. Finally, she was given by the same Christ Jesus dying on the cross as a mother to his disciple, with these words: "Woman, behold thy son" (Jn. 19:26-27).[11]...

III. THE BLESSED VIRGIN AND THE CHURCH

§60. In the words of the apostle there is but one mediator: "for there is but one God and one mediator of God and men, the man Christ Jesus, who gave himself a redemption for all" (1 Tim. 2:5-6). But Mary's function as mother of men in no way obscures or diminishes this unique mediation of Christ, but rather shows its power. But the Blessed Virgin's salutary influence on men originates not in any inner necessity but in the disposition of God. It flows forth from the superabundance of the merits of Christ, rests on his mediation, depends entirely on it and draws all its power from it. It does not hinder in any way the immediate union of the faithful with Christ but on the contrary fosters it.

§61. The predestination of the Blessed Virgin as Mother of God was associated with the incarnation of the divine word: in the designs of divine Providence she was the gracious mother of the divine Redeemer here on earth, and above all others and in a singular way the generous associate and humble handmaid of the Lord. She conceived, brought forth, and nourished Christ, she presented him to the Father in the temple, shared her Son's sufferings as he died on the cross. Thus, in a wholly singular way she cooperated by her obedience, faith, hope and burning charity in the work of the Saviour in restoring supernatural life to souls. For this reason she is a mother to us in the order of grace.

§62. This motherhood of Mary in the order of grace continues uninterruptedly from the consent which she loyally gave at the Annunciation and which she sustained without wavering beneath the cross, until the eternal fulfilment of all the elect. Taken up to heaven she did not lay aside this saving office but by her manifold intercession continues to bring us the gifts of eternal salvation.[15] By her maternal charity, she cares for the brethren of her Son, who still journey on earth surrounded by dangers and difficulties, until they are led into their blessed home. Therefore the Blessed Virgin is invoked in the Church under the titles of Advocate, Helper, Benefactress, and Mediatrix.[16] This, however, is so understood that it neither takes away anything from nor adds anything to the dignity and efficacy of Christ the one Mediator.[17] No creature could ever be counted along with the Incarnate Word and Redeemer; but just as the priesthood of Christ is shared in various ways both by his ministers and the faithful, and as the one goodness of God is radiated in different ways among his creatures, so also the unique mediation of the Redeemer does not exclude but rather gives rise to a manifold cooperation which is but a sharing in this one source. The Church does not hesitate to profess this subordinate role of Mary, which it constantly experiences and recommends to the heartfelt attention of the faithful, so that encouraged by this maternal help they may the more closely adhere to the Mediator and Redeemer.

The exaltation of Mary is the supreme illustration, example, and actuality of how highly God sought to raise man (an extension of the Incarnation itself to creatures). This is part and parcel (as the foremost and most extraordinary instance) of the notion of *divinization* or *deification* or *theosis*—a common motif, particularly in Orthodox thought, Catholic mysticism and spirituality, and the early Eastern Church Fathers, but not by any means confined to them.

Matthias Scheeben (1835-1888), the extraordinary German Catholic mystic and theologian, explains this concept in the detail necessary to avoid huge misunderstandings:

By grace the first man was deified, but he was not made God or turned into God, if we may so speak. It is only in a figurative sense that the Fathers refer to the deified man as God, that is, as a different God by similarity, not by identity, but only in the sense in which we are accustomed to speak of the so-called parhelion or mock sun as the sun. When man, the original bearer and possessor of a purely human nature, became also the possessor and bearer of a share in the divine nature through grace, he did not become another, but remained the same person.

He did not lose himself; he continued to belong to himself. By participation in the divine nature he only acquired a new possession, a new, higher, supernatural character, by which he was transformed into God's image, was made like to God in a supernatural manner, and in consequence of this resemblance necessarily entered into a most intimate union and unity with the divine Exemplar...

God must clothe Himself with human nature, must put it on, as in the deification of man the man must put on the form and character of God. In this event humanity is engrafted in a divine person, as in the other case a shoot of divinity is, so to speak, engrafted in man. Both cases are utterly astounding, supernatural, and mysterious: that a human person share in the divine nature, and that a divine person assume a human nature...

In the Eucharist the truth is realized that the Son of God does more than produce an imitation of His divine life in us; He actually continues it in us. In the Eucharist He brings us into closest contact with the divine source of that life... The mystery of grace, however, is but an imitation and continuation of the myetsry of the Trinity, with which it is connected by the Incarnation. Hence the Eucharist, as the extension of the Incarnation, must also bring us into close relationship with the Trinity.[3]

Biblical indications for *theosis* are abundant:

1) The symbolic equation of Christ and His disciples (even all of mankind) is a most biblical concept:

... whoever receives one whom I send receives me; and whoever receives me receives him who sent me. (John 13:20; cf. Luke 9:48, Mark 9:37, Matthew 18:5—NRSV)

... for I was hungry and you gave me food, I was thirsty and you gave me something to drink [etc.]... *just as you did it to one of the least of these who are members of my family, you did it to me.* (Matthew 25:35,40)

2) In Scripture there is often taught a mystical (but almost literal) identification of the *Body of Christ* (the Church: 1 Corinthians 12:27, Ephesians 1:22-23, 5:30, Colossians 1:24) with Christ Himself. Jesus

---

[3] *The Mysteries of Christianity*, tr. Cyril Vollert, St. Louis: B. Herder Book Co., 1946 (originally 1888 in German), 316-317, 489.

equated Paul's persecution of the Church with persecution of Him (Acts 9:5; cf. 8:1,3, 9:1-2). This is incarnational theology.
3) 2 Peter 1:3-4 is the all-important verse in this regard:

*According as his divine power hath given unto us all things that pertain unto life and godliness, through the knowledge of him that hath called us to glory and virtue: Whereby are given unto us exceeding great and precious promises: that by these ye might be **partakers of the divine nature**...*

(KJV; same clause in RSV / NKJV / ASB / NASB / Wuest; cf. John 14:20-23, 17:21-23)

Other renderings:

Phillips: "... share in God's essential nature"
Today's English Version: "... share the divine nature"
NIV: "participate in the divine nature"
NRSV: "participants of the divine nature"
NEB / REB: "share in the very being of God"
Williams: "sharers in the divine nature"

4) Note also the following cross-exegesis (from RSV):

a) *For in him the whole fulness of deity dwells bodily.* (Colossians 2:9)
b) *For in him all the fulness of God was pleased to dwell.* (Colossians 1:19)
c) *And from his fulness have we all received, grace upon grace.* (John 1:16)
d) *... to know the love of Christ which surpasses knowledge, that you may be filled with all the fulness of God.* (Ephesians 3:19)
e) *until we attain to the unity of the faith and of the knowledge of the Son of God, to mature manhood, to the measure of the stature of the fulness of Christ.* (Ephesians 4:13)
f) *But you are not in the flesh, you are in the Spirit, if in fact the Spirit of God dwells in you. Any one who does not have the Spirit of Christ does not belong to him.* (Romans 8:9)
g) *If the Spirit of him who raised Jesus from the dead dwells in you, he who raised Jesus Christ from the dead will give life to your mortal bodies also through his Spirit which dwells in you.* (Romans 8:11)

h) *What agreement has the temple of God with idols? For we are the temple of the living God; as God said, 'I will live in them...'* (2 Corinthians 6:16)
i) *and that Christ may dwell in your hearts through faith...* (Ephesians 3:17)
j) *for 'In him we live and move and have our being': as even some of your poets have said, 'For we are indeed his offspring.'* (Acts 17:28)
k) *For those whom he foreknew he also predestined to be conformed to the image of his Son, in order that he might be the first-born among many brethren.* (Romans 8:29)
l) *And we all, with unveiled face, beholding the glory of the Lord, are being changed into his likeness from one degree of glory to another; for this comes from the Lord who is the Spirit.* (2 Corinthians 3:18)

(see also John 14:17,20-23, 17:21-23, 1 Corinthians 3:16, 2 Timothy 1:14, 1 John 4:12,15-16)

The Greek word for "fulness" in all instances is *pleroma* (Strong's word #4138). These references also suggest the notion of theosis, or deification. It does not at all imply equality with God, but rather, a participation in His energies and power, through the Holy Spirit.

5) *The Catechism of the Catholic Church* makes frequent mention of *theosis* or *divinization*: see #398, 460, 1129, 1265, 1812, 1988.

Pope John Paul II, in his General Audience of May 27, 1998, spoke about this aspect of theology and spirituality, in his talk entitled, "Spirit Enables Us to Share in Divine Nature" (cited in part):

1. Jesus is linked with the Holy Spirit from the first moment of his existence in time, as the Nicene-Constantinopolitan Creed recalls: "Et incarnatus est de Spiritu Sancto ex Maria Virgine". The Church's faith in this mystery is based on the word of God. "The Holy Spirit", the Angel Gabriel announces to Mary, "will come upon you and the power of the Most High will overshadow you; therefore the child to be born will be called holy, the Son of God" (Lk 1:35). And Joseph is told: "That which is conceived in her is of the Holy Spirit" (Mt 1:20).

The Holy Spirit's direct intervention in the Incarnation brings about the supreme grace, the "grace of union", in which human nature is united to the Person of the Word. This union is the source of every other grace, as St. Thomas explains (S. Th. III, q. 2, a. 10-12; q. 6, a. 6; q. 7, a. 13)...

3. If we ask ourselves what the Holy Spirit's purpose was in bringing about the Incarnation event, the word of God gives us a succinct reply in the Second Letter of Peter, telling us that it happened so that we might become "partakers of the divine nature" (2 Pt 1:4). "In fact", St. Irenaeus of Lyons explains, "this is the reason why the Word became flesh and the Son of God became the Son of Man: so that man, by entering into communion with the Word and thus receiving divine sonship, might become a son of God" (Adv. Haer. III 19, 1). St. Athanasius adopts the same line: "When the Word came upon the Blessed Virgin Mary, the Spirit entered her together with he Word; in the Spirit the Word formed a body for himself and adapted it to himself, desiring to unite all creation through himself and lead it to the Father" (Ad Serap. 1, 31). These assertions are repeated by St.Thomas: "The Only-begotten Son of God, wanting us to be partakers of his divinity, assumed our human nature so that, having become man, he might make men gods" (Opusc. 57 in festo Corp. Christi, 1), that is, partakers through grace of the divine nature.

The mystery of the Incarnation reveals God's astonishing love, whose highest personification is the Holy Spirit, since he is the Love of God in person, the Person-Love: "In this the love of God was made manifest among us, that God sent his only Son into the world, so that we might live through him" (1 Jn 4:9). The glory of God is revealed in the Incarnation more than in any other work.

Quite rightly we sing in the Gloria in excelsis: "We praise you, we bless you... we give you thanks for your great glory". These statements can be applied in a special way to the action of the Holy Spirit who, in the First Letter of Peter, is called "the spirit of glory" (1 Pt 4:14). This is a glory which is pure gratuitousness: it does not consist of taking or receiving, but only of giving. In giving us his Spirit, who is the source of life, the Father manifests his glory, making it visible in our lives. In this regard St. Irenaeus says that "the glory of God is the living man" (Adv. Haer. IV, 20, 7)...

To summarize, then: assuming that the foregoing biblical data and theological speculation establishes the legitimacy of *theosis* or *deification*, it is, therefore, that much more conceivable and plausible that God could and would bestow an extraordinary place upon Mary in His redemptive plan for the human race.

If we are *all* potentially *partakers of the divine nature*, as St. Peter informs us, then how much more so the Blessed Virgin Mary, the Immaculate New Eve, the *Theotokos*? If *all* can be potentially *God's fellow workers*, urged on by God's enabling grace to *work out* our *own salvation*, then why cannot Mary conceivably have been chosen by God to be a dispenser of His salvific grace and Mediatrix?

One can dispute how much biblical data in this regard exists, and argue that Mary as Mediatrix is a quite excessive deduction, but then the Catholic can retort that the Two Natures of Christ and many aspects of the theology of the Holy Trinity involve equal or more amounts of speculation and theology not explicitly spelled out in Holy Scripture.

We maintain, then, in light of all the above, and the inheritance of the Marian Tradition of the Church Fathers, that Mary's function and role as Mediatrix and Co-Redemptrix is neither unscriptural nor opposed to received apostolic Tradition. It is entirely harmonious with both. Theophanes of Nicaea (d. 1381), an Orthodox theologian, tied the concepts of Mediatrix and deification together, somewhat along the lines of the involved analogical argument I have been attempting to make in this final section, and with his words, I shall close:

> Just as she gave our nature directly to God the Word, so God the Word to her directly repaid the deification of all; just as the Son of God through the mediation of his own Mother receives from us our nature, so through her mediation we receive his deification. It is therefore impossible that anyone in any way may become a sharer in the gifts of God other than in the way that we have set forth.[4]

---

[4] *Sermo in Sanctissimam Deiparam*, Lateranum, Nova Series, 1, Rome 1935, V, 55 (Fr. Martin Jugie). In Mark I. Miravelle, editor, *Mary: Coredemptrix, Mediatrix, Advocate: Theological Foundations*, Santa Barbara, CA: Queenship Publishing, 1995, 139.

Appendix One:

My Respect for Protestants

Some people, after reading my apologetic writings, particularly in debate with Protestants, have concluded that perhaps I don't respect Protestants or consider them sincere. Nothing could be further from the truth. To acknowledge these very characteristics is exactly what ecumenism is about—what it presupposes right from the outset. I am careful throughout my writings to assert my great love and respect for my Protestant brethren. Even if I don't state this where I could do so, I assure readers that it is always my assumption and opinion and state of mind.

Just because I may criticize (at times even excoriate) Martin Luther, John Calvin, the Protestant Reformation, or Protestant theology in general or in particulars, does not mean that I have negatively judged any individual person. That doesn't follow at all. I can't know a person's heart. How I view them individually as a Christian and disciple of Jesus is a quite different matter than disagreements as to theology.

I conducted an ecumenical discussion group at my house for four years. Near the end of that time, I did a survey, in which none of the Protestants or Orthodox (when asked) said that they had been offended in all that time. I think this speaks volumes, and I am very gratified by it. Certainly if I had been anti-Protestant, it would have come out in that survey.

Likewise, an evangelical Protestant who has since become a Catholic, read my conversion story *in Surprised by Truth*[1] and picked me out of the eleven whose stories were included, to call on the phone, because (as she told me) she sensed I was not anti-Protestant at all (and this, in a story which recounts how I converted from Protestantism to Catholicism!). That indicates, I think, how highly I regard ecumenism and respectful fellowship, charity, and unity among Christians (based on John 17 and many other biblical exhortations).

Any impression that I am "anti-Protestant" in any way, shape, or form, concerns me very much, and I want to make sure this issue is cleared up. Criticism of ideas and certain beliefs is not intended at all to be personal or "hostile" criticism. I try my utmost to refrain from judging persons and hearts. I have had mine wrongly judged on several occasions and know first-hand how extremely painful that is. I always strive to judge ideas but not people, sins but not the sinners. I'm sure I've failed at times like we all do, but that is my constant goal nonetheless.

---

[1] San Diego: Basilica Press, 1994; edited by Patrick Madrid.

I greatly admire and respect conservative, orthodox Protestantism. I once was an evangelical Protestant, and praise God for that experience, which was greatly beneficial to my spiritual advancement and theological education. I now consider myself an evangelical Catholic.

None of my writings are intended as an attack on the personal integrity of any individual. I do strongly criticize the *ideas* of the Protestant Founders, however, because they were public figures with momentous claims, who ought to be held accountable for their actions and effect on Christianity. I take pains to carefully distinguish between the person and their ideas.

Catholics can benefit greatly from much of Protestantism. I hope to show that the converse is also true. My goal is to build bridges of understanding among Christians of all stripes, who are brothers in Christ (John 17:20-23). Catholics believe that the fullness of apostolic Christianity resides in their Church, but this does not at all mean that great, profound amounts of truth and goodness are not to be found in other Christian communions as well. All validly baptized Christians are our brothers and sisters in Christ, and ought to be accorded the proper amount of respect befitting that status, as well as charity at all times.

Anyone who has spent any amount of time at my extensive website, *Biblical Evidence for Catholicism* (http://ic.net/~erasmus/RAZHOME.HTM) can easily, readily observe, I believe, my respect for Protestantism, by perusing the hundreds of Protestant *links* I provide.

I think it is commonly understood online that a link (like a standard reference citation in a book) does not necessarily imply across-the-board agreement. I choose my links according to a substantial commonality with Catholic doctrine, on whatever subject the link is categorized under. For example, a Protestant apologist or theologian defending the Trinity or the Resurrection of Christ, or presenting philosophical arguments for the existence of God or angels or the devil or heaven and hell (say, an evangelical Protestant who upholds traditional Christian teaching in these areas), will offer virtually nothing a Catholic would disagree with.

So why shouldn't a Catholic utilize sites where we have common ground with our separated brethren, over against our secular, pagan culture? As Catholics, we are called upon to be ecumenical. We have no choice. Evangelicals have been doing a great job in the last generation, in the area of general Christian apologetics. Catholics are just now getting into that again. So I cherish and am thankful and grateful for all the excellent, helpful, worthwhile non-Catholic efforts which agree with Catholic and Christian theology and orthodoxy.

Many Catholic converts wrote excellent books and articles before they converted, which are used by Catholics all the time, because they are orthodox and eloquent: Newman, Chesterton, Thomas Howard, and Malcolm Muggeridge come to mind immediately. Other lifelong Protestants, like C.S. Lewis, and (to some extent) John Wesley, are very close to Catholicism in spirit and doctrine.

In a strict, non-ecumenical point of view, on the other hand, a John Henry Newman sermon from 1839, no matter how brilliant and orthodox, would be considered "unorthodox," as would a Lewis essay on miracles, etc. Very few Catholic apologists (and I know scores of them) would agree with that approach. Truth is truth, wherever it is found, and our Protestant and Orthodox brethren have a lot of it, despite their many errors.

We need to stand with fellow Christians wherever we find common ground, so that we can affect our culture with the gospel of Jesus Christ, and not be defeated by a "divide and conquer" strategy. Whether it's trinitarianism, the bodily Resurrection of Jesus, the inspiration of the Bible, or an opposition to homosexual acts, radical "unisex" feminism, pornography, physician-assisted suicide, abortion, or whatever, we have much in common, and we are called to rejoice in the truths that bind us.

Much truth can be found in, for instance, C.S. Lewis's writing (he remains my own favorite author), as in the writing of many Protestant (not to mention Orthodox) writers, clergymen, and apologists. Catholics are free to acknowledge, and rejoice in, truth. We are sharp enough (or should be) to discern the errors.

Should a Catholic refuse to read Cardinal Newman's *Essay on the Development of Christian Doctrine*? After all, it was written in 1845 when the Venerable Cardinal was still an Anglican. Or should we look down our noses at the even earlier *Parochial and Plain Sermons*, from the 1830s—widely considered the most elegant sermons in the English language? Of course not. A hundred times no...

Most Catholics love and appreciate G. K. Chesterton. But should they eschew his classic work *Orthodoxy*, simply because it was written in 1908, some 14 years before Chesterton became a Catholic? No. Likewise, Malcolm Muggeridge was only a Catholic for the last eight years of his life (from 1982 to 1990)! Chesterton was only formally Catholic for the last fourteen years of his life (I've already been a member of the Catholic Church more than ten years myself!).

Muggeridge himself rejoiced in truth wherever he found it. In one of his last books, written as a Catholic, about his conversion, *Confessions of a Twentieth-Century Pilgrim*[2], he cites approvingly many non-Catholics (as he had always

---

[2] San Francisco: Harper & Row, 1988. As a note of trivia, the title of my conversion story in the bestseller *Surprised by Truth*, was a take-off of this book (though few, if any, seemed to have noticed that). I called my testimony, "Confessions of a 1980s' Jesus Freak." Muggeridge's title in turn hearkened back to St. Augustine's classic *Confessions* and (in all likelihood) John Bunyan's *Pilgrim's Progress*.

done in his writing), such as: William Blake (pp. 17, 45, 49, 69), Thomas Traherne (p. 20), John Milton (p. 35), John Donne (pp. 45, 145), Simone Weil (pp. 44, 51-52), George Herbert (pp. 74, 103-104), Alexander Solzhenitsyn—one of his great heroes (pp. 75, 116-117), Nicholas Berdyaev (p. 88), Fyodor Dostoevsky (p. 98), Jonathan Swift (p. 145), Dietrich Bonhoeffer (p. 146), and Dr. Johnson (p. 148).

Concerning C.S. Lewis[3], what possible objection (apart from perhaps minor disagreements) would a Catholic have to works such as *The Chronicles of Narnia* or, say, *The Problem of Pain*, or *Miracles*, or *The Screwtape Letters*, or *The Four Loves*? Lewis had many Catholic friends in his inner circle—such as J.R.R. Tolkien (the author of *Lord of the Rings*). Many other Catholics are Lewis scholars and experts (Thomas Howard, Peter Kreeft, Walter Hooper).

Would any educated Catholic who knew their faith argue that Hilaire Belloc shouldn't have been best friends with G.K. Chesterton, or cite him as an influence, until the latter converted? Or that this friendship and admiration somehow proves his lack of orthodoxy? I trust that readers can see the sheer silliness of this "guilt-by-association" sort of "reasoning." It breaks down almost immediately upon examination.

It is true that C.S. Lewis rejected Catholicism, and even had (so it seems) a stubborn prejudice against it (one explanation advanced for that is his having been raised in Belfast—J.R.R. Tolkien has stated that Lewis actually admitted this prejudice to him in a private conversation). This doesn't mean, however, that he didn't accept many beliefs which we hold (indeed, this *was* in fact the case), or that his work is worthless. Lewis was highly influenced by Chesterton (he cited *The Everlasting Man* as perhaps the most influential book he ever read). Chesterton was arguably the preeminent Christian popular apologist in the first third of the century, right before Lewis hit the scene.

No properly-catechized Catholic denies that a non-Catholic will have error mixed in with his views. It is a matter of degree. Yet such a person might express himself on particular matters in an orthodox sense, and more eloquently than a Catholic. I think—again—of Newman's Anglican sermons in particular. John Wesley preached many sermons which would be of great benefit to Catholics, as he possessed almost identical beliefs with regard to things like sanctification, regenerative baptism, the perpetual virginity of Mary, Christology, etc.

Even anti-Catholic preachers like Charles Spurgeon or (today) John MacArthur, have many fine and beneficial insights to offer, for the discerning and careful Catholic reader or radio listener. Truth remains truth, even if it is

---

[3] See my widely-cited C.S. Lewis web page: http://ic.net/~erasmus/RAZ26.HTM. The influential evangelical Protestant magazine *Christianity Today* has often mentioned it in its articles concerning Lewis, as the place to go on the Internet for further information.

surrounded by erroneous propositions and statements. We have reason to believe, for example, that the early Church was influenced by Jewish liturgics and sacred architecture. Does that mean that the early Church was therefore Jewish, or compromised, because it was influenced by a non-Christian religious group?

This applies to the New Testament also. It was clearly profoundly influenced by the Old Testament and "Jewishness" (just look at all the quotations), yet no one in their right mind claims that this is a compromise, or improper, because it is recognized that influences can be developed further, with some elements retained, and others rejected.

Likewise with C.S. Lewis's influence on myself. Could Lewis somehow cease to remain an influence on my thinking simply because I took a different ecclesiological path than he did? The entire argument is silly and insubstantial, and works only for someone who has presupposed an anti-ecumenical, quasi-Feeneyite mindset in the first place.

Ecumenism is a great emphasis in the Catholic Church today, especially with Pope John Paul II, and one stressed by Vatican II and the last several popes. What is ecumenism if not attempting to find common ground with our non-Catholic Christian brethren? Internet links are a very concrete way to do that, where there is commonality and agreement. My perspective is completely orthodox and proper within a Catholic framework.

There is far more good in conservative, traditional Protestant writings than bad. We are in the world; we ought to learn to interact with our theological opponents—not avoid them like the plague or pretend they are not there. We can't do an end run around the Church's desire for ecumenism and cooperation where possible. Error is all around us; we are told, that 70% of Catholics disbelieve in the Real Presence, and that 70-80% contracept. These are matters of infallibly defined dogmas and objective mortal sin. So the error is in our midst as well—though not on the level of official teaching, of course.

I have been accused, in particular, of "bashing" or "disliking" or even "hating" Calvinist, or Reformed Protestants. This occurs because I have written quite vigorously (as part of what I would describe as my "apologetic duty") in response to virulently anti-Catholic factions within Calvinism. But this, too, is an inaccurate appraisal of my beliefs.

Actually, I have a rather high view of Calvinism and many Calvinists. I state this in several places on my website. I intensely dislike certain beliefs or strands of Calvinism (particularly supralapsarianism)—as I oppose all error—, but other aspects I highly admire: the scholarly approach, the more historically-oriented view, the retention of sacramentalism, the appreciation for Covenant theology, a superior ecclesiology to many evangelicals, a concern for self-consistency, a high view of the majesty and Providence of God, an exceptional and praiseworthy interest in theology and apologetics, the Lordship salvation view, emphasis on cultural and political aspects of Christianity and Jesus as Lord of all of life, etc., etc..

Francis Schaeffer was and is a huge influence on me, as was Charles Colson, J.I. Packer, Berkouwer and many other Calvinists. I often listen to R.C. Sproul on the radio and receive much benefit from him (I think he is a wonderful teacher). I have Internet acquaintances who attend John Piper's church. I visited a Calvinist pastor and his wife in another state in 1997. I have other Calvinist pastor friends. Many cordial debates with Calvinists are posted on my site. I could go on and on.

It is quite possible to seek to understand something better even if one largely disagrees with it (at least in the sense that it is not superior to Catholicism). Otherwise I couldn't have ever converted to Catholicism. I used to think it was much inferior to evangelicalism (though I never hated Catholicism either), but I actually took the time to learn more about it, and I was persuaded.

That is my attitude towards Protestantism in general. I continue to admire it, and believe that Catholics can learn much from it, for the simple reason that it possesses much Christian and biblical truth, and because individual Protestants (or even denominations) often excel (especially in practice) at particular aspects of the Christian life or theology (e.g., Bible study, prayer, outreach, teen ministry, fellowship) in a way that puts Catholics to shame.

I hasten to add that all of the foregoing would also apply in a general way to my view towards the Orthodox Church, in fact, even more so, as there is much more substantial agreement between Orthodoxy and Catholicism than between Protestantism and Catholicism. I presuppose this at all times, even while issuing strong critiques on individual issues on my website and in my conventional published writings.

The Christian apologist (of whatever stripe), by nature, writes about disagreements; he critiques, and defends and expounds upon what he sincerely and deeply believes are the "superior" views of his own party. But it is incorrect and improper to conclude from this obvious fact, that any given apologist totally lacks all humility, or "hates" or wishes to "bash" personally someone of a different persuasion, or an entire group.

There is a right way to disagree and a wrong way. We are to love at all times, but there are also occasions when we must disagree, in principle. The latter is not exclusive of the former, and indeed, it ought to always incorporate it, if we are to conduct ourselves in a manner worthy of a disciple of Jesus Christ. We all fall frequently, of course, but the biblical guidelines for handling disagreements (doctrinal or otherwise) are clear and straightforward.

> *Rather, speaking the truth in love, we are to grow up in every way into him who is the head, who is Christ, from whom the whole body, joined and knit together by every joint with which it is supplied, when*

each part is working properly, makes bodily growth and upbuilds itself in love. (Ephesians 4:15-16—RSV)

Appendix Two:

My Odyssey From Evangelicalism to Catholicism (Transcript of a Radio Interview) [1]

Al Kresta (A): You're listening to *Al Kresta Live*. With me right now: Dave Armstrong, Catholic apologist and free-lance writer. Dave is also a longtime friend, and I think [he] has one of the best websites out there, if you're interested in the biblical evidence for Catholicism. Dave, good to have you here.

Dave Armstrong (D): Great to be here, Al!

A: We wanted to talk about your story; how you came to know Jesus, and how you came to recognize His Church. It's contained in the volume *Surprised by Truth*. So, take us to the beginning.

D: Well, the beginning is when I was *born*, I guess, which is 1958. So I've been joking that I had my Jack Benny birthday this year: 39. I was raised Methodist; pretty nominal. [My own faith and walk with God] wasn't very vital, and there wasn't much fire there, for whatever reason. So it took really, till 1977 to become an evangelical Christian.

A: How did that happen?

D: Basically, my brother Gerry, getting "saved" around 1971, and the spectacle of his long-haired friends comin' around, carrying Bibles; truth is stranger than fiction! And just observing them; it got me wondering, "what's going on here? These people are talking about Jesus..." I thought you had to be a square [to be a good Christian]. It's kind of funny to look back.

A: The things that were important to you then, yeah...

---

[1] I was interviewed on 8 September 1997 in studio by my longtime friend and former pastor Al Kresta, on his Catholic talk radio program *Al Kresta Live*, on WDEO-AM (990 AM), from Ann Arbor, Michigan. His story of his own return to the Church was also included in *Surprised by Truth* (San Diego: Basilica Press, 1994, edited by Patrick Madrid), and his oral recounting of his "reversion" back to the Catholic Church has been marketed by Karl Keating's Catholic Answers apostolate. He is also editor of an informative Catholic newsweekly, *Credo* (http://www.credopub.com/). The interview was approximately 25 minutes long.

D: Yeah, as a 13-year-old. But a big influence on me was the movies about Jesus that would come on.

A: Really?

D: Like *The Greatest Story Ever Told*. One time we were watchin' that (this would be mid-70s, I guess), and my brother Gerry said "well, Jesus is God." And I didn't even *know* that! That's how ignorant I was. I didn't even know the Trinity. I said, "no, he's the *son* of God!" And he said "no, He's God the Son." So I started thinking about... it gave me a different perspective, watching the movie, even, that this person is God in the flesh.

A: Yeah, I bet; it certainly would. You know, it's characteristic: a lot of kids who are raised in various religious traditions grow up *completely* ignorant of what those traditions formally teach. You were raised Methodist, which of course believes in the tri-unity of God and the deity of Christ, but by the time you hit your teens, anyway, you didn't even know that.

D: At least in the Catholic tradition, generally kids are going to parochial school; they get some kind of catechetical instruction. But I really didn't have that. I didn't have a good Sunday school, or much at all. I think if I had learned *earlier*, some of the things I learned later, that I think I would have had more zeal for being a Christian.

A: So when do you usually date your conversion to Christ, or your commitment to Jesus?

D: That would be 1977, and it took a huge depression that I went through. I was 18 years-old at the time, and God—the way I look at it—God more or less had to put me right on my back to see that I couldn't survive on my own. Because I was under this illusion, "well, you don't need God." I had lived for ten years without going to church—a very secular life; kind of like what you see in England now, where 4% go to church every Sunday.

A: Yeah,... yeah. Once having committed your life to Jesus, were you immediately on fire?

D: Well, for a few days! Then I went back into a lukewarmness for three more years.

A: Wow!

D: I would go to Bible studies, at Messiah Church [an evangelical Lutheran church with an outreach to the inner-city and young people]. That's a very good church. It was a good place to start. But I didn't even go to church on Sunday; I just went to the Bible studies. And I would read things like Hal Lindsey, which interested me because of prophecy.

A: Yes.

D: But in 1980, when I went to Shalom House (where Al used to be the pastor—if people don't know that here); that's when I really started to—I would say—commit myself to Jesus, and since then, it's been pretty constant.

A: Yeah... and that was before I was pastoring there, to give all due credit to [name], who was pastor at the time.

D: Yeah, Al got there six years later...

A: What was your experience like as an evangelical?

D: Well, I *loved* it. I was thinking, driving out today: most conversion stories I hear from Catholics, they don't run down their evangelical experience.

A: Right.

D: They see it as kind of a stepping-stone. So I have great memories and fond memories. I learned all about the *Bible* when I was there, good moral teaching... I just think there was more to it that the Catholic Church can offer, along the lines of sacramentalism and tradition and matters of Church and authority.

A: Yeah. Now, when did it first dawn on you that you wanted something more than you were receiving in this particular evangelical setting?

D: Well, I went about ten years being an evangelical, and involved in counter-cult ministry and my own campus ministry, and then in the late 80s, I started becoming involved in Rescues (Operation Rescue: pro-life activities). Even then, I didn't have a sense that there was "something more that I need, than I have now." So it really goes all the way up to 1990, when I started having a discussion group. I invited two Catholics that I had met in the Rescues, and that started getting me thinking, when they would start answering questions, because I used to think, "Catholics don't have any answers to these questions..." I had very little experience talking to informed Catholics, unfortunately. And then I met one, named John McAlpine, who's a good friend of mine, that could actually answer things that I would ask him. And he just got me curious, and I started studying at that point, in 1990.

A: What were the questions that were most puzzling for you?

D: At that time, being a pro-life activist, I was curious about contraception, where Catholics would be against that—or *supposed* to be against it; the *Church* is against it—and they would make a connection between that and abortion. And I'd try to figure that out: "what connection does *that* have, because one is trying to *prevent* conception; the other is *killing* a child?" And that got me thinking. They'd tell me facts like, "the whole Christian Church was against contraception until 1930."

A: Did that bother you?

D: Yeah, that gave me a start, because I always valued Church history. So, to hear that fact, it was kind of like a bombshell. So I thought, "man, if it was unanimous up till *then*"... I thought it was a stretch to believe that in our century, that we would get a moral teaching *right*, and 1900 years had messed it up... Of all centuries, with all the murder we've had in the 20th...

A: I was gonna say, the bloodiest century in the history of the human race...

D: Yeah, exactly.

A: And all of a sudden we have some grand new moral insight.

D: The light goes on...

A: Yeah; that's good...

D: It's interesting, too, how in 1930, it was the Anglicans, in their conference that year, that changed it, and they talked about "hard cases," just like we've heard in *our* time.

A: Sure.

D: So it's the same kind of mentality: "well, it's only in *hard cases*, and we won't expand it any further than that." But obviously it *has* been.

A: Yeah. We've got three instances that come to mind here: the contraception case, which was argued [on the basis of] hard cases, "so let's permit it here"; then you have Roe v. Wade; "hard cases, well let's permit it here"; and of course the case before us today has to do with assisted suicide: "well, we need it for hard cases." But if the hard case argument has any *historical* meaning, then we know that what was once the *hard* case becomes the *normal* case.

D: Yeah, that's right.

A: So contraception has become well accepted under not just *hard* circumstances, but in almost *all* circumstances—same thing with abortion. And my guess is, you'll have the same thing with assisted *suicide*. Hard cases make bad law... So at the 1930 Lambeth Conference, the Anglican Church goes ahead and permits contraception in tough cases; the first time any Christian Church has permitted the use of contraception. John McAlpine tells you that; you're shocked; you say, "wait a minute! I don't think we've got any grand new moral insights in the 20th century that the Christian Church has missed for the last 1900 years." So that shook you up a bit. What'd you do? What'd you do about that?

D: Basically I didn't have a *defense* for that. I just stood there, silent, at one of the meetings—I don't know if it was during the meeting or after. But I just started thinking about that issue, and I became convinced, that... I tried to work through the distinction between contraception and Natural Family Planning, which is permitted for Catholics. And I came to realize that in one case you're deliberately thwarting a possible conception; you're going ahead and having sex *anyway*, and it's kind of against the natural order. You don't even have to appeal to Church authority to know the wrongness of it, if you reflect on the morality. Then I remember one time, you were at my house, and made this analogy of—I was convinced by then, but it makes sense—comparing that to how when people eat, you have the nutritional aspect and the taste buds. That people would think it strange if you separated one from the other; if you just ate for pleasure or vice versa. And I thought that was good. I don't know if that's original with you, or where it came from.

A: I don't know where it came from, either, but yeah, I do remember that. You weren't yet a Catholic at the time, or were you?

D: No; at that time—the middle of 1990 - I was evangelical. And I remember thinking, "well, if I change my mind on this, I'm kind of a small minority among evangelicals..." And I knew what the implications of that might be... it could develop further, but I still would have said, "well, it doesn't mean I'm gonna be a *Catholic*."

A: Right, right.

D: But I thought it strange that the Catholic Church had, I thought, the best moral theology of any church. So I thought, "how could they be right about *these* things, and be so wrong on Mary and the pope?," and the typical things that evangelicals don't like.

A: Yeah. So really, your entrance; your being wooed into the Catholic Tradition, was through this question of contraception? That's the beginning?

D: The very first thing, yeah.

A: Where does it move from there?

D: That brought to my mind matters of "What is the Church?," because I believed that there was such a thing as **the** Church, with a big "C". And I found it interesting... I was in counter-cult ministry, and they had this habit of talking about, "well, the early Church condemned Arianism in the Council of Nicaea." They'd have this notion of **the** Church. But then somehow that gets lost after *Luther* comes on the scene; all of a sudden now, it seems like evangelicals are reluctant to talk about **the** Church, because they know it usually refers to *us*. We're the only ones who use that terminology (well, the Orthodox, do, too). So I started thinking, "how does that work out?" So I had a view that the early Church was Protestant. It became corrupt with the Inquisition and the Crusades. And then—I mentioned in the book—Luther picked up the ball in the 1500s; it switched over to Protestantism at that point. The Catholic Church was still *Christian*, but it wasn't what I would call the *mainstream*. The evangelicals were really where it was at and the Catholics: they had enough truth, but not enough... they could still be saved, but they were just in a different league—that's how I used to think.

A: Interesting. So, you began to question what it means to be " **the** Church" and how you can consistently use that phrase: "the Church," because, of course, unless you have some sort of visible unity, then how do you know who's in and who's out? Who really *speaks* for **the** Church?

D: Yep.

A: When was that settled for you?

D: At that time—we're still in the middle of 1990—in my discussion group every two weeks, we were talkin', and John and another friend of his named Leno [Poli] (really good Catholics and committed pro-lifers)... it was just observing them: the faith that they had and the answers they would give... But I would try to shoot down the idea of infallibility. I would say, "Ok, you guys can be the Church, or **a** Church, but you're not *infallible.*" I thought that was just totally out of the ballpark. That *couldn't* be: there were too many errors, and there was the Inquisition, and so forth. So I started doing my own study, and even going to Sacred Heart Seminary and trying to shoot down the Catholic Church. So I found the typical things that people bring up, about Pope Honorius, who supposedly was a heretic, but it was all from a kind of jaded viewpoint. As I look back, I wasn't being objective; it was like special pleading: you go in there with an idea and try to just find what fits *in* with it. And so, when I look back at that, I can see that it was sort of a dishonest effort; that there are good Catholic answers to all these so-called charges of heresy. And we see it; it comes around. This kind of stuff is being talked about today, even within the Church. Like Hans Kung and his book *Infallible? An Inquiry.* It's the same kind of thing, [but] there are answers to these things. Catholics just aren't aware of them, by and large.

A: Yeah. And it's part of the problem. How do you go about empowering the laity, so that they *have* this background in history and theology and Scripture. This is a *major* issue, it seems to me, facing the Catholic Church today.

D: Yeah.

A: We've got such grand impetus from Vatican II and from this present pope about the necessary role of the laity in carrying out the priorities of the kingdom of God and of the Church, and yet we find, at the same time, really very few Catholic bookstores; very few places where people can find information. I hope now with the Internet out there...

D: Thank God for that!

A:... people can have access... and get their education, and learn a little bit more about Church history and theology and Scripture.

You're still not in the Church yet... what finally starts pushin' you over the line?

D: One word: [John Henry Cardinal] **Newman**! My friend John became totally exasperated with my constant questions. I was getting into some pretty technical things, and he hadn't done the study, so, understandably, he wouldn't be able to figure out Honorius, and all these things in history. So he said, "why don't you read Newman's *Essay on the Development of Christian Doctrine?*"—which is considered the classic on that subject. And of course, Newman is a genius; he lived in the 1800s. So I started reading that book, and basically it destroyed the whole conception that I had, this notion that the early Church was simple and Protestant, and became *corrupt*... because he develops (no pun intended) the idea that you can have a development as opposed to a corruption. A doctrine can *grow*, but it doesn't have to be a *corruption*, because it remains the same in *essence*. What's happening is that you just *understand* more. So you can find this in Augustine and early Fathers; it's *there*—the *idea* is there, and I think it is the key to Catholic history; why we think we're the apostolic Church, and Protestantism broke off of that, because their doctrines—many of them—didn't develop; they just sprang into existence.

A: So that was for you a turning point in dealing with this idea of "why does the Catholic Church, with this luxuriant overgrowth of custom, and teaching, discipline, and liturgy; why doesn't it look more like what Paul is describing in 1 Corinthians 12-14?"—which looks more like a primitive pentecostal church service.

D: Yeah; yeah, because we had this notion that—probably you did, too—the early Church was this bunch of "Jesus Freaks" runnin' around, meeting in *caves*. You know, they didn't believe in the Eucharist, or any of that kind of hifalutin' stuff. But that's really not what you find... I didn't do this at the time, but since then, I've read the Apostolic Fathers, and you see that it's very "Catholic." They believed in Real Presence, and regenerative baptism—all the things, pretty much, that Catholics believe today, only in more primitive *form*. You didn't have—particularly—the idea of *Scripture Alone / sola Scriptura*. It's just *not there*. People will quote the Fathers, extolling the Bible, and they'll say, "well, see, they're *Scripture Alone*." But no, they're just saying the Bible's a great book (of course, everybody agrees with that).

Catholics think that... The bottom line is the question of authority: who has the authoritative interpretation *of* Scripture? No one's denying that Scripture is God's *Word*. And the Catholic Church has an impeccable record on that score. So it's a question of authority, and the Church Fathers would appeal to apostolic *Tradition*, or succession. They would say, "we trace ourselves back to the Apostles; therefore we have true Christian teaching." And that was the basis of it, rather than *Bible Alone*. Because people would disagree on that basis, as they do today.

A: Once that obstacle is removed for you: the idea of a developing doctrine, what remains?

D: At that point, I told myself, "okay, now I have the Catholic viewpoint of history, so I need to look at the Protestant 'Reformation' and determine, 'what is the Protestant Reformation?'" I had read a little bit about it, but I wanted to get more in depth and maybe read the Catholic views of it—get the other side... Because, there again, you have this myth that Luther came... and somehow the Bible was in chains, and the Church was in darkness, and Luther comes out and brings the Bible to the people... And there's a lot of mythology there, because, for instance, a hundred years before Luther's time, there were, I think it's fourteen versions in German of the *Bible*. By *Catholics*. And yet the popular notion is that no one had the Bible, and they were chained... and that's because of the printing press. You didn't have widespread literacy and Bibles until the *printing press*, and that's only in the 1450s. So, there's a lot of that kind of... it's really anti-Catholic at its core, the idea that the Catholic Church was somehow *suppressing* the Bible.

A: Yeah; putting a deliberately negative spin on these historical circumstances. And there were cases, of course, where you have legitimate debates over what is an acceptable *interpretation*, as the debates between Sir Thomas More and William Tyndale show, where the Church *had* to act, just as any government would act to protect people under its charge; the Church has to act to protect people from bad *translations*. In its lights at the time, they saw Tyndale's translation as a bad translation.

D: Yeah; that's really the Catholic answer to this charge that "you suppress the Bible!" And we say, "we just suppress bad *translations* of the Bible." That's nothing more than fundamentalists do today. They say "this is a liberal translation." It's the same exact thing, but it has that slant to it because they assume that we're somehow anti-Bible, which is *absurd*. We're the ones who preserved it for a thousand years! You know, you hear about these monks and their manuscripts: these beautiful books. So people should just know more about the history; that's really what needs to be done.

A: So then, where do you move, after that?

D: At that time I read a book called *Evangelical is Not Enough*, by Thomas Howard. He's a great writer. I see him as the successor to C.S. Lewis, stylistically. And he showed how the liturgy was... the Catholic Mass had this transcendent quality to it, that transcends time and space. It's a fantastic book. So that kinda gave me a feel for liturgy, which I had virtually no experience with, or that much love for, really, because I was evangelical *low* church. And I read a book, also, called *The Spirit of Catholicism*, by Karl Adam.

A: Oh yeah—one of my favorite books.

D: And that was just *wonderful*. And then at that point, basically it was just a matter of getting over the cold feet and the jitters.

A: Did you have this period of time where you kind of intellectually were persuaded, but somehow the will just wouldn't grasp; wouldn't jump?

D: Yeah—the common thing with most converts is, "I think I *believe* it, but now I have to..." Kind of like getting married: "I have to *do* this, and it just has to be *done*."

A: What finally warmed your heart to move, then?

D: I was reading a little meditation by Newman, called *Hope in God the Creator*. And it just sort of ended with a whimper; whatever resistance was there... I said to myself, "well, no, I'm a Catholic now, I believe everything, so now's the time." So it just happened. And there's a lot of other stuff, but that's basically it.

A: Well, I remember when you were going through that. I had stopped pastoring at the time, and was also moving in the direction of the Catholic Church, and yeah, I had no real resistance to offer you. I thought you didn't have too many options, Dave.

D: That's bad when your former *pastor* has nothing to say...

A: Well, the story is well told in *Surprised by Truth*,... I wanna thank you so much, Dave, for being with me. And we'll talk again.

D: It's been great; been a pleasure.

Appendix Three:

150 Reasons Why I am a Catholic
(Featuring 300 Biblical Evidences Favoring Catholicism)

1. **Best One-Sentence Summary:** I am convinced that the Catholic Church conforms much more closely to all of the biblical data, offers the only coherent view of the history of Christianity (i.e., Christian, apostolic Tradition), and possesses the most profound and sublime Christian morality, spirituality, social ethic, and philosophy.
2. **Alternate:** I am a Catholic because I sincerely believe, by virtue of much cumulative evidence, that Catholicism is true, and that the Catholic Church is the visible Church divinely-established by our Lord Jesus, against which the gates of hell cannot and will not prevail (Mt 16:18), thereby possessing an authority to which I feel bound in Christian duty to submit.
3. **2nd Alternate:** I left Protestantism because it was seriously deficient in its interpretation of the Bible (e.g., "faith alone" and many other "Catholic" doctrines—see evidences below), inconsistently selective in its espousal of various Catholic Traditions (e.g., the Canon of the Bible), inadequate in its ecclesiology, lacking a sensible view of Christian history (e.g., "Scripture alone"), compromised morally (e.g., contraception, divorce), and unbiblically schismatic, anarchical, and relativistic. I don't therefore believe that Protestantism is all bad (not by a long shot), but these are some of the major deficiencies I eventually saw as fatal to the "theory" of Protestantism, over against Catholicism. All Catholics must regard baptized, Nicene, Chalcedonian Protestants as Christians.
4. Catholicism isn't formally divided and **sectarian** (Jn 17:20-23; Rom 16:17; 1 Cor 1:10-13).
5. Catholic **unity** makes Christianity and Jesus more believable to the world (Jn 17:23).
6. Catholicism, because of its unified, complete, fully supernatural Christian vision, mitigates against **secularization** and humanism.
7. Catholicism avoids an unbiblical **individualism** which undermines Christian community (e.g., 1 Cor 12:25-26).
8. Catholicism avoids theological **relativism**, by means of dogmatic certainty and the centrality of the papacy.

9. Catholicism avoids **ecclesiological anarchism**—one cannot merely jump to another denomination when some disciplinary measure or censure is called for.
10. Catholicism formally (although, sadly, not always in practice) prevents the theological relativism which leads to **uncertainties** among Christian laypeople.
11. Catholicism rejects the **"State Church,"** which has led to governments dominating Christianity rather than vice-versa.
12. State Churches greatly influenced the rise of **nationalism**, which mitigated against universal equality and Christian universalism (i.e., catholicism).
13. Unified Catholic Christendom (before the 16th century) had not been plagued by the tragic **religious wars** which in turn led to the "Enlightenment," in which men rejected the hypocrisy of inter-Christian warfare and decided to become indifferent to religion rather than letting it guide their lives.
14. Catholicism retains the elements of **mystery, supernatural**, and the **sacred** in Christianity, thus opposing itself to secularization, where the sphere of the religious in life becomes greatly limited.
15. Protestant individualism led to the **privatization** of Christianity, whereby it is little respected in societal and political life, leaving the "public square" barren of Christian influence.
16. The secular false dichotomy of "church vs. world" has led committed orthodox Christians, by and large, to withdraw from **politics**, leaving a void filled by pagans, cynics, unscrupulous, and the power-hungry. Catholicism offers a framework in which to approach the state and civic responsibility.
17. Protestantism leans too much on mere **traditions of men** (every denomination stems from one Founder's vision. As soon as two or more of these contradict each other, error is necessarily present).
18. Protestant churches (especially evangelicals), are far too often guilty of putting their pastors on too high of a pedestal. In effect, every pastor becomes a "pope," to varying degrees (some are "super-popes"). Because of this, evangelical congregations often experience a severe crisis and/or split up when a pastor leaves, thus proving that their philosophy is overly **man-centered**, rather than God-centered.
19. Protestantism, due to lack of real authority and dogmatic structure, is tragically prone to **accommodation** to the **spirit of the age,** and moral faddism.

20. Catholicism retains **apostolic succession**, necessary to identify true Christian apostolic Tradition. It was the criterion of Christian truth used by the early Christians.
21. Many Protestants take a dim view towards **Christian history** in general, especially the years from 313 (Constantine's conversion) to 1517 (Luther's arrival). This ignorance and hostility to Catholic Tradition leads to theological relativism, anti-Catholicism, and a constant, unnecessary process of "reinventing the wheel."
22. Protestantism from its inception was **anti-Catholic**, and largely remains so to this day (especially certain strains of evangelicalism). This is obviously wrong and unbiblical if Catholicism is indeed Christian (if it isn't, then—logically—neither is Protestantism, which inherited the bulk of its theology from Catholicism). The Catholic Church, on the other hand, is not anti-Protestant.
23. The Catholic Church accepts the authority of the great **ecumenical councils** (see, e.g., Acts 15) which defined and developed Christian doctrine (much of which Protestantism also accepts).
24. Most Protestants do not have **bishops**, a Christian office which is biblical (1 Tim 3:1-2) and which has existed from the earliest Christian history and Tradition.
25. Protestantism has no way of **settling doctrinal issues** definitively. At best, the individual Protestant can only take a head count of how many Protestant scholars, commentators, etc. take such-and-such a view on Doctrine X, Y, or Z. There is no unified Protestant Tradition.
26. **Protestantism arose in 1517**, and is a "Johnny-come-lately" in the history of Christianity. Therefore it cannot possibly be the "restoration" of "pure", "primitive" Christianity, since this is ruled out by the fact of its absurdly late appearance. Christianity must have historic continuity or it is not Christianity. Protestantism is necessarily a "parasite" of Catholicism, historically and doctrinally speaking.
27. The widespread Protestant notion of the **"invisible church"** is also novel in the history of Christianity and foreign to the Bible (Mt 5:14; 16:18), therefore untrue.
28. When Protestant theologians speak of the teaching of early Christianity (e.g., when refuting "cults"), they say "the Church taught..." (as it was then unified), but when they refer to the present they often instinctively and inconsistently refrain from such terminology, since **universal teaching authority** now clearly resides only in the Catholic Church.
29. The Protestant principle of **private judgment** has created a milieu (especially in Protestant America) in which (invariably) man-centered "cults" such as Jehovah's Witnesses, Mormonism, and Christian Science

arise. The very notion that one can "start" a new, or "the true" Church is Protestant to the core.

30. The lack of a **definitive teaching authority** in Protestantism (as with the Catholic magisterium) makes many individual Protestants think that they have a direct line to God, notwithstanding all of Christian Tradition and the history of biblical exegesis (a "Bible, Holy Spirit and me" mentality). Such people are generally under-educated theologically, unteachable, lack humility, and have no business making presumed "infallible" statements about the nature of Christianity.

31. Evangelicalism's **"techniques" of evangelism** are often contrived and manipulative, certainly not directly derived from the text of the Bible. Some even resemble brainwashing to a degree.

32. The gospel preached by too many evangelical Protestant evangelists and pastors is a truncated and abridged, individualistic and ear-tickling gospel, in effect merely "fire insurance" rather than the **biblical gospel** as proclaimed by the apostles.

33. Evangelicalism often separates profound, life-transforming repentance and radical discipleship from its gospel message. The Lutheran Dietrich Bonhoeffer called **this "cheap grace."**

34. The absence of the idea of submission to **spiritual authority** in Protestantism has leaked over into the civic arena, where the ideas of personal "freedom," "rights," and "choice" now dominate to such an extent that civic duty, communitarianism, and discipline are tragically neglected, to the detriment of a healthy society.

35. Catholicism retains the sense of the sacred, the sublime, the holy, and **the beautiful in spirituality.** The ideas of altar, and "sacred space" are preserved. Many Protestant churches are no more than "meeting halls" or "gymnasiums" or "barn"-type structures. Most Protestants' homes are more esthetically striking than their churches. Likewise, Protestants are often "addicted to mediocrity" in their appreciation of art, music, architecture, drama, the imagination, etc.

36. Protestantism has largely neglected the place of **liturgy** in worship (with notable exceptions such as Anglicanism and Lutheranism). This is the way Christians had always worshiped down through the centuries, and thus cannot be so lightly dismissed.

37. Protestantism tends to **oppose matter and spirit,** favoring the latter, and is somewhat influenced by Gnosticism or the Docetic heresy in this regard.

38. Catholicism upholds the **"incarnational principle,"** wherein Jesus became flesh and thus raised flesh and matter to new spiritual heights.

Dave Armstrong

39. Protestantism greatly limits or disbelieves in **sacramentalism**, which is simply the extension of the incarnational principle and the belief that matter can convey grace. Some sects (e.g., Baptists, many pentecostals) reject all sacraments.
40. Some Protestants' excessive mistrust of the flesh ("carnality") often leads to (in evangelicalism or fundamentalism) an **absurd legalism** (no dancing, drinking, card-playing, rock music, etc.).
41. Many Protestants tend to separate life into categories of **"spiritual" and "carnal,"** as if God is not Lord of all of life. It forgets that all non-sinful endeavors are ultimately spiritual.
42. Protestantism has removed the **Eucharist** from the center and focus of Christian worship services. Some Protestants observe it only monthly, or even quarterly; a few, not at all. This is against the Tradition of the early Church.
43. Most Protestants accept a **symbolic Eucharist**, which is contrary to universal Christian Tradition up to 1517, and the Bible (Mt 26:26-8; Jn 6:47-63; 1 Cor 10:14-22; 11:23-30), which hold to the Real Presence (another instance of the antipathy to matter).
44. Protestantism has virtually ceased to regard **marriage** as a sacrament, contrary to Christian Tradition and the Bible (Mt 19:4-5; 1 Cor 7:14,39; Eph 5:25-33).
45. Protestantism has abolished the **priesthood** (Mt 18:18) and the sacrament of ordination, contrary to Christian Tradition and the Bible (Acts 6:6; 14:22; 1 Tim 4:14; 2 Tim 1:6).
46. Catholicism retains the Pauline notion of the spiritual practicality of a **celibate clergy** (e.g., Mt 19:12, 1 Cor 7:8,27,32-3).
47. Protestantism has largely rejected the sacrament of **confirmation** (Acts 8:18, Heb 6:2-4), contrary to Christian Tradition and the Bible.
48. Many Protestants have denied **infant baptism**, contrary to Christian Tradition and the Bible (Acts 2:38-9; 16:15,33; 18:8; cf. 11:14; 1 Cor 1:16; Col 2:11-12). Protestantism is divided into five major camps on the question of baptism.
49. The great majority of Protestants deny **baptismal regeneration**, contrary to Christian Tradition and the Bible (Mk 16:16; Jn 3:5; Acts 2:38; 22:16; Rom 6:3-4; 1 Cor 6:11; Titus 3:5).
50. Protestants have rejected the sacrament of **anointing of the sick** (Extreme Unction / "Last Rites"), contrary to Christian Tradition and the Bible (Mk 6:13; 1 Cor 12:9,30; Jas 5:14-15).
51. Protestantism denies the indissolubility of sacramental marriage and allows **divorce**, contrary to Christian Tradition and the Bible (Gen 2:24;

Mal 2:14-16; Mt 5:32; 19:6,9; Mk 10:11-12; Lk 16:18; Rom 7:2-3; 1 Cor 7:10-14,39).

52. Protestantism doesn't believe **procreation** to be the primary purpose and benefit of marriage (it isn't part of the vows, as in Catholic matrimony), contrary to Christian Tradition and the Bible (Gen 1:28; 28:3, Ps 107:38; 127:3-5).

53. Protestantism generally sanctions **contraception**, in defiance of universal Christian Tradition (Catholic, Orthodox, and Protestant) up until 1930— when the Anglicans first allowed it—and the Bible (Gen 38:8-10; 41:52; Ex 23:25-6; Lev 26:9; Deut 7:14; Ruth 4:13; Lk 1:24-5). Now, only Catholicism retains the ancient Tradition, over against the "anti-child" mentality.

54. Many Protestant bodies (mostly—but not only—its liberal wing) have accepted **abortion** as a moral option, contrary to universal Christian Tradition until recently (sometime after 1930), and the Bible (e.g., Ex 20:13; Job 31:15; Ps 139:13-16; Isa 44:2; 49:5; Jer 1:5; 2:34; Lk 1:15,41; Rom 13:9-10).

55. Many Protestant bodies (largely liberal denominations) allow **women pastors** (and even bishops, as in Anglicanism), contrary to Christian Tradition (inc. traditional Protestant theology) and the Bible (Mt 10:1-4; 1 Tim 2:11-15; 3:1-12; Titus 1:6).

56. Protestantism is, more and more, formally and officially compromising with currently fashionable **radical feminism**, which denies the roles of men and women, as taught in the Bible (Gen 2:18-23; 1 Cor 11:3-10) and maintained by Christian Tradition (differentiation of roles, but not of equality).

57. Protestantism is also currently denying, with increasing frequency, the **headship of the husband** in marriage, which is based upon the headship of the Father over the Son (while equal in essence) in the Trinity, contrary to Christian Tradition and the Bible (1 Cor 11:3; Eph 5:22-33; Col 3:18-19; 1 Pet 3:1-2). This too, is based on a relationship of equality (1 Cor 11:11-12; Gal 3:28; Eph 5:21).

58. Liberal Protestantism (most notably Anglicanism) has even **ordained practicing homosexuals** as pastors and blessed their "marriages," or taught that homosexuality is merely an involuntary, "alternate" lifestyle, contrary to formerly universal Christian Tradition, as the Bible clearly teaches (Gen 19:4-25; Rom 1:18-27; 1 Cor 6:9). Catholicism stands firm on traditional morality.

59. Liberal Protestantism, and evangelicalism increasingly, have accepted **"higher critical" methods of biblical interpretation** which lead to the destruction of the traditional Christian reverence for the Bible, and

demote it to the status of largely a human, fallible document, to the detriment of its divine, infallible essence.

60. Many liberal Protestants have thrown out many **cardinal doctrines** of Christianity, such as the Incarnation, Virgin Birth, the Bodily Resurrection of Christ, the Trinity, Original Sin, hell, the existence of the devil, miracles, etc.

61. The founders of Protestantism denied, and Calvinists today deny, the reality of **human free will** (Luther's favorite book was his *Bondage of the Will*). This is both contrary to the constant premise of the Bible, Christian Tradition, and common sense.

62. Classical Protestantism had a deficient view of the **Fall of Man**, thinking that the result was "total depravity." According to Luther, Zwingli, Calvin, and Calvinists, man could only do evil of his own volition, and had no free will to do good. He now has a "sin nature." Catholicism believes that, in a mysterious way, man cooperates with the grace which always precedes all good actions. In Catholicism, man's nature still retains some good, although he has a propensity to sin ("concupiscence").

63. Classical Protestantism, and Calvinism today, make God (at the very least, arguably, by logical extension) the **author of evil**. He supposedly wills that men do evil and violate His precepts without having any free will to do so. This is blasphemous.

64. Accordingly (man having no free will), God, in classical Protestant and Calvinist thought, **predestines men to hell**, although they had no choice or say in the matter all along!

65. Classical Protestantism and Calvinism, teach falsely the notion of **limited atonement**: that Jesus died only for the elect (i.e., those who will make it to heaven).

66. Classical Protestantism (especially Luther), and Calvinism, due to their false view of the Fall, too often deny the efficacy and capacity of **human reason** to know God to some extent (both sides agree that revelation and grace are also necessary), and oppose it to God and faith, contrary to Christian Tradition and the Bible (Mk 12:28; Lk 10:27; Jn 20:24-9; Acts 1:3; 17:2,17,22-34; 19:8). The best Protestant apologists today simply hearken back to the Catholic heritage of St. Aquinas, St. Augustine, and many other great thinkers.

67. Pentecostal or charismatic Protestantism places much too high an emphasis on **spiritual experience**, not balancing it properly with reason, the Bible, and Tradition (including the authority of the Church to pronounce on the validity of "private revelations").

68. Other Protestants (e.g., many Baptists) deny that **spiritual gifts** such as healing are present in the current age (supposedly they ceased with the apostles).
69. Protestantism has contradictory views of **church government**, or ecclesiology (episcopal, presbyterian, congregational, or no collective authority at all), thus making discipline, unity and order impossible. Some sects even claim to have "apostles" or "prophets" among them, with all the accompanying abuses of authority resulting therefrom.
70. Many Protestants (especially evangelicals) have an undue fascination for the **"end of the world,"** which has led to unbiblical date-setting (Mt 24:30-44; 25:13; Lk 12:39-40) and much human tragedy among those who are taken in by such false prophecies.
71. Evangelicalism's over-emphasis on the "imminent end" of the age has often led to a certain **"pie-in-the sky"** mentality, to the detriment of social, political, ethical, and economic sensibilities here on earth.
72. Protestant thought has the defining characteristic of being **"dichotomous,"** i.e., it separates ideas into more or less exclusive and mutually-hostile camps, when in fact many of the dichotomies are simply complementary rather than contradictory. Protestantism is "either-or," whereas Catholicism takes a "both-and" approach. Examples follow:
73. Protestantism pits the **Word** (the Bible, preaching) against **sacraments.**
74. Protestantism sets up **inner devotion** and piety against the **liturgy.**
75. Protestantism opposes **spontaneous worship** to **form prayers.**
76. Protestantism separates the **Bible** from the **Church.**
77. Protestantism creates the false dichotomy of **Bible** vs. **Tradition.**
78. Protestantism pits **Tradition** against the **Holy Spirit.**
79. Protestantism considers **Church authority** and individual liberty and **conscience** contradictory.
80. Protestantism (especially Luther) sets up the **Old Testament** against the **New Testament**, even though Jesus did not do so (Mt 5:17-19; Mk 7:8-11; Lk 24:27,44; Jn 5:45-47).
81. On equally unbiblical grounds, Protestantism **opposes law to grace.**
82. Protestantism creates a false dichotomy between **symbolism and sacramental reality** (e.g., baptism, Eucharist).
83. Protestantism separates the **individual** from Christian **community** (1 Cor 12:14-27).
84. Protestantism pits the **veneration of saints** against the worship of God. Catholic theology doesn't permit worship of saints in the same fashion as that directed towards God. Saints are revered and honored, not adored, as only God the Creator can be.

85. The **anti-historical outlook** of many Protestants leads to individuals thinking that the Holy Spirit is speaking to them, but has not, in effect, spoken to the multitudes of Christians for 1500 years before Protestantism began!
86. Flaws in original Protestant thought have led to even worse **errors in reaction**. E.g., extrinsic justification, devised to assure the predominance of grace, came to prohibit any outward sign of its presence ("faith vs. works," "sola fide"). Calvinism, with its cruel God, turned men off to such an extent that they became Unitarians (as in New England). Many founders of cults of recent origin started out Calvinist (Jehovah's Witnesses, Christian Science, The Way International, etc.).
87. Evangelicalism is unbiblically obsessed (in typically American fashion) with **celebrities** (TV Evangelists).
88. Evangelicalism is infatuated with the false idea that **great numbers** in a congregation (or rapid growth) are a sign of God's presence in a special way, and His unique blessing. They forget that Mormonism is also growing by leaps and bounds. God calls us to faithfulness rather than to "success," obedience, not flattering statistics.
89. Evangelicalism often emphasizes numerical growth rather than individual **spiritual growth**.
90. Evangelicalism is presently obsessed with **self-fulfillment**, self-help, and oftentimes, outright selfishness, rather than the traditional Christian stress on suffering, sacrifice, and service.
91. Evangelicalism has a truncated and insufficient view of the place of **suffering** in the Christian life. Instead, "health-and-wealth" and "name-it-and-claim-it" movements within pentecostal Protestantism are flourishing, which have a view of possessions not in harmony with the Bible and Christian Tradition.
92. Evangelicalism has, by and large, adopted a worldview which is, in many ways, **more capitalist than Christian**. Wealth and personal gain is sought more than godliness, and is seen as a proof of God's favor, as in secularized American thought, over against the Bible and Christian teaching.
93. Evangelicalism is increasingly tolerating **far-left political outlooks** not in accord with Christian views, especially at its seminaries and colleges.
94. Evangelicalism is increasingly tolerating **theological heterodoxy** and liberalism, to such an extent that many evangelical leaders are alarmed, and predict a further decay of standards of orthodoxy.
95. **"Positive confession"** movements in pentecostal evangelicalism have adopted views of God (in effect) as a "cosmic bellhop," subject to man's frivolous whims and desires of the moment, thus denying God's absolute

sovereignty and prerogative to turn down any of man's improper prayer requests (Jas 4:3; 1 Jn 5:14).

96. The above sects usually teach that anyone can be **healed** who has enough "faith," contrary to Christian Tradition and the Bible (e.g., Job, St. Paul's "thorn in the flesh," usually considered a disease by most Protestant commentators).

97. Evangelicalism, by its own self-critiques, is badly infected with **pragmatism**, the false philosophical view that "whatever works is true, or right." The gospel, especially on TV, is sold in the same way that McDonalds hawks hamburgers. Technology, mass-market and public relations techniques have largely replaced personal pastoral care and social concern for the downtrodden, irreligious, and unchurched masses.

98. **Sin**, in evangelicalism, is increasingly seen as a psychological failure or a lack of self-esteem, rather than the willful revolt against God that it is.

99. Protestantism, in all essential elements, merely borrows wholesale from Catholic Tradition, or distorts the same. All doctrines upon which Catholics and Protestants agree, are clearly Catholic in origin (Trinity, Virgin Birth, Resurrection, 2nd Coming, Canon of the Bible, heaven, hell, etc.). Those where Protestantism differs are usually distortions of Catholic forerunners. E.g., Quakerism is a variant of Catholic Quietism. Calvinism is an over-obsession with the Catholic idea of the sovereignty of God, but taken to lengths beyond what Catholicism ever taught (denial of free will, total depravity, double predestination, etc.). Protestant dichotomies such as faith vs. works, come from nominalism, which was itself a corrupt form of Scholasticism, never dogmatically sanctioned by the Catholic Church. Whatever life or truth is present in each Protestant idea, always is **derived from Catholicism**, which is the fulfillment of the deepest and best aspirations within Protestantism.

100. One of Protestantism's foundational principles is *sola Scriptura,* which is neither a biblical (see below), historical (nonexistent until the 16th century), nor logical (it's self-defeating) idea:

101. The **Bible is not exhaustive**; it doesn't contain the whole of Jesus' teaching, or Christianity, as many Protestants believe (Mk 4:33; 6:34; Lk 24:15-16,25-27; Jn 16:12; 20:30; 21:25; Acts 1:2-3).

102. *Sola scriptura* is an abuse of the Bible, since it is a use of the Bible contrary to its explicit and implicit testimony about itself and **Tradition.** An objective reading of the Bible leads one to Tradition and the Catholic Church, rather than the opposite. The Bible is, in fact, undeniably a Christian Tradition itself!

103. The NT was neither written nor received as the Bible at first, but only gradually so (i.e., early Christianity couldn't have believed in *sola*

Scriptura like current Protestants, unless it referred to the OT alone). At first, **oral tradition** was primary.

104. **Tradition** is not a bad word in the Bible. Gk. *paradosis* refers to something handed on from one to another (good or bad). Good (Christian) Tradition is spoken of in 1 Cor 11:2; 2 Thess 2:15, 3:6, and Col 2:8. In the latter it is contrasted with traditions of men.

105. **Christian Tradition**, according to the Bible, can be oral as well as written (2 Thess 2:15; 2 Tim 1:13-14; 2:2). St. Paul makes no qualitative distinction between the two forms.

106. The phrases **"word of God"** or "word of the Lord" in Acts and the epistles almost always refer to oral preaching, not to the Bible itself. Much of the Bible was originally oral (e.g., Jesus' entire teaching- He wrote nothing—St. Peter's sermon at Pentecost, etc.).

107. Contrary to many Protestant claims, Jesus didn't condemn all tradition any more than St. Paul did. E.g., Mt 15:3,6; Mk 7:8-9,13, where He condemns corrupt **Pharisaical tradition** only. He says "your tradition."

108. Gk. *paradidomi*, or **"delivering" Christian, apostolic Tradition** occurs in Lk 1:1-2; Rom 6:17; 1 Cor 11:23; 15:3; 2 Pet 2:21; Jude 3. *Paralambano*, or "receiving" Christian Tradition occurs in 1 Cor 15:1-2; Gal 1:9,12; 1 Thess 2:13.

109. The concepts of **"Tradition," "gospel," "word of God," "doctrine,"** and "the Faith" are essentially synonymous, and all are predominantly oral. E.g., in the Thessalonian epistles alone St. Paul uses three of these interchangeably (2 Thess 2:15; 3:6; 1 Thess 2:9,13 (cf. Gal 1:9; Acts 8:14). If Tradition is a dirty word, then so is "gospel" and "word of God"!

110. St. Paul, in 1 Tim 3:15, puts **the Church** above Bible as the grounds for truth, as in Catholicism.

111. Protestantism's chief "proof text" for *sola Scriptura*, 2 Tim 3:16, fails, since it says that the Bible is profitable, but not sufficient for learning and righteousness. Catholicism agrees it is great for these purposes, but not exclusively so, as in Protestantism. Secondly, when St. Paul speaks of "Scripture" here, the NT didn't yet exist (not definitively for over 300 more years), thus he is referring to the OT only. This would mean that NT wasn't necessary for the rule of faith, if *sola Scriptura* were true, and if it were supposedly alluded to in this verse!

112. The above eleven factors being true, Catholicism maintains that all its **Tradition is consistent with the Bible**, even where the Bible is mute or merely implicit on a subject. For Catholicism, every doctrine need not be found primarily in the Bible, for this is Protestantism's principle of *sola Scriptura*. On the other hand, most Catholic theologians claim that all

Catholic doctrines can be found in some fashion in the Bible, in kernel form, or by (usually extensive) inference.

113. As thoughtful evangelical scholars have pointed out, an unthinking *sola Scriptura* position can turn into **"bibliolatry,"** almost a worship of the Bible rather than God who is its Author. This mentality is similar to the Muslim view of Revelation, where no human elements whatsoever were involved. *Sola Scriptura*, rightly understood from a more sophisticated Protestant perspective, means that the Bible is the final authority in Christianity, not the record of all God has said and done, as many evangelicals believe.

114. Christianity is unavoidably and intrinsically **historical**. All the events of Jesus' life (Incarnation, Crucifixion, Resurrection, Ascension, etc.) were historical, as was the preaching of the apostles. Tradition, therefore, of some sort, is unavoidable, contrary to numerous shortsighted Protestant claims that *sola Scriptura* annihilates Tradition. This is true both for matters great (ecclesiology, trinitarianism, justification) and small (church budgets, type of worship music, lengths of sermons, etc.). Every denial of a particular tradition involves a bias (hidden or open) towards one's own alternate tradition (e.g., if all Church authority is spurned, even individualistic autonomy is a "tradition," which ought to be defended as a Christian view in some fashion).

115. *Sola scriptura* literally couldn't have been true, practically speaking, for most Christians throughout history, since the movable-type printing press only appeared in the mid-15th century. Preaching and oral Tradition, along with things like devotional practices, Christian holidays, church architecture and other sacred art, were the primary carriers of the gospel for 1400 years, due to **widespread illiteracy.** For all these centuries, sola Scriptura would have been regarded as an absurd abstraction and impossibility.

116. Protestantism claims that the Catholic Church has **"added to the Bible."** The Catholic Church replies that it has merely drawn out the implications of the Bible (development of doctrine), and followed the understanding of the early Church, and that Protestants have "subtracted" from the Bible by ignoring large portions of it which suggest Catholic positions. Each side thinks the other is "unbiblical," but in different ways.

117. *Sola Scriptura* is Protestantism's "Achilles' Heel." Merely invoking *sola Scriptura* is no solution to the problem of authority and certainty as long as multiple interpretations exist. If the Bible were so clear that all Protestants agreed simply by reading it with a willingness to accept and follow its teaching, this would be one thing, but since this isn't the case by a long shot, *sola Scriptura* is a pipe-dream at best. About all that all

Protestants agree on is that Catholicism is wrong! Of all Protestant ideas, the "clarity" or **perspicuity** of the Bible is surely one of the most absurd and the most demonstrably false by the historical record.

118. Put another way, having a Bible does not render one's private judgment infallible. **Interpretation** is just as inevitable as tradition. The Catholic Church therefore, is absolutely necessary in order to speak authoritatively and to prevent confusion, error, and division.

119. Catholicism doesn't regard the Bible as obscure, mysterious, and inaccessible, but it is vigilant to protect it from all **arbitrary and aberrant exegesis** (2 Pet 1:20, 3:16). The best Protestant traditions seek to do the same, but are inadequate and ineffectual since they are divided.

120. Protestantism has a huge problem with the **Canon of the NT**. The process of determining the exact books which constitute the NT lasted until 397 A.D., when the Council of Carthage spoke with finality, certainly proof that the Bible is not "self-authenticating," as Protestantism believes. Some sincere, devout, and learned Christians doubted the canonicity of some books which are now in the Bible, and others considered books as Scripture which were not at length included in the Canon. St. Athanasius in 367 was the first to list all 27 books in the NT as Scripture.

121. The Council of Carthage, in deciding the Canon of the entire Bible in 397, included the so-called **"Apocryphal" books**, which Protestants kicked out of the Bible (i.e., a late tradition). Prior to the 16th century Christians considered these books Scripture, and they weren't even separated from the others, as they are today in the Protestant Bibles which include them. Protestantism accepts the authority of this Council for the NT, but not the OT, just as it arbitrarily and selectively accepts or denies other conciliar decrees, according to their accord with existing Protestant "dogmas" and biases.

122. Contrary to persistent Protestant myth, the Catholic Church has always **revered the Bible**, and hasn't suppressed it (it protested some Protestant translations, but Protestants have often done the same regarding Catholic versions). This is proven by the laborious care of monks in protecting and copying manuscripts, and the constant translations into vernacular tongues (as opposed to the falsehoods about only Latin Bibles), among other plentiful and indisputable historical evidences. The Bible is a Catholic book, and no matter how much Protestants study it and proclaim it as peculiarly their own, they must acknowledge their undeniable debt to the Catholic Church for having decided the Canon, and for preserving the Bible intact for 1400 years. How could the Catholic Church be "against the Bible," yet at the same time preserve and revere the Bible

123. profoundly for so many years? The very thought is so absurd as to be self-refuting.
123. Protestantism denies the **Sacrifice of the Mass**, contrary to Christian Tradition and the Bible (Gen 14:18; Ps 110:4; Isa 66:18,21; Mal 1:11; Heb 7:24-5; 13:10; Rev 5:1-10; cf. 8:3; 13:8). Catholicism, it must be emphasized, doesn't believe that Jesus is sacrificed over and over at each Mass; rather, each Mass is a representation of the one Sacrifice at Calvary on the Cross, which transcends space and time, as in Rev 13:8.
124. Protestantism disbelieves, by and large, in the **development of doctrine**, contrary to Christian Tradition and many implicit biblical indications. Whenever the Bible refers to the increasing knowledge and maturity of Christians individually and (particularly) collectively, an idea similar to development is present. Further, many doctrines develop in the Bible before our eyes ("progressive revelation"). Examples: the afterlife, the Trinity, acceptance of Gentiles. And doctrines which Protestantism accepts whole and entire from Catholicism, such as the Trinity and the Canon of the Bible, developed in history, in the first three centuries of Christianity. It is foolish to try and deny this. The Church is the "Body" of Christ, and is a living organism, which grows and develops like all living bodies. It is not a statue, simply to be cleaned and polished over time, as many Protestants seem to think.
125. Protestantism **separates justification from sanctification,** contrary to Christian Tradition and the Bible (e.g., Mt 5:20; 7:20-24; Rom 2:7-13; 1 Cor 6:11; 1 Pet 1:2).
126. Protestantism pits faith against works (*sola fide*), which is a rejection of Christian Tradition and the explicit teaching of the Bible (Mt 25:31-46; Lk 18:18-25; Jn 6:27-9; Gal 5:6; Eph 2:8-10; Phil 2:12-13; 3:10-14; 1 Thess 1:3; 2 Thess 1:11; Heb 5:9; Jas 1:21-7; 2:14-16). These passages also indicate that salvation is a process, not an instantaneous event, as in Protestantism.
127. Protestantism rejects the Christian Tradition and biblical teaching of **merit**, or differential reward for our good deeds done in faith (Mt 16:27; Rom 2:6; 1 Cor 3:8-9; 1 Pet 1:17; Rev 22:12).
128. Protestantism's teaching of extrinsic, imputed, forensic, or **external justification** contradicts the Christian Tradition and biblical doctrine of infused, actual, internal, transformational justification (which inc. sanctification): Ps 51:2-10; 103:12; Jn 1:29; Rom 5:19; 2 Cor 5:17; Heb 1:3; 1 Jn 1:7-9.
129. Many Protestants (especially Presbyterians, Calvinists and Baptists) believe in **eternal security**, or, perseverance of the saints (the belief that one can't lose his "salvation," supposedly obtained at one point in time).

This is contrary to Christian Tradition and the Bible: 1 Cor 9:27; Gal 4:9; 5:1,4; Col 1:22-3; 1 Tim 1:19-20; 4:1; 5:15; Heb 3:12-14; 6:4-6; 10:26,29,39; 12:14-15; 2 Pet 2:15,20-21; Rev 2:4-5.

130. Contrary to a prevalent Protestant myth, the Catholic Church doesn't teach that one is saved by works apart from preceding and enabling grace, but that faith and works are inseparable, as in James 1 and 2. This heresy of which Catholicism is often charged, was in fact condemned by the Catholic Church at the Second Council of Orange in 529 A.D. It is known as **Pelagianism,** the view that man could save himself by his own natural efforts, without the necessary supernatural grace from God. A more moderate view, Semi-Pelagianism, was likewise condemned. To continue to accuse the Catholic Church of this heresy is a sign of both prejudice and lack of knowledge of the history of theology, as well as the clear Catholic teaching of the Council of Trent (1545-63), available for all to see. Yet the myth is strangely prevalent.

131. Protestantism has virtually eliminated the practice of **confession** to a priest (or at least a pastor), contrary to Christian Tradition and the Bible (Mt 16:19; 18:18; Jn 20:23).

132. Protestantism disbelieves in **penance**, or temporal punishment for (forgiven) sin, over against Christian Tradition and the Bible (e.g., Num 14:19-23; 2 Sam 12:13-14; 1 Cor 11:27-32; Heb 12:6-8).

133. Protestantism has little concept of the Tradition and biblical doctrine of **mortifying the flesh,** or, suffering with Christ: Mt 10:38; 16:24: Rom 8:13,17; 1 Cor 12:24-6; Phil 3:10; 1 Pet 4:1,13.

134. Likewise, Protestantism has lost the Tradition and biblical doctrine of **vicarious atonement, or redemptive suffering** with Christ, of Christians for the sake of each other: Ex 32:30-32; Num 16:43-8; 25:6-13; 2 Cor 4:10; Col 1:24; 2 Tim 4:6.

135. Protestantism has rejected the Tradition and biblical doctrine of **purgatory**, as a consequence of its false view of justification and penance, despite sufficient evidence in Scripture: Is 4:4; 6:5-7; Micah 7:8-9; Mal 3:1-4; 2 Maccabees 12:39-45; Mt 5:25-6; 12:32; Lk 16:19-31 (cf. Eph 4:8-10; 1 Pet 3:19-20); 1 Cor 3:11-15; 2 Cor 5:10; Rev 21:27.

136. Protestantism has rejected (largely due to misconceptions and misunderstanding) the Catholic developed doctrine of **indulgences,** which is, simply, the remission of the temporal punishment for sin (i.e., penance), by the Church (on the grounds of Mt 16:19; 18:18, and Jn 20:23). This is no different than what St. Paul did, concerning an errant brother at the Church of Corinth. He first imposed a penance on him (1 Cor 5:3-5), then remitted part of it (an indulgence: 2 Cor 2:6-11). Just because abuses occurred prior to the Protestant Revolt (admitted and

rectified by the Catholic Church), is no reason to toss out yet another biblical doctrine. Too often, Protestantism burns down a house rather than cleanse it; it "throws the baby out with the bath water."

137. Protestantism has thrown out **prayers for the dead,** in opposition to Christian Tradition and the Bible (Tobit 12:12; 2 Maccabees 12:39-45; 1 Cor 15:29; 2 Tim 1:16-18; also verses having to do with purgatory, since these prayers are for the saints there).

138. Protestantism rejects, on inadequate grounds, the **intercession of the saints** for us after death, and the correspondent invocation of the saints for their effectual prayers (Jas 5:16). Christian Tradition and the Bible, on the other hand, have upheld this practice: Dead saints are aware of earthly affairs (Mt 22:30 w/ Lk 15:10 and 1 Cor 15:29; Heb 12:1), appear on earth to interact with men (1 Sam 28:12-15; Mt 17:1-3, 27:50-53; Rev 11:3), and therefore can intercede for us, and likewise be petitioned for their prayers, just as are Christians on earth (2 Maccabees 15:14; Rev 5:8; 6:9-10).

139. Some Protestants disbelieve in **Guardian Angels**, despite Christian Tradition and the Bible (Ps 34:7; 91:11; Mt 18:10; Acts 12:15; Heb 1:14).

140. Most Protestants deny **angelic intercession** for us, contrary to Christian Tradition and the Bible (Rev 1:4; 5:8; 8:3-4).

141. Protestantism rejects **Mary's Immaculate Conception**, despite developed Christian Tradition and indications in the Bible: Gen 3:15; Lk 1:28 ("full of grace" Catholics interpret, on linguistic grounds, to mean "without sin"); Mary as a type of the Ark of the Covenant (Lk 1:35 w/ Ex 40:34-8; Lk 1:44 w/ 2 Sam 6:14-16; Lk 1:43 w/ 2 Sam 6:9: God's Presence requires extraordinary holiness).

142. Protestantism rejects **Mary's Assumption**, despite developed Christian Tradition and biblical indications: If Mary was indeed sinless, she would not have to undergo bodily decay at death (Ps 16:10; Gen 3:19). Similar occurrences in the Bible make the Assumption not implausible or "unbiblical" per se (Enoch: Gen 5:24 w/ Heb 11:5; Elijah: 2 Ki 2:11; Paul: 2 Cor 12:2-4; the Protestant doctrine of the "Rapture": 1 Thess 4:15-17; risen saints: Mt 27:52-3).

143. Many (most?) Protestants deny **Mary's perpetual virginity**, despite Christian Tradition (including the unanimous agreement of the Protestant founders (Luther, Calvin, Zwingli, etc.), some Protestant support, and several biblical evidences, too involved to briefly summarize.

144. Protestantism denies **Mary's Spiritual Motherhood** of Christians, contrary to Christian Tradition and the Bible (Jn 19:26-7: "Behold thy mother"; Rev 12:1,5,17: Christians described as "her seed.") Catholics

believe that Mary is incomparably more alive and holy than we are, hence, her prayers for us are of great effect (Jas 5:16; Rev 5:8; 6:9-10). But she is our sister with regard to our position of creatures vis-a-vis the Creator, God. Mary never operates apart from the necessary graces from her Son, and always glorifies Him, not herself, as Catholic theology stresses.

145. Protestantism rejects the **papacy**, despite profound Christian Tradition, and the strong evidence in the Bible of Peter's preeminence and commission by Jesus as the Rock of His Church. No one denies he was some type of leader among the apostles. The papacy as we now know it is derived from this primacy: Mt 16:18-19; Lk 22:31-2; Jn 21:15-17 are the most direct "papal" passages. Peter's name appears first in all lists of apostles; even an angel implies he is their leader (Mk 16:7), and he is accepted by the world as such (Acts 2:37-8,41). He works the first miracle of the Church age (Acts 3:6-8), utters the first anathema (Acts 5:2-11), raises the dead (Acts 9:40), first receives the Gentiles (Acts 10:9-48), and his name is mentioned more often than all the other disciples put together (191 times). Much more similar evidence can be found.

146. The Church of Rome and the popes were central to the governance and theological direction and **orthodoxy** of the Christian Church from the beginning. This is undeniable. All of the historical groups now regarded as heretical by Protestants and Catholics alike were originally judged as such by popes and/or ecumenical councils presided over and ratified by popes.

147. Protestantism, in its desperation to eke out some type of historical continuity apart from the Catholic Church, sometimes attempts to claim a lineage from **medieval sects such as the Waldenses, Cathari, and Albigensians** (and sometimes earlier groups such as the Montanists or Donatists). However, this endeavor is doomed to failure when one studies closely what these sects believed. They either retain much Catholic teaching anathema to Protestants or hold heretical notions antithetical to Christianity altogether (Catholic, Protestant, and Orthodox), or both, making this Protestant theory quite dubious at best.

148. Catholic has the most sophisticated and thoughtful Christian **socio-economic and political philosophy**, a mixture of "progressive" and "conservative" elements distinct from the commonplace political rhetoric and Machiavellianism which typically dominate the political arena. Catholicism has the best view of church in relation to the state and culture as well.

149. Catholicism has the best **Christian philosophy and worldview**, worked out through centuries of reflection and experience. As in its theological reflection and development, the Catholic Church is ineffably wise and profound, to an extent truly amazing, and indicative of a sure divine stamp. I used to marvel, just before I converted, at how the Catholic Church could be so right about so many things. I was accustomed to thinking, as a good evangelical, that the truth was always a potpourri of ideas from many Protestant denominations and Catholicism and Orthodoxy (selected by me), and that none "had it all together." But, alas, the Catholic Church does, after all!

150. Last but by no means least, Catholicism has the most sublime **spirituality and devotional spirit**, manifested in a thousand different ways, from the monastic ideal, to the heroic celibacy of the clergy and religious, the Catholic hospitals, the sheer holiness of a Thomas a Kempis or a St. Ignatius and their great devotional books, countless saints—both canonized and as yet unknown and unsung, Mother Teresa, Pope John Paul II, Pope John XXIII, the early martyrs, St. Francis of Assisi, the events at Lourdes and Fatima, the dazzling intellect of John Henry Cardinal Newman, the wisdom and insight of Archbishop Fulton Sheen, St. John of the Cross, the sanctified wit of a Chesterton or a Muggeridge, elderly women doing the Stations of the Cross or the Rosary, Holy Hour, Benediction, kneeling—the list goes on and on. This devotional spirit is unmatched in its scope and deepness, despite many fine counterparts in Protestant and Orthodox spirituality.

Appendix Four:

Catholicism and Orthodoxy: A Comparison

AN APPRECIATION OF ORTHODOX SPIRITUALITY

Orthodox Christianity possesses the seven sacraments, valid ordination, the Real Presence, a reverential understanding of Sacred Tradition, apostolic succession, a profound piety, a great history of contemplative and monastic spirituality, a robust veneration of Mary and the saints, and many other truly Christian attributes. Catholics (including myself) widely admire, in particular, the sense of the sacred and the beauty and grandeur of the Orthodox Divine Liturgy (which—it should be noted—is also present in the many Eastern Rites of the Catholic Church), as the great Catholic author Thomas Howard eloquently illustrates:

> When I walk into an Orthodox Church... one is immediately aware that one has stepped into the presence of what St. Paul would call the whole family in heaven and earth. You have stepped into the precincts of heaven!... I love the Orthodox Church's spirit. I think the Orthodox Church many, many centuries ago, discovered a mode of music and worship which is timeless, which is quite apart from fashion, and which somehow answers to the mystery and the solemnity and the sacramental reality of the liturgy.[1]

In pointing out the differences between Orthodoxy and Catholicism, no disrespect is intended towards my Eastern brethren in Christ; this is simply a "comparison and contrast" for the purpose of educating inquirers who are interested in both Christian communions. My Catholic bias will be evident and should not come as a surprise to anyone. Nevertheless, I devoutly hope that I succeed in avoiding the shortcomings of triumphalism or lack of charity. And I certainly do not wish to misrepresent Orthodox views in any fashion.

Catholics must believe that Orthodoxy is a part of the universal Church (commensurate with the Second Vatican Council and many recent papal encyclicals on ecumenism in general or Orthodoxy in particular). That fact alone

---

[1] "A Conversation With Thomas Howard and Frank Schaeffer," *The Christian Activist*, vol. 9, Fall/Winter 1996, 43.

precludes the justification of any condescension, animosity, or hostility, which is especially sinful amongst Christians (Galatians 6:10).[2]

ONENESS AND ECCLESIOLOGY (CHURCH GOVERNMENT)

The Nicene Creed, adhered to by most Christians, contains the phrase, "One, holy, catholic, and apostolic Church." From a Catholic ecclesiological perspective, Orthodoxy—strictly speaking—is not "one" Church, but a conglomerate of at least seventeen, each with separate governance. The *Encyclopedia Britannica*,[3] states that, "Since the Russian Revolution there has been much turmoil and administrative conflict within the Orthodox Church." Although Orthodox theology is fairly homogeneous, nevertheless, a Catholic would respectfully reply that none of these "autocephalous" churches can speak with the doctrinal definitiveness which existed in the Church before 1054, and which indeed still resides in the papacy and magisterium of the Catholic Church.

THE PAPACY

Catholics assert that Orthodoxy's rejection of the papacy is inconsistent with the nature of the Church through the centuries. No one denies the existence of the papacy in some form in the early period. Orthodoxy, however, regards the authority exercised by popes historically (or which should have been exercised) as simply that of a primacy of honor, rather than a supremacy of jurisdiction over all other bishops and regional churches. To counter that claim, Catholics point to biblical Petrine evidences and the actual wielding of authority by renowned popes such as St. Leo the Great (440-61) and St. Gregory the Great (590-604), honored as saints even by the Orthodox.

The papacy, according to Catholic Tradition, is a divinely-instituted office, not merely (as Orthodoxy considers the papacy and Roman supremacy) a political and historical happenstance. Rome was apostolic, and preeminent from the beginning of Christianity, whereas Constantinople (the seat of the Byzantine Empire) was not.

CAESAROPAPISM

---

[2] See: *Ut Unum Sint—That They May Be One, Orientale Lumen—The Light of the East* (encyclicals of Pope John Paul II), and Common Declaration of Pope John Paul II and Patriarch Bartholomew I (29 June 1995).
[3] 1985 edition, vol. 17, 867.

Orthodoxy (and Eastern Catholic Christianity, from roughly the second half of the first millennium) has been plagued with caesaropapism, which, in effect (in terms of exercised power and de facto jurisdiction, if not actual Orthodox doctrinal teaching), places the state above the church—somewhat similar to early Lutheranism and Anglicanism.

In Catholicism, on the other hand, it is significantly easier to maintain the notion that the Church is regarded as above all states (which Orthodoxy also formally believes), and is their judge, as the carrier of God's Law, which transcends and forms the basis of man's law. The papacy is the bulwark and standard and symbol whereby this dichotomy is supported. Patriarchs—oftentimes—were put into power by the Emperors in the East according to their whim and fancy and were all too frequently little more than puppets or yes-men. Noble exceptions, such as a St. John Chrysostom or a St. Flavian, more often than not had to appeal to Rome in order to save their patriarchates or necks or both.

ECUMENICAL COUNCILS

Orthodoxy accepts the first seven ecumenical councils (up to the Second Council of Nicaea in 787), but no more. From a Catholic perspective, this appears incoherent and implausible. Why have an agreed-upon system in which Councils are central to the governance of the Church universal, and then all of a sudden they cease, and Orthodox Christians must do without them for 1200 years?

DOCTRINAL DEVELOPMENT

Likewise, Orthodoxy accepts the doctrinal development which occurred in the first eight centuries of the Church, but then allows little of any noteworthiness to take place thereafter. For instance, the *filioque*, i.e., the doctrine that the Holy Spirit proceeds from the Father and the Son, rather than from the Father alone (which the West added to the Nicene Creed), was rejected by the East, and has been considered by the Orthodox a major reason for the enduring schism, yet Catholics would reply that it was a straightforward development of trinitarian theology (one of many accepted by both East and West).

Aspects of doctrines such as the Blessed Virgin Mary and purgatory (not defined doctrine, although the Orthodox pray for the dead), which experienced a measure of development in the Middle Ages and after, are not recognized in Orthodoxy. For example, Orthodoxy doesn't define the Marian doctrines of the Immaculate Conception and the Assumption, but it should be noted that Orthodox individuals are free to believe these without being deemed "heretical."

Catholics feel that Orthodoxy is implicitly denying the notion of the Church (past the eighth century) as the living, developing Body of Christ, continuously led into deeper truth by the Holy Spirit (John 14:26; 16:13-15).

MODERNITY

Catholics would argue that Orthodoxy has not come to grips with modernity and the new challenges to Christianity that it brings, in terms of how to effectively communicate the gospel to modern man. The Catholic Church renewed itself along these lines in the Second Vatican Council (1962-65). One need not compromise doctrine in order to deal with the modern situation. Pope John Paul II does not do so in his stream of extremely relevant and cogent encyclicals on present-day issues such as moral theology, labor, the family, the role of women, the place of laypeople, etc.

Although, as a result of this undertaking (i.e., due to a corruption of the nature of the Council by ambitious heterodox Catholics), the Catholic Church suffers from a modernist crisis within its own ranks, this too will pass, and Orthodoxy is not immune from such things altogether. Signs of a revival of orthodoxy in the Catholic ranks are increasing, and the nonsense will fade away like all the other crises and heretical movements in the past. The long-term benefits of the strategy to confront the culture boldly and with fresh insight and innovation (within the bounds of traditional Catholic orthodoxy) will be evident in the years to come.

CONTRACEPTION

Orthodoxy, although praiseworthy in its generally traditional stand for Christian morality, differs from Catholicism over the question of the propriety and morality of contraception, which was universally condemned by all branches of Christianity until 1930. Thus, Catholics feel that they (almost alone today) are more in accord with apostolic Christian Tradition on this point, and that an acceptance of contraception is a giving in to humanistic sexual ethics. Catholics regard it as a mortal sin, whereas much of Orthodoxy does not even forbid it. To be fair, it is true that some of the more "conservative" or "traditional" branches of Orthodoxy have retained the traditional view, but the very fact of plurality in such a grave moral issue is highly troubling.

DIVORCE

Catholics also believe that Jesus and the apostles, and ancient Christian Tradition, considered a valid sacramental marriage between two baptized

Dave Armstrong

Christians as absolutely indissoluble. An annulment is essentially different from a divorce in that it is the determination (based on a variety of possible reasons) that a valid sacramental marriage never existed. Orthodoxy accepts second and third marriages, with, however, a measure of penitential sadness commensurate with a falling short of the Christian ideal, and feels that this is a tragic pastoral necessity, in light of the fallen human condition.[4]

---

[4] For many more articles and essays and dialogues concerning Orthodoxy and its relationship to Catholicism, see my web page (to my knowledge, the most extensive treatment of Orthodoxy from a Catholic perspective on the Internet): http://ic.net/~erasmus/RAZ23.HTM.

About The Author

Dave Armstrong is a Catholic writer, apologist, and evangelist, who has been actively proclaiming and defending Christianity for more than twenty years. Formerly a campus missionary, as a Protestant, Dave was received into the Catholic Church in 1991, by the late, well-known catechist and theologian, Fr. John A. Hardon, S.J.

His conversion story was published in the bestselling book *Surprised by Truth* (edited by Patrick Madrid; San Diego: Basilica Press, 1994). Dave's articles have appeared in many Catholic periodicals, including *The Catholic Answer*, *This Rock*, *Envoy*, *Hands On Apologetics*, *The Coming Home Journal*, *Credo*, and *The Latin Mass*.

His large and popular website, *Biblical Evidence for Catholicism* (http://ic.net/~erasmus/RAZHOME.HTM), has been online since March 1997, and received the 1998 *Catholic Website of the Year* award from *Envoy Magazine*. (Dave was also nominated for *Best New Evangelist* by the same magazine: the only nominee who appeared in both categories). His biblical commentary on Philippians and Colossians is to be included in a major reference work, *Catholic Apologetics Study Bible*, edited by prominent Catholic apologist Robert Sungenis, and his first book, *A Biblical Defense of Catholicism*, was published by 1stBooks Library in 2001.

Dave's writing has been enthusiastically endorsed by many leading Catholic apologists, including Dr. Scott Hahn, Fr. Peter M.J. Stravinskas, Marcus Grodi, Patrick Madrid, Steve Ray, Fr. Ray Ryland, and Fr. John A. Hardon, S.J.

He married Judy Kozora in 1984; they have four children (three boys and a girl), and live near Detroit, Michigan.

Printed in the United States
68101LVS00004B/132